"Good enough"
isn't enough . . .

"Good enough" isn't enough . . .

Nine Challenges for Companies That Choose to Be Great

Alan Weiss

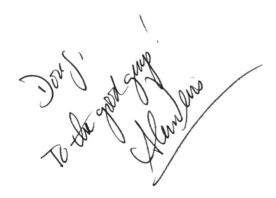

AMACOM
American Management Association
New York • Atlanta • Boston • Chicago • Kansas City • San Francisco • Washington, D.C.
Brussels • Mexico City • Tokyo • Toronto

Special discounts on bulk quantities of AMACOM books are available to corporations, professional associations, and other organizations. For details, contact Special Sales Department, AMACOM, an imprint of AMA Publications, a division of American Management Association, 1601 Broadway, New York, NY 10019.
Tel.: 212-903-8316. Fax: 212-903-8083.

This publication is designed to provide accurate and authoritative information in regard to the subject matter covered. It is sold with the understanding that the publisher is not engaged in rendering legal, accounting, or other professional service. If legal advice or other expert assistance is required, the services of a competent professional person should be sought.

Library of Congress Cataloging-in-Publication Data

Weiss, Alan
    Good enough isn't enough— : nine challenges for companies that choose to be great / Alan Weiss.
        p.   cm.
    Includes index.
    ISBN 0-8144-0505-3
    1. Management.   2. Industrial management.   3. Total quality management.   4. Industrial management—United States Case studies.
    5. Business failures—United States Case studies.   6. Corporate turnarounds—United States—Case studies.   I. Title.
    HD31.W432   1999
    658—dc21   99-30096
                                                                              CIP

Printing number

10   9   8   7   6   5   4   3   2   1

For my high school sweetheart and wife,
the same person for over 30 years

Contents

Preface

In 1982, Tom Peters and Bob Waterman created one of the first business book blockbusters with *In Search of Excellence*.[1] Nearly two decades later, like Diogenes, we are still searching. And like that cynic's quest for an honest man, our hunt for excellence seems unending. Perhaps it should be.

I've been a consultant for a quarter of a century. From the early 1970s to the new millennium, I've explained to my wife over dinner what I've seen, experienced, and recommended within client organizations. Her reactions have been consistent over the years: "But isn't that simply common sense? Why do they need you for that?" Aside from being an effective ego deflator, the questions have intrigued me. Why am I paid so much, so frequently, by so many, to tell them what's so screamingly obvious?

Let me make my disclaimer here. There are superb organizations extant in the United States, and you'll read about many of them in the pages that follow. But there simply aren't enough. Most businesses—and you can include here nonprofits, institutions, trade associations, government agencies, and any other organizational entities, large or small—aren't run as well as they could and should be. While we see the visible detritus of the worst of them in Chapter 11 bankruptcy, layoffs, "reengineering," executive changes, lawsuits, and headlines, we generally miss the nuances. The fact is, most organizations that appear healthy have nagging coughs and sometimes hidden, chronic, debilitating diseases. They show a profit that should be much larger. They work too hard to compensate for lost clients who needn't have departed. They unnecessarily cut productive employees to atone for

---

1. Thomas J. Peters and Robert H. Waterman, *In Search of Excellence: Lessons from America's Best-Run Companies* (New York: Harper & Row, 1982).

costs that ran out of control. It's this "hidden" inefficiency, this unseen incompetence, that plagues most organizations and, therefore, haunts us all in higher costs, lost jobs, and lower quality. It's as though corporate executives have adopted Boswell's philosophy about the dog that walks on its hind legs. The creature doesn't do it well, but we should appreciate that the deed is done at all.

That might be sufficient for walking dogs, but it's not the highest standard for American businesses. In fact, the trend has been all wrong since Peters and Waterman wrote their book. We've not only eschewed the search for excellence, we've satisfied ourselves with "getting by" in an unprecedented economic boom. The pole vault has given way to the limbo.

I've assembled nine challenges herein primarily for business that also apply to society (where many of the root causes reside). They originate not only in my observations from thousands of organizations, but also from identifying (sometimes, metaphorically, on my knees with a flashlight in my teeth) the weak links and Achilles' heels of some of the best-run organizations. Some of the challenges are common sense, such as creating accountability, and some are honest looks at dishonest phenomena, something my friends at Hewlett-Packard call "putting the dead rat on the table." One of those fetid rodents, for example, is the "touchie-feelie" industry and its priesthood. And some of them are about good old-fashioned sloth. "Close enough for government work" has become a performance criterion rather than a satirical dismissal.

My responses and solutions to the challenges appear within each chapter except the last chapter, which focuses solely on solutions. Since you presumably have paid for the book, this is not a consultant's free advice, and, therefore, ought to be considered prior to being disregarded. It's time to stand like a rock, as Jefferson would have said, in the stream rushing toward mediocrity. Unlike truth, which ultimately seeks out and reveals even the most evasive liar, excellence is not a hunter. It's the quarry, and *we* need to be ruthlessly hunting *it*.

As with all people who sound an alarm to rivet the attention of the public, there is the dual possibility of being either Chicken Little or Paul Revere. I'll leave that judgment to the reader.

—Alan Weiss
East Greenwich, RI, May 1999

Acknowledgments

My sincere thanks to all of the clients of Summit Consulting Group, Inc. over the last fifteen years. Their trust, collaboration and generosity were fundamental to my ability to learn, practice and improve my craft. In particular I'm indebted to Paul Cottone, former CEO of Mallinckrodt Veterinary; Fred Kerst, retired CEO of Calgon; Marilyn Martiny, Director of Knowledge Management at Hewlett-Packard; Art Strohmer, retired Executive Director of Human Resources at Merck; Mike Magsig, former CEO of Cologne Life Reinsurance; Barbara Schisani, Senior Vice President at Merck Medco Managed Care; Connie Bentley, former CEO, and Matt Galik, Vice President, both of Times Mirror Training Group; Lowell Anderson, CEO of Allianz Life; Pat Scott, retired Training Director at GE; Jerry Abarbanal, Senior Vice President, Nancy Newman, Vice President, and Jessica Rogers Dill, Vice President of Professional Development, all at State Street Corporation; and Ron Gartner, retired Training Director at Mercedes-Benz. Thanks for helping to put the kids through school.

I could not have written two new books over the past year in conjunction with a heavy speaking and consulting schedule without the help of my crack research team, Claire McCarthy, Laurie Marble, Paul Dunion, and Phoebe Weiss. My thanks for their collaboration and attention to detail. It's also time that someone thanked the readers, and my thanks go to Evelyn and David Gubitosi, who faithfully read every word, every time. I try not to let them down.

The book's entire concept and early description were painstakingly assembled completely over the Internet with an understanding and perceptive editor, Noah Shachtman. Without his interest and persistence the work would not exist.

And I'm greatly comforted by the love of Danielle, Jason, and my first wife, Maria, who also happens to be my current and only wife, through these past thirty years.

Finally, to my close collaborator and fellow bon vivant, L.T. Weiss, whose unerring editorial assistance has been an integral part of my work through eight books. To him I can never adequately express my profound gratitude.

Prologue

As the millenium occurs, the year ahead certainly looks dazzling. This must be Nirvana.

Why write a book about raising standards now, when the economy is booming, the stock market has reached the previously unimaginable 11,000 level, unemployment is at a twenty-four-year low, and the United States is the last remaining superpower? Because we are all, by an accident of history and circumstances, firsthand observers to the greatest test of national character since World War II.

We have generated record corporate profits, a seemingly limitless trajectory on the stock exchange, vast riches for the securities industries, and wonderful statistics for government economic reports. We have achieved the mysterious alchemy of low inflation and low unemployment. Alan Greenspan is getting more newspaper coverage than George Steinbrenner and Donald Trump combined. This *must* be Nirvana.

Beneath this glowing sphere of economic prosperity is a hollow core, and the distance from the hollow to the surface is often nothing more than the patina of the latest inflation statistic or politician's braggadocio.[1] Look around you and, no matter what your political persuasion, paraphrase Ronald Reagan's famous question: Are your neighbors, friends, business acquaintances, suppliers, and customers better off today than they were four

---

1. One could argue about the real nature of the success we seem to be enjoying. The latest government economic statistics indicate a *decline* in corporate growth, despite downsizing, reengineering, restructuring, and the rest of the academics' magic pills. Annual non-farm productivity growth averaged only 0.4 percent between 1992 and 1996, less than half of the 1.1 percent growth that occurred between 1973 and 1992. For the record, that same growth was 2.8 percent on average between 1947 and 1973.

years ago? If you bother to measure factors such as retirement savings, job security, real increases in income, hours worked, discretionary time, the educational system, reliability of products and services, *quantity* of successful businesses, and a myriad of others, you'll be in for anything ranging from mild shock to stupefying surprise.

This is not a Doomsday book, or the kind of contrarian work that appears during good times to appeal to the professional cynics amongst us.[2] It is an objective view of business and the related social environment with this philosophy: There is no better time to change than when in a position of strength. Change wrought out of desperation is invariably poorly conceived and frantically implemented. My advice to readers is no different from my advice to my Fortune 500 clients: When you're strong, *you should take an introspective, even harsh look at the way in which you operate, interact with others, and make basic decisions,* because the easiest time to successfully implement profound change is when you are strong and have the luxury of failing in a good cause. Risk-taking is never so "safe."

It's also never been so timely. The Europeans, at the moment, in the absence of the cold war threat to their eastern regions for the first time since World War II, are becoming increasingly introspective. France, Switzerland, Germany, Italy, and other nations are examining their approaches to business support, social policy, global involvement, policies on immigration, and the accuracy of the historical record. It's time for the United States to also gaze inward and not simply accept our current, supreme good fortune as our natural divine right or inheritance by default.

Not long ago, United Parcel Service settled a bitter dispute with its union. Despite a small resurgence, unionism in the United States is at its lowest point since the 1950s, with real

---

2. Although if I wanted to write the Doomsday version, I would have cited the fact that the gross domestic product has grown only 2.7% from 1993 to 1996, and the productivity growth that Alan Greenspan predicted as recently as July 1997 doesn't appear to be on the horizon, according to government economic data. Pretax profits in industries purchasing, say, expensive software are legally but basically inflated through the practice of depreciating costs over several years rather than writing them off the year of purchase, as was once more common. Billions poured into technology has yet to manifest itself in return on that investment. But let's give all of that the benefit of these doubts.

growth only in the public sector. One of the working person's most potent weapons, unionism, has grown archaic and rusted through its own corruptibility and misuse. No one is about to cite the union movement as a stellar example of ethics and lofty ideals. And UPS has a history of fine employee relations (all of their officers started their careers on the trucks). The employees own the company, whose stock is not publicly traded. UPS is thirty-seventh on the current *Fortune 500* list and was fourth among that magazine's 1996 list of "most admired companies." Yet this strike was really about character and ethics, and how corporations view people.

A full-time, average UPS worker earns almost $20 an hour, plus benefits. A part-time, average UPS worker earns about $9 an hour. And the part-timers receive fewer benefits than the full-timers, so the real differential in employment costs is far greater than $11 an hour. This has been worth hundreds of millions to the UPS bottom line over the past few years and will continue to be for the years ahead.

Almost 110,000 UPS workers are part-time, out of a complement of just over 180,000. That's almost two-thirds of the total workforce of a company employing one of every 400 workers in the entire country. Since 1993, UPS has added 43,000 new jobs, of which only 8,000—less than 20%—have been full-time.

Work the math and you can begin to appreciate what the union is fighting (whether its leadership realizes it or not), and it's much more than merely the full-time jobs at UPS. It is the very model of the "economic miracle" we currently enjoy.

But at what real cost?

We have *many fewer* successful businesses than ever before, because the great success of a relative few has largely relied on the acquisition or destruction of the many, in industries as diverse as airlines, hardware, newspapers, booksellers, computers, entertainment, and travel agents. We have larger numbers of people employed but in more menial jobs or in jobs with less benefits than ever before. If the employment statistics measured *quality* of work life, *confidence* in employment, and *loyalty* to one's work, we'd see a different picture. The odds are enormous that you either are part of this new reality or know at least two people who are. That's how pervasive the change in our economic model has become. We've accepted "dress down" days as a benefit while giving up major health benefits as a concession. There is something wrong with this picture.

The real challenges can be viewed through the transparent difficulties of organizations such as Compaq Computer, Kodak, Amtrak,[3] Archer Daniels, TWA, and Prudential. With the exception of Amtrak's monopoly, there are organizations excelling in each of the markets of my examples (i.e., Dell, Fuji, Cargill, Continental, and Northwestern Mutual). Those I've cited—and scores more like them—are the victims of poor leadership, dilatory board performance, misguided consultants, inappropriate executive compensation policies, desperate resorts to legal remedies, and a host of other ills detailed in this book. Apple has, arguably, the finest technology and most rabid customer base in the industry, yet inept leadership and an unresponsive board had brought its survival into question. While IBM and Merck successfully replaced CEOs using people from outside their industries, AT&T failed dismally and Kodak is desperately treading water. Prudential, once a "rock" on which to rely, has engaged in more questionable ethical practices over the past decade than a circus sideshow. Where was leadership? What happened to excellence?

With little or no competition, this country must raise its standards to create its own new challenges, embracing the notion that all citizens have a right to work and to profit from our collaborative success. In business and industry, our leadership must understand and act upon the fact that people are assets not expenses, and that downsizing, reengineering, and all the other euphemisms from the academics who have never run a business have simply been excuses to reduce employment to atone for past management mistakes and poor marketplace strategies (and pad executive compensation through expense reduction). That approach entails both a myopic view and a callous act. Business leadership is accountable to grow the enterprise through higher standards of performance, not redeem their own mistakes on the bottom line by throwing people out of work.

Are our organizations being led with a telescope or a microscope? My observations and findings are that it's a mixture of

---

3. Don't regard this as an immediately "easy target." Amtrak has highly profitable northeastern corridor operations that it has been unable to replicate or even take much advantage of. Amtrak leadership could bankrupt Microsoft if they got their hands on it.

both, but with far too much of the latter and far too little of the former.

What CEO Robert Allen and the board of AT&T did to a great American company—in terms of decreased shareholder profits, massive layoffs of good people, and undignified ousters of presumed heirs apparent who just might have changed the system—was nothing less than an epic case study in ineptitude. Yet few seemed to care. It's time to start caring, before we all reap what such leadership is sowing. That, too, is a test of character.

If our future model is that which is exemplified by UPS—grow the bottom line by paying people less and less for the same work—woe is us. That model is not only ethically flawed but also destined to produce little loyalty, scant innovation, and poor service. No organization I've ever seen has unhappy employees and happy customers. Extrapolate that model into our research labs, our sales forces, and our financial centers, and you have the recipe for complacency, arrogance, and, ultimately, demise.

That's the hollow to our current economic bubble. An evanescent surface may be all that's keeping us airborne. Yet it doesn't have to be this way and wasn't always so.

Our "character test" lies in the fact that the hollow core is not an inescapable factor of our times, but rather a phenomenon created by our leadership. I've separated the issues into nine challenges that we must resolve. They include relatively recent developments, such as the plethora of consultants who come to study a problem and then stay on to become part of it; the "touchie-feelie" brigade that effectively forestalls focus on pragmatic action through psychological snake oil and emotional patent medicine; the perceived legal "safety net" that has replaced ethics, judgment, and common sense with legal remedies far more insidious than the dilemmas they address; corporate boards that have served as high-rise resorts for the uninterested, unresponsive, and unconscious, rather than true sources of governance; executive compensation that palpably does not reward performance but rather position; and a general decline in standards so that poorer and poorer performance—in society and in business—is interpreted as the model. After all, it's always easier to lower the bar than it is to improve performance. But good enough simply isn't enough.

What happened to excellence? Read on, and find out. This is not nirvana.

"Good enough"
isn't enough . . .

Introduction
How Good Companies Get That Way; How Great Companies Stay That Way

---

THE DIFFERENCE BETWEEN CONTENT AND PROCESS

Why are some organizations simply better than others? This question is not as easy to answer as it is to ask. Very few companies are successful over the long haul. In fact, the life span of organizational success is ephemeral, more like a fruit fly than a tortoise.

If you were, in fact, to examine the "best" organizations of the past, those written up in *In Search of Excellence*, or on *Fortune's* "Most Admired" lists, or any other expert citation, you would find a mixed lot. To cite just one recent example, Rubber Maid, repeatedly chosen in the past as one of the finest organizations in existence, was sold in 1998 to a company no one ever heard of for a stock price below what it was selling for in 1991.[1] Under CEO Stanley Gault for over a decade, the company was a model for shareholder return, innovative employee policies, and masterful relationships with the media. Upon Gault's retirement in 1991, his successor, Wolfgang Schmitt, simply ran the place into the ground. Manufacturing quality declined, service standards went unmet, customers turned elsewhere.[2]

---

1. It was purchased by Newell, of Freeport, Illinois. The stock was at 38 in 1991, and hasn't been there since. See "How Rubbermaid Managed to Fail," *Fortune*, 23 November 1998, 32.

2. In December 1998, the company had to recall over 60,000 toboggans because of defects resulting in injuries to riders. See "Rubbermaid recalls defective toboggans," *Providence Journal*, 2 December 1998, 2.

Over the course of most of a decade, senior executives and board members sat around watching the company's demise. That, in and of itself, is not surprising. Such somnolence could have been seen at GM, IBM, DEC, Kodak, and any number of other corporate giants. However, GM's and IBM's boards eventually shook themselves out of their torpor, fired some executives, and got the train running on time again. The board at Rubbermaid quiescently allowed the train to derail and turn over.

Conversely, Chrysler was one of the worst-run operations in the world before Ioccoca, and its stock tumbled to $3 while he was wading around trying to drain the swamp, simultaneously avoiding the alligators. In 1999, Chrysler was the most profitable of the American auto makers, and it merged with Daimler-Benz, perhaps the most revered of all auto companies, to become one of the great global businesses. Daimler/Chrysler stock sells in a range between 95 and 102 at this writing. In the early 1980s, Lee Iaccoca dramatically revived Chrysler, and in the late 1990s, Bob Lutz did it all over again. Iaccoca came from Ford; Lutz, from GM. They were both allowed to "escape," and they altered the auto world as a result.[3]

If you were a risk-averse investor, saving for your children's education or your own retirement fifteen to twenty years ago, the best bet between Rubbermaid and Chrysler would have clearly been Rubbermaid. And you would have been dead wrong.

Highly successful companies may achieve that status by dint of their products and services, *but they don't remain in that lofty air because of their products and services.* They stay there because of the manner in which they are led and managed. IBM achieved its initial success because of expertise in punch cards for primitive information processing. If its managers had believed the company to be in the punch card business, neither they nor the company would be around today.[4] Since that time, IBM has had its ups and downs, but not because of lack of prowess in research, manufac-

---

3. See "A Gut Check from Detroit," *Management Review,* December 1998, 15, for a review of a book describing Lutz's particular contributions, often overshadowed by Iaccoca's earlier heroics.

4. Don't laugh at this seeming absurdity. Not one of the companies manufacturing vacuum tubes successfully entered the transistor business. They thought they were in the tube manufacturing business instead of the electronic communication business.

turing, sales, or, perhaps most important, "brand name." It has had its problems because it has not evaluated its markets properly, has lost key people, has failed to recruit and/or tolerate "new blood" and non-IBM-blue initiative, and has lost the trust of its buyers.

Kodak successfully moved from largely chemical-process film processing to electronic processing. However, it also engaged in some bizarre acquisitions (e.g., a pharmaceutical company), failed to counter competitive threats, and lost its unassailed dominance in the local retail stores. Yet Continental Airlines, once the laughingstock of every serious management writer (including this one), flew a 180-degree turn under CEO Gordon Bethune, who has managed to transform employee apathy, poor performance, and executive indifference into a thriving, on-time, highly competitive airline.

It is *content* that often determines whether an organization can ascend to the exalted ranks of "hot commodity," favorite of Wall Street, media darling, and consumer magnet. But it is *process* that determines whether it can stay there for long and endure both the foreseeable obstacles (competition, growth pains, rising expectations) and the surprise landmines (new technology, global dependencies, volatile economies). A "new" technology, such as instant photography, which has never been accomplished before, can produce immediate ascendancy. But the process by which the company is led and managed will determine long-term success. Polaroid has had an exciting technology but has been a dull company. On the other hand, scores of organizations have tried to do what Continental has done in a "commodity-like" industry, but you can count the successes on the fingers of one hand (while wishing desperately that terrible service providers like Northwest would somehow get the message).

At the moment, Amazon.com has had short-term stock fluctuations running the gamut from $126 to $185, after having split three-for-one in late 1998. The company is written about every day. It is innovative and exciting. With its new approach to handling book (and other) sales and orders on the Internet, it immediately reached a capitalization surpassing its two main competitors, Barnes & Noble and Borders, combined. (One wonders if Barnes & Noble might try to remove the greatest thorn ever thrust into its side by resorting to an old GE tactic: Buy the place.[5] They did buy Ingram, the huge wholesale book distributor.)

During all this excitement, Amazon.com never, ever, showed one penny of profit. It is a new company excelling in the minds of investors because of its novel use of technology and innovative positioning (and sheer bravado). Will it stand the test of time? It will do so by continually changing the way it is being led and managed. The original qualities have generated the start-up needs of volume, cash, recognition, and momentum. But you don't stay at the top of the pack while you're losing two dollars for every one you bring in. And, the last time I looked, you can't make up for that with volume.

Content—innovative technology, market positioning, appeals to consumer needs, ease-of-use, and related benefits—can get you into the dance. But it's process—alignment of goals behind a common vision, recruiting and retaining talent, balancing customer and shareholder interests—that keep you dancing in time to the music. Great companies get that way because they learn how to evolve and perpetuate their success, not fall victim to it.

THE REASON ORGANIZATIONS OFTEN CAN'T SEE THE OBVIOUS

There probably aren't too many leaders who say, "We'd really prefer not to be market leaders, not to continually improve standards, not to dynamically grow for the long term." So why don't more of them do it? It would seem that merely awareness and constant challenge would be sufficient to generate a positive attitude and resultant innovation. (And, indeed, a great many companies have platitudes for accomplishment on every employee's desk, hung from the rafters in the cafeteria, and emblazoned on much of the bare wall space. "Team work is the only kind of work." "Success is up to each one of us." "Don't let a good idea go bad." There's even a company, called "Successories," that is in the business of manufacturing such treacly cheerleading, using wall plaques, lapel buttons, and other office dust-collectors.)

---

5. An apocryphal but accurate description of GE strategy in the early days of Jack Welch was described for me during my work with that company as, "If we can't beat 'em, buy 'em."

The great organizations, those which thrive over time, don't get lost in their press clippings, don't assume that success is ever permanent, and don't become wed to "the way we do things around here." Poorer organizations try not to tamper with success, refrain from rocking the boat, and congratulate themselves a lot. If you watch the great football coaches, you'll notice they are never happy, no matter how impressive their team's momentary success. In any game, there was always a block that was missed, a pass that went astray, an assignment poorly undertaken. The great coaches are always looking for an opportunity to coach, to improve, to attain a grander height. In the history of the National Football League, only one team, the Miami Dolphins, has ever completed an undefeated season. And that success didn't last all that long, since the very next year they were dethroned as the champs.

Bill Parcells, a tough, irascible, hard-to-like coaching genius, took three different lowly (at the time) franchises—New York Giants, New England Patriots, New York Jets—and made them into winners. He won two Superbowls with the Giants, and lost one with the Patriots. After his departure, the Giants foundered and the Patriots struggled. Neither maintained the excellence they had seen under Parcells. The man was never content with a victory. He realized that the goal was the final win in the final championship game. Anything short of that was limited success. He would not get sidelined by short-term victories or temporary gratification.

Organizations too often take their eye off the ball. They seem to get caught up in their own success and inadvertently (or, worse, advertently) listen only to themselves, follow solely their own procedures, look exclusively to their own past.

Hewlett-Packard is a good example. This has been a fine company, overall, a case in which the wonderful American stereotype of "begun in the founders' garage" is true. It stumbled badly some years ago under CEO John Young (after Bill Hewlett and Dave Packard voluntarily ceded personal control), but rebounded nicely under his successor, Lew Platt. The stock was attractive, the talent was rich and diverse, and the company's image was radiant. But it was not so forever.

If the CEO didn't change (Platt is still there at this writing), then what happened? Well, organizational success is about leadership *and* management. Platt was the right leader at the right time, but HP has not grown and evolved beyond his dramatic turnaround.[6] And that's a function of a particularly HP culture that has worked well for it in the past, but now needs to be jettisoned.

HP has grown through the aid of a remarkably nonconfrontational culture. Meetings at HP are generally cordial, convivial, pleasant environments in which participants genially support common goals.[7] It is virtually unheard of for colleagues to disagree strongly in formal meetings, and it would be unthinkable to disagree with a superior's initiative or remarks. Such behavior is not within the boundaries of "The HP Way," which is the official description of the organization's culture (and the name of the hardcover book provided by the company).

Disagreements, of course, do exist, and they have traditionally been worked out behind the scenes in a series of informal meetings without agendas at which people air their grievances or objections, determine how to resolve them or live with them, and decide what can be safely discussed, examined, and analyzed, and what is off limits. The result is a peculiar kind of gentle ballroom dance, in which partners smile and compliment each other's abilities, and the steps are performed exactly in time to the music. However, although people touch, no one embraces, and although the dance is completed, it is not recalled with any great pleasure.

The pragmatic results of such nonconfrontation and superficial camaraderie are that radical ideas are seldom heard, risk aversion is safe behavior, and finding subterranean ways around the system consume a lot of time.

HP is a truly global company, and spends a lot of time on strategy and planning. Those pursuits are purportedly highly inclusive, attempting to embrace all levels and all areas. One would hope that the time for painful honesty would occur when a multibillion dollar global giant is attempting to establish the nature and direction of its business for the immediate future. As in all companies, there are rigorous planning processes, planning de-

---

6. Everything is relative. Some years ago, the Cadillac Division of General Motors won one of the prestigious quality awards for improvement. The irony is that Cadillac's quality had been so poor that dramatic, relative improvement was simple. Consistency at the top, not stumbling out of the ashes, is what should be rewarded.

7. The author has worked with thousands of people within HP at various sites over a period ranging from 1972 through 1998.

partments, corporate strategists, and other functionaries to ensure that the job is done well.

The job is done, but not well. When I visited the country managers of HP's Asian operations, I learned to my shock that each of them was unilaterally ignoring corporate strategy, doing what was best in his or her own backyard. Their general manager, in the same room, was aware and approving.

"But you take part in the formulation of this strategy," I protested, "and you're given an opportunity to review it before it's finalized. Why do you simply accept it and ignore it?"

"Because it would cause too much of a career problem to say what we really believe, and there are no repercussions for ignoring it, as long as we make our numbers," replied several members of the group, with the rest nodding assent.

HP has failed to change its nonconfrontational corporate culture to suit the times. At the very moment the company leadership requires honesty, risk taking, and "push back" (another HP daily term) on initiatives, it is still "trapped" by the prior successes of a congenial, don't-rock-the-boat culture. Great companies remain great by evolving their culture, not by cementing it in place and memorializing it. For the first time in my memory, HP is experiencing defections at a high level and an involuntary loss of talent. Lew Platt has shown some signs of getting tough. Unfortunately, it's not his ability to confront, nor his comfort level in so doing, that's at issue.

THE TEN KEYS TO ENDURING SUCCESS

The authors of *In Search of Excellence*, who began a genre in terms of critically assessing management, took something of a retrospective beating a few years after publication, because critics began to note that some of their "excellent" companies had stumbled.[8] Yet the authors never made a claim about permanence. They, in fact, applied a set of processes (e.g., "stick to the knit-

---

8. Thomas J. Peters and Robert H. Waterman, Jr., *In Search of Excellence* (New York: Harper & Row, 1982). Some of their historically questionable choices would be DEC, Texas Instruments, Wang Labs, National Semiconductor, K-Mart, and Delta Airlines. But some of the enduring, successful selections would include Disney, Merck, Wal-Mart, 3M, and Intel.

ting," "management by walking around," etc.) that, whether you agreed with them or not, were criteria against which their subject organizations were rated. They took the equivalent of a snapshot, not a movie.

One of the reasons that academics have been so successful in creating management interventions du jour from ivied towers[9] into which the real world has never penetrated is that business leaders have been desperately seeking a formula for success. Ironically, they need only look to their own colleagues who have been able to maintain excellence over extended periods of time and ask, "What is it that they are doing?"

Here are the ten most important processes I've observed, spanning thousands of organizations for over twenty-five years, which account for long-term success irrespective of the content of the organization. Here's how great organizations *stay that way.*

1. Alignment of *Everyone's* Objectives in Support of Corporate Goals

I walked into a regional office of GRE Insurance in Syracuse, New York, just as I've walked into hundreds of other regional offices for scores of other insurance companies over the years.

"Hi," I said to the smiling receptionist, "I'm Alan Weiss and I'm here to see Tom."

"Yes, we're expecting you. I'll let him know you're here."

"How are things?" I asked, an innocuous question that sometimes leads to insights about the local organization that management isn't always quick to reveal.

"Well, pretty good," she replied, "our loss ratio has been above our goal for the entire month."

Whoa! This was different. The receptionist's response to "How are things?" wasn't about the weather, the vacation policy,

---

9. My very favorite is Michael Hammer writing a best-selling book on "reengineering," then following with another best-selling book explaining how he had been wrong in the first one! I teach a graduate program each semester at the University of Rhode Island, and one of the full-time faculty teaches a required MBA course which actually focuses solely on Hammer's original book, every class, all semester. This is the equivalent of spending $10 to go to the movies just to watch the ads for the refreshment stand, and leaving before the main feature.

or the Syracuse football team, but was about the positive nature of the *loss ratio?*[10]

Most senior managers focus strictly on the business side of the enterprise: strategy, tactics, daily execution. But the outstanding ones also focus on the cultural side: values, behaviors, performance. Only by managing the latter can you support and perpetuate the former. Organizational "culture" has taken on sacrosanct nuances, as if we should all be out in the desert beating on drums and intoning the names of our ancestors. In fact, corporate culture is merely the set of beliefs that governs behavior. Consequently, it is eminently changeable and malleable, and can be influenced to support legitimate business goals. The trouble is that too many managers are out there beating drums and intoning "stewardship" and "servant leadership" and "customer focus" and other evanescent, empty phrases that mean nothing to the rank and file.

That Syracuse office manager knew that a key component of success rested in a positive loss ratio. So he explained that to everyone. He showed how everyone's bonus ultimately depended on that measure of profitability. He made it easy for people to check the numbers daily. He openly solicited ideas to positively influence it. This is not rocket science. But it is alignment.

2. Demonstrated Willingness to Confront Issues and to Disagree

Hyatt executives always receive a great media splash when they take a day to serve as baggage handlers, front desk clerks, and room service deliverers. But how else can you tell what's really going on?

I've sat through countless meetings in which $5 million in corporate salaries was sitting around a table serving as an echo chamber for the boss, the "yes man" raised to a very expensive art form. No one in that room, save the consultant who points out the bizarre dynamic, is helping the shareholders one iota. I can get scared, timid, pushovers for one-tenth of that salary who will be just as efficient and respectful in saying, "What a great idea!" I can also guarantee that any boss who never questions the

---

10. Loss ratios are comparisons, basically, of premium dollars versus claims payments. You want to be taking in more money than you're paying out, above and beyond other operating costs.

fact that he or she is never questioned is either deaf or a fool. I can find fools a lot more cheaply as well.

I was once one of forty presidents who ran companies owned by the insurance tycoon W. Clement Stone. He made his millions through the sales of industrial life insurance with penny premiums, invested wisely, surrounded himself with astute financial talent, and sold out to larger companies. He had mistaken that very specialized talent for universal wisdom. He intended to change the world through "positive mental attitude," the business pursuit of which never made him a dime, and cost him some of those millions.

The presidents would be convened in the ballroom on the top story of his mansion. He would present a peculiar idea under the general heading of (honest, who could make this up?) "Mr. Stone's Universe," and every president around the table would, one by one, testify to the vast wisdom of trying to move the building six feet to the left, make everyone ambidextrous, or whatever the latest notion was. I was the lone dissenter for most of this nonsense. I didn't last long in that universe.

Organizational chains of command tend to paint the most positive face on disaster, disguise discontent as helpful support, and pretend that banners in the cafeteria will take care of everything. Compare this with Jack Welch at GE who, throughout his shepherding of one of the most complex and most successful organizations in the world, has regularly stood in "the pit" at the training center at Crotonville and demanded that the best and the brightest throw their sharpest and toughest questions at him.

Welch has been surprised too many times to be complacent, whether from bribes to Israeli defense officials, staged auto gas tank explosions on NBC, price fixing with diamond companies, or ill-advised ventures into the securities industry. He demands honesty and openness. Roy Vagelos was the same during the period he guided Merck, one of the surest bets in the stock market and one of the world's great pharmaceutical enterprises, through unexcelled growth and returns.

It is ironic that we often regard executives who demand honesty and candor as "tough" and "intimidating," two sobriquets that Welch, Vagelos, and, for that matter, Bill Parcells, all have endured.

3. Exemplary Behavior

An entrepreneur owner of a $20 million company hired me because his organization had grown but had stalled. He had the inside track, through his technology, on mechanisms that filled assembly line products with fluid. The products were sound and well regarded, but sales initiatives had been lost, service was mediocre, and profits were flat.

"Find out," he said, "if I'm hiring the wrong people or training the right people the wrong way. I can take the critique."

With small businesses I demand payment in advance, and then wait for the check to clear the bank before rendering any opinions. It's a good thing I do. The owner was hiring good people, had provided a highly competitive benefits package, and the company was above average in both salary and physical work environment. The trouble was that he ran a "do as I say, not as I do" shop. There was no smoking allowed on the property, except for him and his wife. There were clear management and supervisory accountabilities in place, but he ignored them and made changes directly on the front line. He had a growth strategy and succession plan for the business, but refused adamantly to share them with even his direct reports. He opened anyone's mail he cared to open. I wouldn't have been surprised if the phones were tapped, since he seemed to know an awful lot about conversations I was having with individuals on a one-on-one basis, the content of which I doubted they would have shared voluntarily with the boss.

When I confronted him about his dysfunctional behaviors, he nearly had to implement his "secret" succession plan on the spot, because I thought he was having a heart attack. He asked me to leave, which I did. He asked me to return his money, which I didn't.

No one in organizational life believes what they read and hear, no matter how prominently posted or how often repeated. People believe only what they *see*. Hence, the role of the exemplar is the strongest influence on daily behavior in any organization.

When there's a cutback, and the CEO takes a hefty pay cut or benefit reduction to show that everyone must jointly suffer, the grumbling is mitigated. When Bob Allen, as CEO of AT&T, tried to throw 40,000 people out the door in a downsizing effort required by his own poor decisions, and refused to take even a dime's reduction in his multimillion dollar compensation package, employees went to the barricades. Even AT&T's complacent board had finally had enough and eventually forced him out.

When I see executives walking the floors of their retail stores, meet airline executives flying on their company's planes, recognize that the auto dealer owner occupies a cubicle just like everyone else down on the sales floor, and watch executives who take customer calls gladly without functionaries who serve as screeners against the great unwashed, I know that I'm in an organization where people lead by example.

Words are empty. Actions carry weight.

4. Realistic Customer Interactions

News flash: the customer is not always right. Some customers cost you money. Employees know this.

The recent emphasis on "customer-driven" organizations is absurd. Customers shouldn't set strategy. That's why we have (purportedly) executives. Customers always know what they want, but don't always know what they *need*. If that weren't the case, we'd never have the Walkman or Post-It Notes, since we never knew that we wanted these things. But, oh, did we need them.

The Cross Pen Company has been famous through the years for replacing its pens for *any* defect, no matter how bizarre. People who dropped the writing implements into their lawnmowers[11] had them replaced, free of charge, by the ever-understanding Cross Pen Company. As a shareholder in Cross, I would not be amused. And, in fact, Cross is facing very tough times in the late 1990s, dropping its dividend for the first time in its history.

Retailer Nordstrom's has developed the ultimate brand image for customer service. They live up to it. Employees are empowered to offer exceptional service, accept returns, and be extraordinarily creative in responding to customer desires or complaints. However, even Nordstrom's—as have retailers everywhere—has begun to look with a jaded eye on some customers. Dresses that are brought back "because they don't fit" or "don't

---

11. These are, presumably, people who need to make notes of their mowing patterns.

look as good out of the store" are no longer routinely accepted if the sales personnel can see deodorant stains, wine spills, food bits, or other signs of a party experience on the garment. If you talk to retail store salespeople, as I have, you'll hear a wild assortment of stories about clothing returns, including items such as love notes, party invitations, and even condoms left in a pocket or discreet hiding place and forgotten.

The airlines have become quite pragmatic about customer service. They will refuse people drinks if they appear to be drunk. They'll enforce a limited carry-on policy if planes are too full or boarding too cumbersome. Delta and United recently installed carry-on sizers in front of their security equipment at a few airports. If the bag can't fit through, then it can't go through security and must be checked.

Employees are in an awkward position, and often an impossible one, when they are told to accede to customer requests, no matter what they are. And organizations are disrupted, unfocused, and placed at a competitive disadvantage when they decide (consciously or unconsciously) to mindlessly do what their customers demand. Most customers want the airlines to increase seat dimensions dramatically, lower prices, serve better food, and fly on time no matter what the weather conditions.

It's a safe bet that the airline attempting to meet those demands would be the most popular, and shortest-lived, operation in the world.

5. Perspective in Crisis

The Union Carbide catastrophe in Bhopal, India, and the Exxon Valdez calamity off the Alaska coast are, thankfully, rare occurrences. They are so infrequent, in fact, that we can name them singularly (Tylenol tampering, Ford Pinto gasoline tank explosions, etc.).

Organizational "crises" are usually about more trivial, albeit important, matters: a key client deserts, someone has embezzled, profits are taking a plunge, there is a buyout rumor, top talent is going to the competition, technology is out of date. These are actually rather normal organizational happenings. If each one is allowed to become an out-of-proportion threat, then the organization will come to a screeching halt more often than someone just learning to drive with a manual transmission.

Stellar organizations alert employees (and customers, if need be) to bad news, just as readily as they do good news. They tell everyone what they know and what's being done. They solicit suggestions, and provide communication avenues for people who want to check the status.

I was staying in a Four Seasons Hotel in Washington, D.C. when the fire alarm went off in the middle of the night. No one alerted guests in any manner. A call to the front desk, when the lines were not busy, generated this response: "We think it's a false alarm caused by the carpet cleaners. Please stay where you are." Meanwhile, some guests were hitting the stairs in their night-wear, while others casually stood in the corridors having a drink.

In a Hyatt resort property in Florida, a nighttime fire alarm was immediately followed by a hotelwide intercom announce-ment that there was a small fire in the kitchen. The fire depart-ment was standing by and, while the danger was small, guests were asked to evacuate to a designated area across from the main entrance. We were back inside the building thirty minutes later, having felt very well cared for.

State Street Bank in Boston was faced with a possible acqui-sition by Bank of New York a few years ago. Employees were con-stantly kept informed through E-mail, written memos, and personal presentations by CEO Marshall Carter. His frequent management meetings were packed, and they were videotaped for distribution around the global institution. When I conducted a survey of the communications efficacy of the organization, the handling of the Bank of New York attempt was universally cited as the company's finest communication moment, and as the key reason that productivity remained high. People felt they were well informed and would stay that way, and everyone went back to work.

6. Elimination of Poor Performers

Other than excessive and meaningless meetings, nothing soaks up more executive time than the attempt to "save" and otherwise develop poor performers. Senior people should focus on developing those people *who are already performing at a high level and high standard.* These are the employees who have demon-strated ability, motivation, and success. They represent the largest return on the developmental investment. Alas, the process is usually just the opposite: The high performers are left to fend for themselves, while the poor performers soak up everyone's energy and money.

One of my clients was a $600 million division of a multibillion dollar conglomerate. The CEO asked me to help with team building among his direct reports. "Pay special attention to John," he said, "because he's the weak link. He's holding the team back, so if we solve that problem, we'll make real progress."

John was the senior vice president of strategic planning. Working with him one-on-one, I quickly found him to be highly political (he would offer no opinions on anything until he found which way his boss was leaning), poor to the point of incompetent in terms of strategy (he had no track record elsewhere and couldn't even define his own goals), and ready to blame his colleagues for all errors (he was nearly paranoid about the vice president of operations deliberately undermining the company).

I told the CEO that John was hopeless and ought to be removed. The CEO balked, claiming that no one should be readily lost "on his watch." I put in another thirty days with no progress with John, and once again made my recommendation to the CEO, who was still reluctant to surrender his "savior" role.

"Jim," I asked, "how much time are you spending on John's behavioral problems, refereeing his petty disputes, and putting right the ill will he's causing around the company?"

"I don't know," said Jim, "maybe 20 percent of my time. Say a day a week. But I think he's worth it."

"And what would your board say if they knew that a fifth of your time, salary, and energies were going not into acquisitions, long-term strategy, and enhancing customer relationships, but instead into saving a guy who is his own worst enemy?"

Jim knew exactly what the board would say, and John was gone before the end of the week. The company never missed him, and his entire position was eliminated as unnecessary. If organizations are not weeding out the bottom 5 percent of performers every year, through termination, forced retirement, or transfers, then they are condoning mediocrity. Ignore that poor performance long enough, and the organization becomes mediocre.

7. Commitment to Doing the *Right* Thing

As a practical matter, our system is based on certain ethical principles. You agree to provide me with a certain product or service, of a certain quality, at a certain time, for a certain price. I agree to pay for that product or service with a certain instrument, in a certain manner, at a certain time. Without that mutual trust and integrity the system breaks down. Russia, for example, is not having a difficult economic time solely because of a lack of hard currency or an antiquated infrastructure, but also because that basic ethical dynamic has never existed there under communism. When you're trying to cheat someone as an economic way of life, you can bet that there are a lot of people simultaneously trying to cheat you. You're better off in the casinos.

Our tax system is in the mess it's in because there are so many loopholes and "gray areas" that tend to proliferate, in which taxpayers and tax preparers try to work the system to their advantage. It's only a short step from there to bending the black-and-white rules, and another leap to outright fraud. (Claiming that you gave more to charity than you actually did is fraud, not a gray area.) Disrespect for one law or one rule creates disrespect for all laws and all rules. In the Reagan years, Betsy Blooming-dale, an exceedingly rich woman and personal friend of Nancy Reagan, was caught redhanded trying to smuggle newly pur-chased furs past U.S. customs officers by the amateur expedient of having cut the labels out and claiming them as used. When a rich woman tries to cheat to save a few bucks, then shouldn't we all?

Great organizations have clear values that manifest them-selves in *everyone's* behaviors. When I ask employees during my random walks through organizational passageways, "What do you do in the absence of policy and precedent?" the responses are varied. In poor organizations they say, "I protect myself," or "I make sure I meet my numbers," or "I blame accounting." In good organizations they say, "I ask my boss," or "I ask someone who's been here longer," or "I act as conservatively and safely as pos-sible."

In the great organizations they say, "I do the right thing." Doing the right thing will never cause long-term problems, and while it can cause momentary discomfort or short-term loss, when an entire company and its employees act that way, there is never a chance that the sexual harassment that existed for so long at Astra or the racial comments and behaviors at Texaco could endure. You don't need banners in the cafeteria when employees habitually do the right thing.[12]

8. Focus on Output, Not Input

The old saw is that no one buys a drill because they need a drill. What they need is a hole. Consequently, don't attempt to thrill me with the merits of the drill, show me the beauty of the result.

Too many organizations measure task and input. During a consulting assignment for the *Los Angeles Times* advertising department, I found that the measures and rewards for salespeople were focused on number of sales calls, attendance in the office when not seeing prospects, the accurate and punctilious completion of paperwork, and similar tasks. These things were all easy to measure. They were also largely irrelevant.

The only things that matter are results properly arrived at (see point seven above). I've actually seen "outstanding" ratings given to employees for arriving at the office before everyone else and putting the coffee on. If you analyze the normal performance reviews at organizations, you'll find that most employees are "above average" even though the organizational performance is only "average" (or below). How can that be? Is the leadership squandering the fruits of the outstanding labors of the masses? No, leadership is simply providing a sop by providing artificially high ratings.

The salesperson who says "My job is to make sales calls" is a frightening sight to behold. The salesperson who says, "My job is to bring in new business" is the player I want on my team. The *Los Angeles Times* had bred a group of salespeople who could sail along quite well *without dramatic business acquisition* by merely complying to the task measures and taking orders from exiting (and dwindling) accounts. The increased competition from the

---

12. I sometimes despair for our times. In late 1998, a freelance writer and columnist by the name of Michelle Cottle writing in no less than the *New York Times* advised that an employee should keep her mouth shut about anti-Semitic remarks, because calling attention to them would just hurt her career. See "Positive Ways to Move On," Working Column, 11 October 1998.

Internet, alternative newspapers, and cable television hadn't so much as dented the system.

When you call a company, some receptionists will immediately put you on hold, or merely wordlessly transfer you, or won't volunteer any help if you're not sure whom you want. Others will volunteer assistance, graciously say "please" and "thank you," and even stay on the line to ensure that the call goes through. The difference between the two approaches is not in salary, benefits, work environment, or training on the equipment. It is in mental orientation. In the first case, the receptionist is being employed to answer the phones, which the employee does, period. In the second instance, the receptionist is employed to ensure that customers receive proper service, callers are directed to the right parties, and delays are minimized.

When the newspaper carrier carelessly throws the paper under cars and bushes, it's because the job is perceived as merely the task of getting the paper to the house. When the paper is always in the same place in front of the door, it's because the job is perceived as "providing excellent customer service." That applies to officers, managers, and professionals just as much as receptionists and newspaper carriers. Great organizations focus on output.

9. Supportive Employee Environment

I've never seen a company with unhappy employees and happy customers. It doesn't work that way. Nor is money the answer to every motivation problem. If you have an unhappy employee (over perceived discrimination, poor advancement prospects, lack of training, harsh supervisors, etc.) and you throw more money at the individual, what you create is a wealthier, unhappy employee.

When FedEx pilots threatened to strike during the 1998 holiday season, the company's nonunion employees (the pilots are the only ones who are organized) staged a huge rally at the Memphis headquarters, pledging to deliver every package at the company's existing standards with the pilots or without them. The pilots quickly backed down, and their union is now severely weakened. Fred Smith, FedEx founder and CEO, has been an employee zealot from the outset. He understands that to have a great company you have to have a great employee environment.

At one point in a past more distinguished than its present, Delta Airlines, acknowledged as having the finest service of any U.S. carrier, was presented with a spanking new Boeing 727 *by its employees,* who had voluntarily provided a small percentage of their paychecks to buy it. Delta lost that employee support during a vicious cost-cutting campaign in the 1990s, and its service plummeted. The airline is now trying to rebuild that trust, which is much harder once it's been sacrificed on the altar of short-term profits.

It's no accident that the *Business Week* and *Fortune* surveys of "the best companies to work for," or "the best companies for minorities," or "the best companies for women" are usually also listings of the most successful and profitable companies on the landscape. The reason is that firms do not make and lose money every day as a result of decisions in the executive suite. They make or lose money daily based on tens of thousands of decisions made by employees who are constantly interacting with the customer, product, and service, or are in support of those who are. When those employees feel supported, integral to the system, and valued, they tend to make decisions as if they are owners. When they feel alienated, threatened, and immediately replaceable, they tend to make decisions as if they are visitors.

People virtually never take their rental cars to be cleaned, nor do they check the oil when they're forced to get gas. Employees need to be more than temporary occupants of their vehicle.

10. Innovative Mentality

This entire book is about the reality that "good enough" is not enough. The nine categories above, representing as they do the *processes* that organizations exhibit when they achieve *and maintain* outstanding performance, must be engaged in with a "test the envelope" kind of mentality. You can't be "as good as" the competition[13] because that never leads to market leadership. You have to be consistently better.

---

13. One of the primary fallacies in the mindless espousing of "benchmarking" and "best practices" is that these analyses of the competition delimit you to their standards. If one has to have a trendy label, "leapfrogging" would be more appropriate to represent an organization trying to do more than merely match its best competition.

William Penn once observed, "no cross, no crown." Contemporarily, we say, "no risk, no reward." But we intone it rather than practice it.

Marketplace leadership is not about perfection, it's about success. Great companies often make great errors. But they recover. Intel produced some flawed chips. Mercedes-Benz had to redesign its new European economy car when it consistently overturned in road trials. Bulgari has had some watches fail. Jay Leno and David Letterman sometimes bomb. The industry that brought us *Gone With the Wind* and *The Godfather* also brought us *Ishtar* and *Heaven's Gate*.

Love it or hate it, Microsoft has proven to be a company doing most of the things on my list very well. The result is two-fold: market dominance and a huge government antitrust suit. Innovation, in all aspects of an organization's processes, is a key to long-term, consistent success. However, it takes courage and commitment—and the ability to withstand legitimate risk as well as unfair attack—to sustain it.

I was called in by the British Standards Institute to help them survive and thrive in the new European community. This organization was charged with setting the standards in Britain for everything from cement to electrical connections, but no one was certain how it would fare when pan-European standards would be introduced. After two weeks of grueling work, an assortment of teams had come up with very innovative alternatives to preempt the competition and attempt to lead the new, larger market.

After sitting through the teams' presentations, the managing director (equivalent to our CEO) stood up and said, "If these ideas are really so good, I'm sure our competitors are already working on them. The fact that we have seen no indication of that tells me that the ideas probably aren't that good."

We could hear the air escape from the room, and the prospects for the British Standards Institute evaporate with them. Great companies take prudent risk—the Chrysler minivan, the Swatch watch, the Walkman, Schwab's discount brokerage—in order to achieve and maintain market leadership. That requires a certain measure of courage. But success is never final, and failure is seldom fatal.

It's courage that counts.

Challenge One

Raise the Bar, Don't Lower It

Train for the Pole Vault, Not the Limbo

There's an ancient story about a snail that climbs up on the back of a tortoise. As the latter ambles past, an observer can hear a tiny sound from the snail. Leaning closer, the observer hears the snail yelling, "Wheeeee . . ."

Everything is relative.

The Educational Testing Service (ETS) in Princeton, New Jersey, has "recalibrated" its testing, at the request of the National College Board, which owns the test, so that more recent Scholastic Aptitude Tests—long a yardstick used by college-bound students and their prospective schools—now provide higher scores. Whereas breaking the 1000 barrier was once considered good and a score of, say, 1300 superb (the test's maximum is 1600), today aspiring scholars can crack 1000 by doing the equivalent of a hundred points lower years ago. ETS says that the reconfiguration was necessary to better reflect the modern averages. The organization has sent a conversion chart to its customers that "raises" the old scoring to new levels for accurate comparisons. However, its critics say that it was done to make more people feel good about their results and to provide the opportunity for more students to create the illusion of better performance, despite their actual aptitude.

Society and business abound with such examples. Consider the following:

▲ About ten years ago the influx of Japanese industries into northern New Jersey and New York created a surge in Japanese expatriates residing in the former state's exclusive bedroom communities just outside of Manhattan. The school systems, already among the best around, accepted hundreds of serious, hard-working, highly disciplined Japanese students. An ideal addition, wouldn't you say? Well, not for the parents of the American students, who watched in horror as the Japanese kids threw the grading curves out the window and quickly took over the top spots. The American parents lobbied to lower the standards, so that their children could still be included among the highest performers in grades, even without performing as well. Apparently the idea of studying harder, investing more time, and meeting this new, higher standard was one whose time hadn't come.

I find company management attempting to make the same case all the time: Their people should receive higher bonuses despite their relative ranking in the performance evaluation system because of "extenuating circumstances" and "unforeseen competitive actions." People in business tend to spend more time, money, and energy attempting to circumvent the system than they do trying to simply succeed within it.

▲ Automated phone systems and voice mail options are superficially advanced technology to handle calls more efficiently. In some cases, they manage to do just that, and a human being with the right information and qualifications emerges from the ether at the other end of the help line. But more often, these devices simply *prolong* the waiting time, providing an appearance of progress as a customer circumnavigates the menu choices, but actually generating no better response whatsoever. Call Maryland Bank of North America (MBNA) or Fleet Mortgage Group or the outfit that owns your VISA card and you'll probably find bewildering options, lengthy waits, and mediocre service. The elaborate technology is cheaper and easier than staffing phone lines with a sufficient number of well-trained, personable customer service people. The classic scenario: You're asked to key in your 27-digit account number, followed by a five-minute wait, after which the service representative's first question is, "May I please have your account number?"

▲ A school board in Rhode Island passed a regulation stipulating that no student could play football if he failed a class academically. One failure, the board reasoned admirably, indicated that the youth required more time studying for a long-term future and less time on the short-term focus of organized athletics. The parents of weak students on the team rebelled, and demanded that their sons be allowed to play with at least one failing grade. Another school system dropped its traditional listing of the top ten scholars—as measured by objective grade point averages—in the yearbook, because other students would feel inferior by dint of their exclusion, irrespective of performance that didn't warrant inclusion.

Some firms have stopped giving out top sales awards, preferring to award teams, if they award anyone, so as not to make less stellar performers feel bad by comparison. There's nothing wrong with recognizing excellent teamwork, but there's also nothing wrong with recognizing superb individual performance. *The people who claimed that it doesn't matter whether you win or lose were not winning at the time they said it.*

▲ No matter where you are reading this book, the odds are that your phone call to directory assistance will not be answered by anyone familiar with your state, let alone your city. First, you will probably receive the option to name your city and desired listing for an automated voice.[1] If you wait for the directory assistance operator, you'll find that he or she is sitting somewhere in Phoenix or Des Moines, even though you're in Pennsylvania. In my original ignorance I said to one who couldn't find a restaurant listing, "Come on, it's right across from City Hall." She replied, "Sir, I'm in Arizona—*which* City Hall?"

▲ John Silber, erstwhile gubernatorial candidate in Massachusetts and president of Boston University, suggested not long ago that every child graduating from high school should demonstrate his or her accomplishments by passing a standardized test, not unlike the bar exam, but much, much easier. If a child failed, the diploma would be withheld until such time as the child could pass.[2] The State Board of Education battled the notion so furi-

---

1. Here's a technique to go directly to a human being: Press any number on the keypad when you get the automated request and you'll be routed to an operator. You're getting value from this book already.

2. See Mike Barnicle, "Good ideas aren't enough—gotta be cute too," *Providence Journal*, 24 December 1996, B5.

ously that Silber had to soften it, and the probabilities are that it will never go further. The mechanic who changes your oil must pass a test, and your hairdresser must be licensed, and even your supermarket gets inspections by the Board of Health, but your kids can get out of school without any assurance that they've actually learned anything useful once the strains of "Pomp and Circumstance" fade away (or that they even know what "Pomp and Circumstance" is).

▲ Robert Allen, before being forced out as CEO, and the board of AT&T, of whom we shall hear much more later, fired John Walter. This was their second consecutive cashiering of a president and heir apparent to Allen; Walter had been hand selected by the board from outside the industry, invested with all due hype and panoply, and lasted less than a year. Walter picked up $26 million for his departure, the equivalent of about $92,000 per day actually on the job. If a sales vice president hired and fired two consecutive sales managers in that fashion, his or her own competence would be questioned and the incumbent perhaps removed. The resultant outrage finally meant the end for Allen, a leader who consistently atoned for his own strategic mistakes by firing employees to maintain profit margins. An analogous situation occurred at Apple Computer, where Gil Amelio received $7 million with his pink slip, the second Apple CEO to be jettisoned in two years.[3] All of these cashiered princes left with a barrel full of the shareholders' money. No one is accountable at the upper levels for the sheer incompetence of these decisions. That level and rate of failure wouldn't be tolerated at the local charity golf tournament.

These same attitudes of protecting poor performance rather than providing the means to improve performance, and the resulting paucity of innovation and risk taking, have permeated all kinds and all sizes of institutions and enterprises. And we are often afraid to talk about it, even when business results are at risk.

This corporate "political correctness" mania has implications far beyond the normal issues with which it is usually associated, such as religion, minorities, women, gays, the disabled, and other

---

3. Apple lost $1.5 billion—that's *billion*—during his tenure, which is not easy to do.

members of the workforce and society. We have become loath to hurt anyone's feelings, and any indication that one person isn't performing as well as another has become equivalent to hurting their feelings. Incredibly, hurt feelings have become the basis for litigation, so avoiding them has taken on the same urgency as avoiding defective products and dangerous conditions. That's right—preventing others from feeling bad about themselves is now a business, as well as societal, priority.

A few examples:

Protecting poor performance reaches its apotheosis in business planning. The planning processes in most businesses are laughable. They consist of a bottom-up number, really nothing more than a best guess, which is deliberately conservative to pro tect the performer (the salesperson) from too tough a quota. (Think about it—if the impact of the number you turn in can be the difference between being fired for underperforming and earning incentive compensation for overperforming, just how aggressive are you going to be?) These intentionally misleading plans go up the line until the executives are faced with the difficult decision of trying to determine who is lying the least. Sometimes the entire plan is thrown out and, in the darkness of misinformation that results, ridiculously high quotas are assigned to everyone. But, more often, endless negotiations are held to arrive at numbers that everyone can barely live with, *irrespective of what the market actually merits.*

The avatar of this standard mangling occurred at Apple Computer, when the entire field force turned in highly conservative estimates in light of a performance system which paid handsome incentives for beating the forecast. The salespeople diligently turned in low numbers, only slightly improved by a sales management cadre also compensated for beating the plan. The company, in a nightmare of poor controls, had neither the market savvy nor the internal procedures to assess the accuracy of the plan, so it was accepted. Such plans, of course, affect more than projected revenues. They have a nasty habit of influencing manufacturing, inventory levels, promotion, and other minor facets of a business. The result was that Apple was unable to fill an overwhelming slew of orders. A great deal of the potential business was lost, many future long-term customers went elsewhere, existing customers were alienated, and Apple finally fired its CEO, though not for the last time.

This same, antiquated, don't-rock-the-boat approach to planning is currently used in most organizations. The results aren't often as catastrophic or obvious, but they are sapping productivity and undermining profitability annually, nonetheless. This is part of the "hollow core" of businesses that are enjoying a rising market but should be performing far better than they are. *Anyone can manage well in good times.* Strong economies make heroes out of mediocrities. It takes brilliant leadership to manage above and beyond the level reached within a general halcyon environment.

CLOSE ENOUGH FOR GOVERNMENT WORK IS NOT CLOSE ENOUGH

Even in the nongovernment world, we do seem to be under the impression that "close" is good enough. Legendary Kentucky basketball coach Adolph Rupp said that if winning doesn't really matter, why does anyone bother to keep score? Why, indeed?

No organizations I know hold the position that some prejudice, a little bias, and occasional harassment are tolerable in the workplace. Their policies on these issues are zero tolerance, as they should be. No one would dare claim that occasional bigotry is all right, as long as it's not the rule. Why, then, do we take the position—organizationally and personally—that a little poor performance, a soupçon of poor service, and a touch of missed commitments are tolerable?

Let's say that Toyota produces about 800,000 cars a year. Suppose it accepted a 0.5 percent error rate going out the door. One half of one percent of its vehicles would have defects noticeable to the customer (let alone potentially dangerous). That's a total of 4,000 vehicles that create at least 4,000 unhappy purchasers of their product. If the average time, labor and materials for rectifying the defects and restoring customer satisfaction were just $300 per car, the company would incur over a million dollar hit on its profit line to make things right. Toyota would never accept that, but others might.

For example, when Ford bought Jaguar, it sent a team of engineers to England to study the Jaguar manufacturing process. Although Ford might not have been the *ne plus ultra* of fanatic quality, the group was still shocked by what it found. At the end of the Jaguar assembly line was a team of mechanics whose specific job it was to correct defects in the just-produced cars. Jaguar, it seems, did not believe in building quality into the job, but rather thought it was a contingent action to deal with inevitable mishaps in the manufacturing process. Even the most die-hard Jaguar aficionados would admit that the car's mechanical history had been the equivalent of a nervous breakdown. It wasn't hard to understand why.

Toyota believes in zero defects. Jaguar believed in inevitable defects as necessary evils. Toyota is a thriving company while Jaguar, even with a distinct marque and rabid loyalty, needed a new buyer to save it.

How High Can We Go: Standards as Rewards and Not Measures

Standards don't relate solely to tangibles, levels of service, or quality, as the last example illustrates. They also relate to values, philosophy, and the ethics of doing business. In fact, these standards may be the most powerful of all, so when they decline, the very walls begin to tremble.

For example, it's always been ironic to me that organizations can muster the "courage" to fire 20,000 people at a time through the euphemism of "downsizing" but cringe in terror at the thought of confronting even a few poor performers.[4] In the former case of mass terror, neither the government nor the lawyers get much concerned about the slaughter, but in the latter case the entire organization's legal expertise becomes dedicated to explaining why poor performers have to be retained.

Actually, the lawyers are just doing their jobs, because in most cases the poor performers haven't been treated like poor performers, haven't been informed that they're poor performers, and haven't been compensated as though they're poor performers. Their managers have either neglected to give them a performance evaluation or have engaged in the spineless vanilla evaluation that essentially says, "Keep up the good work, whatever it is."

There are so many poor performers showing up at work each

---

4. See my book *Our Emperors Have No Clothes* (Franklin Lakes, N.J.: Career Press, 1995), for an extensive discussion of the horrors and productivity fallacies of downsizing as a strategy.

day without a clue about their actual lack of contribution that productivity inevitably suffers because:

▲ Poor performance goes unpenalized.
▲ Poor performers don't receive the opportunity to improve, perpetuating the poor performance.
▲ Better performers see the poor performance going unpenalized, and consciously or unconsciously lower their own performance to easier levels.
▲ Greater and greater amounts of management time are dedicated to rework and repair of failed work required by the poor performers.
▲ Expense cutbacks often result from the lowered profits engendered by poor performers.
▲ Expense cutbacks usually impede better performers and/or prevent better performers from being hired.
▲ In a bizarre tropism, the organization leans, like a plant seeking the sun, toward poorer and poorer performance through its own momentum.

The ultimate result in very poor performing organizations is downsizing to try to save profit on the expense line, which itself results in:

▲ Poor performance from those who remain and who feel guilty about departed colleagues.
▲ Poor performance from those who remain and who try to "hide" to avoid being downsized themselves in the future.
▲ Poor performance from the top remaining performers, who are now focused on finding better and more secure work elsewhere.

Hence, the organizational inability to confront immediate, sub-par performance will, systemically, create an inevitable inertia toward increasingly worse performance until senior management starts to stare blankly at the walls and mutter, "How did we get here?" They got there through the cowardice of an evaluation system which provides ratings rather than real measures. Dilbert, where are you when we need you?

The performance review forms in most organizations contain

the equivalent of a 1-to-5 scale, with these typical definitions (taken from an actual rating sheet):

1: Unacceptable performance requiring termination.
2: Fails to meet expectations and requires development.
3: Meets expectations.
4: Exceeds expectations.
5: Consistently performs at the very top levels of the job.

These ratings, of course, are a joke. The forms might as well be preprinted with "4" on all of them, and let's all get back to work.

No one today will accept the equivalent of a 3, "meets expectations." It's considered to be a slap in the face, an affront to one's dignity, the Yugo of ratings. And that's because management is consistently afraid to provide employees with honest feedback. After all, how are most American organizations performing today? I'll tell you how—they are meeting expectations at best, and some are failing to do even that. The current, explosive economy is hiding most of the flaws.

Where would you rank most organizations, private or public, large or small, profit or nonprofit? I think that the distribution would resemble a normal bell curve, with the preponderance smack in the middle.

If all those firms are meeting expectations, then it stands to reason that most of their employees, from top to bottom, are doing likewise, with the same small exceptions at either end of the bell curve. Yet that's not how those people are rated. The equivalent of 4 has become the norm, with commensurate expectations for salary, bonus, and whatever promotions remain in post-downsized America. We've not only allowed people to have their fantasies, we've encouraged them, because management has been afraid to establish true measures of performance, monitor against them regularly, and provide feedback to the performers. (How many people have performance reviews *more* than annually, unattached to some performance number or raise? Very, very few, that's how many. Performance reviews should be frequent, informal, and ongoing.)

A few years ago I worked with Calgon in Pittsburgh. At the end of one year in which the company had shown a good profit but hadn't met its performance goals for its parent, the CEO and I were reviewing the numbers.

"It kills me," he said, "to have to go to our owners having finished at only 90 percent of the profit target. We owed it to them and ourselves to have exceeded that goal, and we simply didn't perform as well as we could have."

"What I can't figure out, Fred," I noted, "is this large item for executive incentive. It's slightly over $900,000, and that's a significant drain on your bottom line. What does it represent?"

"That's the executive incentive program I inherited. This year, since the team didn't make the profit goal, they collect about 90 percent of the full potential."

"Let me understand this. You're showing up before your parent board of directors and telling them that you're spending close to a million bucks on incentive for a team *that missed their goal?*"

"It's crazy, isn't it? That's the way they've done it here."

As the doctor says, then stop doing that.

At Mallinckrodt Veterinary, Paul Cottone, a new CEO, found that his people had come to expect the "exceeds expectations" accolade as normally as they would expect the health plan to re-imburse them for a doctor's visit. Performance wasn't exactly a key determinant. He recognized the problem when the perform-ance reviews came back with glowing recommendations for an organization that had just managed to eke out an acceptable year. The organization was at a 3, and the cumulative ratings were at a 4.[5]

The next year we reeducated the organization, and it was the equivalent of "cold turkey" withdrawal. We demanded a "zero tolerance" policy, in that everyone would have clear performance goals with the understanding that meeting them was a require-ment of the job and constituted "meets expectations," which was a fine rating that the overwhelming preponderance of employees would find on their evaluation form if it were a year in which the company made plan, and nothing more. Standards were estab-lished for exceeding expectations and for failing to meet expecta-tions, and there would inevitably be more of one or the other if

---

5. Most secretaries in a variety of organizations have told me that they routinely get 4s and even 5s in lieu of salary increases. Since they rarely participate in any bonus plan, and their raises are so minuscule, their bosses give them top ratings despite their actual performance as a sop to keep them happy. Consequently, many companies have highly rated secretaries even when they have poor clerical work.

the company's fortunes rose or fell. Three categories, clear goals, zero tolerance for exceptions. The following sequence occurred:

▲ A lot of people moaned and groaned.
▲ Most of their managers moaned and groaned and carried others' objections upward.
▲ The managers were turned around and told to toe the company line or find other work.
▲ The system was applied fairly and objectively, albeit not without further moaning and groaning.
▲ The system worked well. Ratings actually reflected contribution, and increases and promotions were based upon that contribution. No one wasted any time trying to "work the system."
▲ The organization's investment in people is now commensurate with the performance of its people. The performance evaluation system has become a legitimate management investment with a strong return, rather than an energy-draining "necessary evil" that consumed resources.

The notions of "equal finish" and false equity have to end. Otherwise an equal start doesn't matter.

SOLUTIONS: RAISE THE BAR AND STOP CREEPING UNDER IT

Disdain for excellence must be replaced with the pursuit of excellence, and all of the reward, gratification, and respect that the latter merits.

Twenty years ago the U.S. Marine Corps was famous for taking anything that could walk and turning it into a lean, mean fighting machine. The marines never retreated, and only once in their history was the order given to "hold ground" and not advance. This is an organization that survived on brute force and manic discipline. But it's moving forward on higher standards and innovative approaches in an increasingly technological world.

Marine Commandant, Lt. Gen. Charles Krulak, said the Corps needs "intellectual agility."[6] Consequently, recruits are get-

6. See Richard J. Newman, "The few, the proud, the smart, the moral," *U.S. News & World Report*, 16 December 1996, 33–34.

ting harder to find. Nevertheless, the Marines have raised the bar, not lowered it. They teach values that might not have been inculcated earlier in a recruit's life: teamwork, sacrifice, decision making, and a focus on objectives. The command structure seems to have understood that you can raise standards, even in tough times (fewer volunteers, poorer recruiting pools, lack of a major threat to our national security) by working harder to find the right people, preparing them well, and showing zero tolerance for exceptions.

There are at least four major areas in which the pursuit of excellence can be accelerated. We need to learn from the Marines.

1. Organizations Have to Set Standards That Are Stretches, Not Accommodations

Since Gordon Bethune took over Continental Airlines, he has installed incentive systems that are based on beating the standards for luggage delivery, on-time performance and customer complaints. The airline has metamorphosed under his leadership. Southwest Airlines has a CEO in Herb Kelleher who leads by example, establishes tough standards (they can turn a plane around in fifteen minutes or less) and supports those goals consistently (he uses a single variety of aircraft to minimize parts, training, and confusion). "Stretch goals" are set by leaders who can view the organization holistically and provide for a consistent set of support resources, all aligned to reach and exceed that new goal.

In general, employees should receive a base salary, based upon expected performance, that represents a decent lifestyle in the geographic area of employment (i.e., ability to pay a moderate mortgage, drive a midsized car, take a week's vacation). All other remuneration, which represents the opportunity for an enhanced lifestyle (private schooling, a vacation home, a luxury car) should be based upon achievement above and beyond that which is expected. Whether on the production floor, in the field force, in the research lab, or in finance, incentive compensation must be based on a combination of exceeding performance requirements and the organization, commensurately, exceeding its plans. (See Chapter 7 for a discussion of executive compensation, a situation so ghastly as to merit a separate section and a suitable cooling-off space.)

Not long ago I worked with a CEO puzzling over whether to

adhere to a promised 4 percent merit increase or reduce the amount to 2.5 percent, given an underperformance by the organization.

"Larry," I said, "this is not a merit increase."

"Of course it is," he explained. "We plan for it at the beginning of the year, and it's built into the plan. The problem is that we won't make our profit number if we distribute the entire amount."

"The word *merit* means 'earned.' This is just an award, an arbitrary increase, a 'feel good' raise. Not everyone has performed equally well, not everyone has performed with merit and, in fact, if you're missing your profit numbers you probably don't have a whole lot of 'merit' out there."

"What are you suggesting?"

"Don't give the raise at all, and certainly don't plan it like this again. If you give people more money each year for doing nothing more than their jobs (or less, in this case), that's exactly what you'll get in return."

People should be paid for their expected performance, and receive incentive for performance above and beyond what's expected.[7]

2. Pretend You're a Customer

Organizations routinely neglect to "shop their own businesses" often enough. Internal perceptions are rarely congruent with customers' perceptions because they are filtered though the lenses of people whose interest is in not trying harder. Every executive should spend 5 percent of his or her time calling the service numbers, shopping in the outlets, returning something for repair, applying for a credit card, and generally testing the system from "the other side." When I implement this with clients they are almost always shocked at what they find. This activity is far more important than endless staff meetings filled with people who tell you what you want to hear and hide the worst news by using smoke, mirrors, and smooth talk.

---

7. And remember that the presence of money is never a true motivator, although its absence is often a demotivator. If you give more money to an unhappy employee, you create a wealthier, unhappy employee.

Hyatt Hotel executives are known for the day they spend each year exchanging places with luggage handlers, front desk clerks, and curbside greeters. While it's largely symbolism, it's also an attempt to find out what customers are experiencing and employees are hearing. However, it's better to go one step beyond and *be* a customer. Why are executives so shocked to read the latest, expensive reports on service, dependability, and responsiveness compiled by expensive consultants when they could find out for themselves any time they truly wanted? I remember telling a pharmaceutical division president that the division receptionist was a royal pain to deal with. He was aghast.

"She must be having a bad day. Or maybe *you're* having a bad day," he archly suggested.

"Well, she's like that every time I visit you. When was the last time you called her on the phone without revealing who you are?"

"I never have occasion to call her."

"Well, pick up the phone and let's make an occasion."

A week later she was transferred to other duties. It's often not the volition that's missing, it's the awareness.

One manufacturing president whom I advised to do this was aghast to find out *he couldn't reach himself* by phone! The voice mail system and a coterie of gatekeepers and protectors kept shunting him off to alternatives at lower levels. The impression of the "customer" was that the president was aloof, unreachable, and uninterested. The system was changed the next day.

3. Avoid the "Extended Fix"

When something goes wrong continually, we shouldn't fix it—we should improve it. Weak links aren't meant to be shored up. The whole chain should be replaced. Too many businesses keep applying Band-Aids over Band-Aids. Pretty soon, they look like a mummy, and move about as nimbly as Boris Karloff used to, draped in centuries of rotting bandages and dissolving chemicals.

If something has to be fixed repeatedly, don't give merit badges to the people with their fingers in the dike. Ask why no one has built a better water management system. When our friends at the postal service couldn't really guarantee to get anything, anywhere reliably the next day, Fred Smith didn't respond by starting FedEx with the mundane notion of finding better optical scanners, hiring better people, or using different zip codes. He decided that the existing delivery system was as patched as it could get without crumbling under the weight of its own repairs. So he implemented a hub-and-spoke system that allows a package from New York to get to Detroit the next morning by going through Memphis.

In Massachusetts, the division of motor vehicles, usually the favorite target of anyone who hates bureaucracy, has set up local storefront offices that have diminished waiting times and even offer alternative poses for the dreaded license picture. In Rhode Island, the motor vehicle bureau's people handle the problem of long lines by putting up additional ropes and stanchions to control the crowds. Do we really need a high-priced consultant to tell us who serves the public better, and which agency might receive more tax funding with less outcry?

A key aspect of rewarding the pursuit of excellence rather than the restoration of mediocrity is in rewarding *behavior*, and not simply "victories." If we only award the victorious (a new account brought in, a new system implemented) then people will tend to be quite conservative in their actions. After all, if only a "win" will gain reward, then I want to wait until conditions are most assured for the victory, which will be very seldom indeed. But if you reward the behavior, even if the victory isn't imminent, you show people the right route.[8]

If a salesperson creates a superb client presentation, brings in heavy artillery from the corporate office, generates references from analogous organizations, but still loses the business because the client chose a vice president's cousin for the job, that salesperson should be lauded for a magnificent effort, not condemned for failing to shoot the cousin. When a bus driver is late finishing a route because several senior citizens had chosen the wrong bus and required detailed instructions to find the correct one, that driver should be praised for the sound use of judgment.

I was browsing in a Cadillac dealership once in which I was

---

8. You might be thinking that this is contradictory to earlier tenets about paying people for performance above and beyond expectations. But the "reward" I'm speaking of is nonfinancial, as are most rewards at work. Recognition, visibility, key assignments, more latitude of action and similar provisions provide the reward necessary for those daring to try new things.

the only customer. Four salespeople lounged around, two talking, one reading, and one drinking coffee. Not one approached me. I finally had to ask for help from an entirely unhelpful salesman. Yet the dealership proudly proclaimed on the wall the "sales leaders of the month." I wonder how much higher those sales totals would be if the sales manager were out there praising the people who ran to offer assistance and greet customers, and penalizing those who chose not to. The sales leader of the month was the best of a mediocre lot. Successful organizations seldom examine how much more successful they could be if they focused on behaviors that lead to success and not just the "victory" created by success. Many car dealerships folded after years of profitable business because the traditional clientele whose predictable return for a new car every few years made the salespeople into mere order takers either died off or were lured away by the (mostly foreign) competition.

Several of my clients have implemented an annual award for "the best idea that didn't work." Sometimes it's presented, complete with loving cup or trophy, at an employee awards banquet, and sometimes it's presented with a gift certificate at the employee's desk. In either case, it's a direct reinforcement from the executives that an idea might not have come to fruition, but the thinking behind it is what the organization needs and values.

4. Regularly Raise the Bar of Achievement

Hewlett-Packard, critiqued earlier, deserves credit where credit is due because of its prevailing philosophy: Find an area that is working really well in meeting its goals and then tear it apart to find out how it can do still better. The intent is to continually raise the bar, and to raise it in areas where it's already high. You don't set world records—in this case, become a world-class organization—by helping people who are clearing 12 feet to clear 12½ feet. You do it by clearing the world record height, over 20 feet, with your best people.

Figure 1-1 shows the difference between restoring performance to past levels of mediocrity and raising the bar to new heights. Most problems cause a brief panic that prompts management to "get it fixed." Ascending to the old, acceptable level is considered progress, and the problem solvers move on to the next "fix." Hewlett-Packard raises the bar even when there aren't any

Figure 1-1. Restoring mediocrity versus raising the bar.

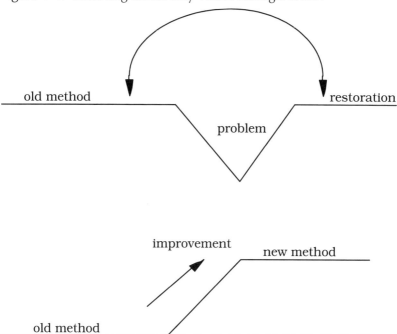

problems. But even the presence of problems can create an effective trigger.

Several years ago, Mercedes-Benz of North America asked me to visit various dealers to find those who were providing outstanding service in the perception of their customers. At the time, Lexus and Infiniti were eating Mercedes' lunch, and thoroughly outperforming it in customer satisfaction surveys. Mercedes intelligently reasoned that some of its dealerships were providing superior service, and such standards could be emulated elsewhere. In other words, why reinvent the wheel?

What we found was shockingly simple. There were some outstanding Mercedes dealers in the service area, and the franchise owners reported consistently that they owed their continually improving service standards to problems. Nick Viti, one of those franchise owners, told me that problems were an opportunity to improve and to shine.

"We don't just seek to fix a problem," said Nick at the time. "We want to understand what would restore the customer's confidence in us, show the customer that we are responsive and will spare nothing to correct the situation, then understand what we can do to improve the process that caused the failing."

(This makes eminent sense to me. When room service arrives accurately and on time at your hotel, you don't call your spouse to exclaim that the room service was delivered properly. But if your order was delivered inaccurately, or late, or cooked poorly, and the hotel provides a new dinner at no charge or reduces your room rate, you'll probably remark about their gracious response to the problem.)

All dealerships were placing paper mats on the floors of the cars to protect the interiors during servicing. But some high-performing ones had the technicians remove the mats in the presence of the customer, to show that they were in place and to dispose of them without the customer having to do so later. All dealerships provided loaner cars, but the high-performing ones picked up and delivered, by having employees drive loaner cars home and leave them at customer houses first thing the following morning when cars were picked up for servicing.

Every employee in these high-performing franchises was encouraged and recognized to come forward with suggestions. Every day the operation gained a few inches on the bar. Every day meetings were held to discuss further improvements. And every day, customers referred friends and acquaintances to the showrooms. *Improve by 1 percent a day, and in 70 days you're twice as good.* I call this "the 1 percent solution" (TM). Yet few organizations gain that daily 1 percent because they're overwhelmed trying to fix problems and restore standards to the old levels.

We inordinately reward the fixing of problems and restoration of past performance levels, and neglect to reward, or even support, raising the bar to new heights. While it's important to praise the firefighter who risks life and limb to douse the flames, it's even more important to recognize the fire marshal who determines new ways to prevent fires and consequent loss of life and property. In our organizations we can use the occurrence of problems to search for new levels and new practices. The idea is not to be satisfied at the restoration level but to seek the new level that represents true improvement, as shown graphically in Figure 1-2.

I wrote to Robert Booth when he became the new president of Hammacher Schlemmer, the high-end catalog company, to tell him how egregiously poor their backordering, billing, and cus-

Figure 1-2. Using a problem to reach new levels.

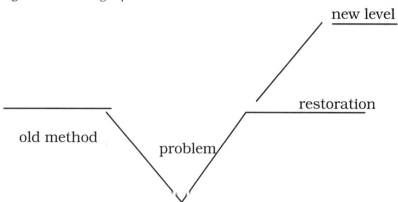

tomer service functions had been performing. He called me personally to apologize, and told me that he understood my reluctance to continue being a customer. He told me things would change, and acknowledged the problems.

He wrote to me six months later. He explained how he had empowered lower level managers, who quickly located and corrected flaws in the ordering and planning processes. Back-orders had been reduced by two-thirds. There were still problems, he said, and they served to motivate everyone concerned to find better ways to get things done. He invited me to give them another try whenever I was ready.

I have. There's a person who is raising the bar and pursuing excellence.

HOW RAISING THE BAR RAISES PERFORMANCE

We don't work on the basis of perfect planning systems. In fact, the variables of technology, competition, global economies, consumer perceptions, media influence, and government regulation—to name just a few—create havoc with every strategic plan and every set of projections and assumptions about the market. However, the worst, most insidious nature of the planning process is that it may work. In other words, the trouble with a plan is that you may just hit it.

I've been in any number of organizations in which the powers-that-be announce that "Next year we will grow by 12 percent in the Northeast." It's accepted and chanted as the corporate mantra, spoken with the fervor of the converted zealot. The phrase appears on company memos, in E-mail, and on secret decoder rings. And, more times than we'd suspect, that organization does, indeed, meet its 12 percent growth goals in the Northeast. The trouble is, the company should have grown by 32 percent, given the market and state of the competition. But it only grew by 12 percent *because that is what it had prepared itself to do.*

While working for State Street Corporation, the huge Boston-based, global financial and investment institution, I had occasion to deliver my observations to CEO Marsh Carter on several occasions. State Street had been enjoying compound annual growth of about 22 percent for Carter's entire tenure at the helm.

"It's a great position to be in," he observed modestly. "We are striving to continue to meet it for our shareholders and for the investment community."

"I'm curious," I said, "in how you know the number should be in the low twenties. Since you're dominant in certain aspects of custody, are moving rapidly to newer technology platforms, and are growing in investments that suit a growing elderly population, how do you know your growth number shouldn't be 30 percent, or 34 percent, or even 40 percent?"

Marsh Carter, a decorated Vietnam veteran and one of the most intellectual of all the CEOs I've every worked with, regarded me for a few seconds, finally smiled, and said, "We don't."

Great organizations have to continually test the envelope. They have to push their upper limit of performance because, literally, they don't know how good they are. Here are some criteria that separate out the good but complacent organizations from the continually unsatisfied great ones:

Good Companies	Great Companies
▲ Maximize the things they do to remain at high levels of performance and protect their positions.	▲ Find out what brought them to high levels of performance, and use those processes to raise the bar still higher.
▲ Meticulously develop all underperforming employees.	▲ Fanatically reward and foster the most productive and innovative employees.

▲ Minimize risk and maximize benefit.

▲ Analyze and improve poorly performing departments and subsidiaries.

▲ Promote overwhelmingly from within to demonstrate loyalty and build morale.

▲ Understand what the customer wants.

▲ Separate idea generators from the implementers of new initiatives.

▲ Voraciously solve problems.

▲ Stick to what they know well and focus on core competencies.

▲ Create strategies that serve as templates and road maps to the future.

▲ Engage aggressively in prudent risk.

▲ Analyze and improve top-performing departments and subsidiaries.

▲ Promote using a combination of internal and external people, to ensure new ideas.

▲ Understand what the customer needs.

▲ Encourage idea generators to implement their own initiatives.

▲ Voraciously look for new opportunities.

▲ Readily look at unassociated areas which may have non-obvious synergies.

▲ Use strategy as a framework which can be adjusted and fine-tuned continually.

How Do You Raise the Bar When You're in Trouble to Begin With?

One of the great management stories of the last part of the twentieth century isn't Microsoft or GE or Amazon.com. It's Continental Airlines.

When Gordon Bethune took over, the airline was mired in problems, including poor customer service, desperately unhappy employees, and chaotic attempts to "fix" the operation. At one point, someone in an executive pair of shoes decided that there should be "no frills" flights, with one, low-fare economy class, while the airline continued to compete simultaneously with full-fare carriers. The corporate brain trust actually believed it could concurrently compete with Southwest Airlines and American Airlines. Of course, it could do neither. The result was scheduling migraines, with "no-frills" all-economy equipment showing up at gates that were boarding full-fare, first-class customers for five-hour flights. Continental had become the joke of the industry.

As CEO, Bethune did not focus solely on fixing those problems. It was simple to end the conflicting levels of service and to stop trying to be all things to all people. Any first-year MBA student could have done that, and any consultant worth a damn would have recommended it in the first twenty minutes of an assignment. An average CEO would have stanched the hemorrhaging, and tried a modest improvement or two, but basically would not have rocked the boat for fear of still more customer, employee, and investment desertions.

Bethune did something breathtakingly brilliant and bold. He looked at the key indices that constituted airline success with the public and, commensurately, for profitability. Not surprisingly, they included metrics such as on-time arrival and bags delivered on time. He told the employees on no uncertain terms that Continental was going to be an industry leader in these areas, and that employees would share in the success, since only they could account for it. Bethune stated that every Continental employee would receive a direct cash bonus if the airline finished in the first or second position in these measures according to FAA statistics.

He did this based on the achievement, not on a bean-counter's subsequent measure of the impact on profitability. Great leaders have to show confidence in their plans, and he was confident that if Continental could raise the bar in those areas, profit would result. Within a year, Continental had not only become number one in those and other performance areas, but had turned around the morale of its workforce, become the darling of Wall Street, generated the highest rating for its frequent flier program in *Frequent Flyer Magazine*'s survey of its readership, and improved its in-flight service to the point where it is now regarded as one of the best in the business.[9]

Our approach to problems is to solve them. However, that's not good enough. Nick Viti, cited above, used problems as his

---

9. At one point, Bethune felt that Continental's placement in one of the indices was lower than it should have been due to a competitor's fudging of its numbers. When the FAA refused to change the standings based on Bethune's protests, he rewarded his people as if they has been in the number one position and unilaterally announced that they actually were.

springboard to better serve customer needs. Gordon Bethune used problems to leapfrog to new levels of performance. We've become obsessed with fixing and moving on, rather than fixing *and moving up.*

How Do You Raise the Bar When You're Doing Just Great?

Ever since 1929 there's been a struggle to just get close to Babe Ruth's baseball record of 60 home runs hit in one season. The record stood for thirty-four years, one of the most enduring and unassailable in all of sports. Some years, tantalizingly, a player or two would hit 52, or 56, or even 58. But not every year, and not many players. Finally, Roger Maris hit 61 in 1961.

Suddenly, in 1998, two players, Sammy Sosa of the Cubs and Mark McGwire of the Cardinals, *both* surpassed the mark in the same season, each *ahead* of the pace that Ruth had maintained,[10] with McGwire ultimately shattering the record by 16 percent with a total of 70 home runs in a single season. The sports world (and much of the non-sports world) was captivated by a seemingly unapproachable level of performance exceeded by two different people, with one of them not just edging past it but completely eclipsing it.

This isn't as unusual as it sounds, even in sports in which records are measured in fractions of seconds or centimeters, or by subjective figure-skating judges from unknown countries. When Bob Beamon broke the then-record for the long jump in the late 1960s, he did so by *feet*, not inches. Some said it was a once-in-a-lifetime jump. But hadn't Beamon been training for the long jump every day for years? He never trained to exceed the prior record by just two inches; he trained to jump *as far as he possibly could.* Mark McGwire didn't take batting practice and undergo fitness training so that he could hit one home run more than Babe Ruth. He was trying to hit as many as he could, and he was trying to hit one every time he came to bat.

Beamon and McGwire are gifted athletes. They don't train to maintain their particular status quo. They train to continually improve, sometimes breaking prior "bests" by dramatic degrees. The same principle holds for great organizations. They can't

---

10. They hit more home runs than Ruth in fewer games and fewer at-bats.

"train" to maintain their current level of excellence, even if that standard is an industry leader at the moment. They have to "train" to break their own records every day. That means that organizational leadership must constantly—daily, unceasingly— examine factors such as these:

- ▲ Why are our best operations performing that way? How can they perform even better? How can we take what they do and transfer it to other areas not performing as well?
- ▲ How can our reward system be improved to create more initiative? How can we use our employees' talent still better?
- ▲ What might our customers need that they don't realize? How can we "surprise" our customers with products or services that they aren't expecting, representing a very high-value relationship between them and our company?
- ▲ How can we use technology to take something we're doing well now to still another level?
- ▲ How can we improve our communications with the marketplace so that our market intelligence is more insightful, more anticipatory, and more accurate?
- ▲ What can we do with our financial resources that will propel us to greater marketplace advantage?
- ▲ What is changing today—in society, government, technology, global commerce, belief systems—that we should be exploiting?

Organizations that achieve greatness temporarily can experience the greatest of falls if they allow that temporary success to become an opiate for their infallibility. Nike can attest to that; IBM experienced it; Sears went through it; Boeing was mired in it in the late 1990s; GM can't seem to escape it. The key is not to pad the executive compensation funds and batten down the hatches when you're on top. The key is to take the risks and set the ever-higher standards that one expects of an industry leader.

Hewlett-Packard has had a history of tearing apart its best operations to try to improve them still more. Jack Welch has demanded that every GE division be number one or two in its marketplace. Harold Geneen, as CEO of the old ITT conglomerate, wanted a minimum of 5 percent net after-tax return from every subsidiary. 3M's strategy is that at least 25 percent of revenues have to be generated by products that didn't exist five years prior.

It's far easier to operate from a position of strength. When companies (or divisions or departments or subsidiaries) are leading the pack, they can't become defensive and seek to protect their rear. That's the time to critically reexamine what they currently do to seek out a still better way to do it. Experiment and failure are not nearly so costly when the organization is in a strong, profitable position. Change, however, is never as effective and is always much more difficult from a position of weakness and desperation.

WHAT IF YOU ATTEMPT TO RAISE THE BAR AND IT FALLS ON YOU?

Not all changes attempts are successful. The Nehru jacket comes to mind, along with Quadraphonic sound, midi-skirts, and Beta-format video recorders. There are two aspects of failure to consider.

First, we'll go back to William Penn. Unless you're willing to take risks, there are no rewards. The Edsel might have failed and disappeared unappreciated, but Ioccoca learned about the growing demand for "lifestyle" cars, and produced the Mustang out of the debacle. Post-It Notes arose out of the failure of a new glue to adhere permanently. Xerox was born as a new company because IBM rejected the offer to buy the technology, citing it as impractical and unwanted.

Organizations often tout a "freedom to fail" philosophy that doesn't ring true: Employees have the freedom to fail, all right, *once!* After that failure, they get whacked. If Bob Allen could make a $300 million error in a failed attempt to get into the computer business while CEO of AT&T, if Jack Welch can survive a dismal effort to get into the securities business during his watch at GE, if Bob Crandall survived his inappropriate discussions of fare structure with another airline CEO when he was trying to rationalize prices while running American, then I guess we can attest that mistakes do happen. As long as the attempt was in the best interests of the company, its customers, and shareholders, then failure is understandable and forgivable.

A far worse kind of failure is sloth. That occurs daily, in organizations in which employees at all levels are told, formally and informally, "don't rock the boat." If you try something new and it fails, you're history. "Not invented here" is the company fight song. If you're not actively trying to improve the operation, then the place is, in fact, retrogressing. It's impossible to merely fight a "holding action" in the organizational arena today, because advances in technology, increasing customer demands, shifting world markets and a host of other independent variables are forever affecting the landscape. To "defend one's turf" and try to remain happily immobile is to slip backward.

Only aggressive, innovative organizations can maintain the high ground, much less move to higher ground, in today's conditions. And those conditions are going to get tougher and tougher. If Kodak, Sears, IBM, GM, Prudential, and Delta Airlines can seriously stumble, then so can anyone. And not everyone has their resources or original market positioning to enable a gradual return to prominence.

The second factor in the raised bar's potential to fall on your head is to ensure that you're raising it correctly. Prudent risk doesn't mean wild gamble. Innovation doesn't mean "let's throw what we can against the wall." Clever positioning doesn't mean latching on to the fad du jour.

Here is a checklist for change. Consider this the operations manual or the instruction sheet for raising the bar.

1. Capitalize on Success

If you, a competitor, a vendor, or a customer are dramatically successful in some area of the business, it's an invitation to innovate. However, more companies simply assume that "doing more of the same thing" is innovating. It's not. It's simply doing more of the same thing, and that's a brainless response to success. (You don't need highly paid people to say, "We're doing well there, so let's do more of it.") When the airlines were overwhelmed with response to the frequent flier programs, hotels and rental car companies quickly developed affiliations. When it was determined that voice mail could effectively take messages and satisfy callers (most of the time), it was quickly adapted to take orders.

Instruction: When you're good at something, don't stop there.

2. Capitalize on Failure

Sometimes the bar falls. Always wear a hard hat. Then find out why it fell and raise it even higher on the next attempt. Don't simply repair weak links, use them to create higher levels of lift.

Fred Smith founded FedEx on the postal service's weak link of not being able to deliver anything, anywhere reliably the next day. He didn't seek to compete with them on their own terms. He created a hub-and-spoke method that enabled overnight delivery to work. The Edsel gave birth to the Mustang. The inability of major airlines to cater to non-business travelers seeking low fares created Southwest Airlines.

Instruction: When something isn't working, try to reach the same objective with a completely different alternative.

3. Engage a Sponsor

Ideas are ephemeral, until someone with a budget comes along and says, "Hey, I like that," in which case they become business plans. Raising the bar requires a backer who usually possesses three traits: The backer has a budget to support the idea (or can acquire it); can draw people to the cause through leadership, charisma, brute force, or other redeeming characteristics; and can tolerate setback and delay. The sponsor is the person (or people) who protect the idea from the forces of sloth. When IBM successfully developed the first personal computers, it did so by assembling a team of executives whose charge was to protect the development team from the rest of IBM. Some insightful managers realized that their own culture would otherwise kill the nascent idea.

Instruction: It's best to have as many sponsors as possible, but you need at least one in front clearing the way, and another behind protecting your rear.

4. Utilize Technology

There is virtually nothing immune to technology today, although that's not always good. Voice mail, E-mail, cell phones and their brethren can all be major productivity enhancers as well as huge energy drains. Technology can't be used for its own sake, but it should be utilized for the sake of the idea and the customer. Internet listings and purchase opportunities are becoming a normal part of commerce. Hertz will now include electronic navigational aids in your rental car for a slightly additional fee. You can raise the bar manually, but it's a lot easier and usually more powerful to use technology to help.

Instruction: *Merging technologies provides synergies that leapfrog the competition. Don't make it complicated, but do make it comprehensive.*

5. Maximize Your Timing

Never wait until you've plateaued to make your next move. Always make it on the way up. This is called, "jumping the S-curves." Any product, service, or relationship, if of any quality, will grow dramatically, but eventually plateau. This is because technology surpasses it, the competition usurps it, or the consumer simply grows tired of it. You should make the "leap" (the next move, the bar raising), while you're still in the ascendancy, not after you've plateaued. Don't milk every ounce of advantage from your position, but use your growth to springboard you to the next level, the next S-curve, as shown in Figure 1-3. No one in

Figure 1-3. Leaping the S-curves.

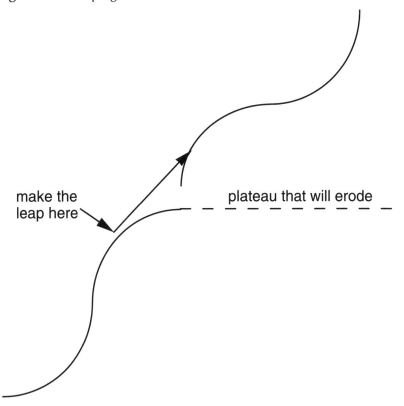

make the
leap here   plateau that will erode

the vacuum tube business successfully entered the transistor business that replaced it. Microsoft, however, has smoothly jumped from one S-curve to the next, never allowing itself to wallow in its past successes.

Instruction: *If you find that the climb has gotten easier, it's probably because you're on level ground. Look up.*

After reading this chapter, some of you might have concluded that Microsoft, used as an example at the very end, actually embodies a great deal of the traits, actions, and philosophies required to continually raise the bar. That's quite true. And in 1998 they were sued by the government. A sign of the times?

> An individual walking down the street came upon a friend stooped over the sidewalk. "What are you looking for?" he inquired.
>
> "I'm looking for my car keys. I must have dropped them earlier."
>
> "Where exactly do you think you dropped them?"
>
> "Somewhere down the block, near the restaurant where I had dinner."
>
> "Then why are you looking for them here?"
>
> "Because the light is better here."
>
> *There's no sense going to better lighting if the area is not relevant to our search. It's better to work in what light we have. It might be tough to find what we're looking for, but it's there someplace.*

Challenge Two
Create Accountability
No One Rallies Behind Generals Who Fall off Their Horses

There is no hidden, unseen "they" in corporations, plotting to undermine and subvert every well-intentioned effort, yet that pronoun is used more than any other. "They" won't let me do it. "They" don't have a clue. "They" are the ones at fault. I once conducted a strategy session for the top officers of National Westminster Bank in New York City. At one point, discussing a particularly innovative new idea, the consensus among the group was "they would never allow it." Was it the CEO? No, he was very supportive. Was it the government? No, it wasn't a regulatory matter. Was it the employees? No, they would probably welcome it.

"I've got news for you," I explained, "YOU ARE 'THEY!' " Even top-level people resort to the omnipresent "they" to excuse inaction, indecisiveness, and sloth.

There are great companies and organizations that believe the opposite, of course. They believe that the executives are there to make sometimes difficult calls but that, even in areas of ambiguity, there are ethical compasses and moral rudders. George Merck, the iconographic figure in Merck & Company's corporate history, said once that if you do good, good will follow. That is, if the company does what's right for the physician and the patient, there's no reason to think that those criteria won't provide for a decent return for the shareholders. George Merck's words are included in Merck's annual report, his intent is embodied in the research and production of profound products for human health, and his company has achieved one of the most dramatic examples of annual compound profit growth of any business on the planet.

There is no "they." There are no people with green eyeshades and sleeve protectors locked away in a dusty room controlling everyone's fate (not even in the law schools).

I once worked with a huge and prosperous diversified financial services firm. The CEO, reasonably enough, expected that his top management should be able to translate the corporate strategy into operating realities for their troops. When that translation seemed to be garbled, he ordered up a series of 20-person sessions for his entire senior team of over 100, to help create alignment and a uniform technique. I facilitated every one of those sessions, and we didn't exactly break the land-speed record for gaining accountability. Almost everyone felt that it was the CEO's problem along with his four top reports, and *they* weren't providing enough detail, *they* were not presenting a uniform message, *they* were not a solid team, and *they* would have to fix it.

With one group—all talented, intelligent people in a successful business—I ventured down a different path. I said, "Forget strategy. What if you decided to implement a common E-mail system [the absence of which created chronic communications problems]? Assuming for the moment that all twenty-two of you agreed 100 percent on both the objective and the alternative, how would the system be implemented and how long would it take?"

The group started to debate which of them or their colleagues would make the call, who would have to be involved, how the budget might be obtained, and so on. Finally, there was a lull. "Well?" I asked, "who's got the ball on this?" They stared at the ceiling then stared at their fingernails. "Come on," I insisted, "who's in charge here?"

"It would seem," offered one senior vice president after what appeared to be agonizing internal debate, "that the CEO would have to make that call."

"The CEO?!" I shouted incredulously. "Do you mean that the CEO has to make the decision on E-mail and no one in this room can do that? He's sitting downstairs in his office expecting you to make those calls. That's why nothing's getting done in terms of new initiatives, strategic or otherwise!" Everyone agreed it was a good time to take a break.

Not too long ago I stayed in a Hyatt Hotel that had a guest services "hot line." A card near the telephone proclaimed:

Hyatt Hotline
No problem too big or too small!
Call the Hyatt Hotline:
For instant response
dial extension 21.

I did not have a room service menu. I immediately realized that this was a job for the Hyatt Hotline. I dialed extension 21.

"Hyatt Hotline. How may I help you?"

"This is Alan Weiss, room 732. I don't have a room service menu."

"I'm sorry, but we don't handle that. Try banquets, extension 19. Thanks for calling the Hotline."

As the line went dead I was busy trying to figure out what level of emergency would merit the attention of the Hyatt Hotline. Perhaps nuclear war?

The prevailing attitude of the Hyatt Hotline was not one of service and "no problem too big or too small," but rather TNMJ: That's Not My Job. TNMJ has become the scourge of American organizations[1] and it has sapped the vitality out of most of them.

The Ritz-Carlton chain provides that any employee can approve an expense of up to $2,500 to resolve a guest's problem on the spot. A luggage handler, reservations agent or restaurant worker can thereby immediately offer something to assuage an outraged guest. There is no need to involve management in the

---

1. Lest you think this is a uniquely American affliction, take small solace in the fact that it's often much worse elsewhere. The United Kingdom is a land of particularly indifferent service. In most hotels, the equivalent of the concierge—the "hall porter"—is a distinguished-looking person who feels the job requires nothing more than that appearance. One affable chap once sent my bags to the airport in another person's limo, remarking to me that "It's up to the guests to watch their luggage, not me."

vast majority of instances. In response to complaints about excess noise, a poor meal, a prolonged wait for a car, and other hotel nemeses, guests can be offered an upgraded room, free meal, complimentary parking, or whatever it takes, and it usually takes considerably less than $2,500.

Do employees sometimes offer a benefit worth $1,000, when $500 would have satisfied the guest? Probably, but so what? The benefit of solving a guest's legitimate problem on the spot is a huge cost saver, as well as a customer pleaser. When resolutions have to escalate to higher management levels, two complicating factors immediately come into play: First, there is a longer wait for resolution and the commensurate increased frustration and anger. Second, a much higher satisfaction threshold is established when the guest is dealing with hotel management.

Ritz-Carlton's policy is really a highly pragmatic and cost-efficient business tactic. It resolves the problem more quickly, provides for guest satisfaction on the spot before the issue can fester, and saves money by preventing personnel at higher salary levels from having to enter the fray. Most superb service approaches entail these two inescapable elements:

1. They empower people at the point of service.
2. They are reinforced because they actually save money daily.

TOUGHER THAN ROCKET SCIENCE: EXECUTIVE ATTENTION

In a famous case some years ago, AT&T decided to launch a customer service effort, and instructed its directory assistance operators to be polite, helpful, and solicitous to callers. They emphasized this with reinforcement from supervisory personnel and distributed literature. But how did AT&T actually measure the performance of directory assistance operators? You guessed it—by the number of calls handled per hour. Civility takes much longer than abruptness, and the operators soon learned that courtesy wasn't going to help their job security.

The acceptance of mediocre performance isn't always a personal, deliberate choice. Sometimes it is systemically mandated. The psychologists call this phenomenon "cognitive dissonance."

It means telling me to expect one thing while I'm actually experiencing something quite different. It results in unbreakable paradoxes, which probably began with the classic, ancient admonition:

To all employees:

The beatings will stop as soon as morale improves.

Thank you for your help in this matter.

Service excellence isn't rocket science, but it does require a specific kind of hard, corporate work: executive attention.

A bank CEO told me that his overarching priority was to improve shareholder value. "But I can't expect my employees to carry this abstract notion around with them every day. So I have to focus on the alignment of their daily goals with my longer-term objectives."

He did this by recognizing and rewarding those pursuits that reinforced improvement in shareholder value. For example, he found that opening IRA rollover accounts, providing auto loans, and establishing home equity lines of credit were actions that were both highly profitable and immensely gratifying to the local branch managers, who were providing short-term, tangible help to customers they saw on a daily basis. The CEO provided strong reward and high recognition for growth in those areas. That short-term, pragmatic help to the customer was reflected, however, in long-term, high-value benefit to the bank and its stock in a variety of ways:

- ▲ Customer loyalty in the face of pervasive mail inducements from competitors
- ▲ The "benefit of the doubt" when unavoidable long lines were encountered in the bank
- ▲ Unsolicited referrals from customers and resultant new business

▲ The ability to provide competitive but not the best interest rates available[2]
▲ Long-term investments on deposit
▲ Loyalty that extended to customer's children as they reached maturity
▲ Inherent trust in the continual product and service offering that the bank marketed, creating an "easy sell"

"My job is to ensure that every employee, right down to the receptionists, are doing jobs that totally support our corporate direction. If I'm not doing that, who will?" Good question.

The reward systems (or lack of them) in organizational life often undercut improvements in performance. If there is no reward and no penalty, then any response is an equal response. In consulting, we call these "undifferentiated responses" or "low-quality responses" because any response—any alternative—is as good as another. If you take your Toyota in for service, the service manager, technicians, and even cashiers are attentive, polite, crisp, and professional. They never miss a request and they'll carefully explain all of the work they intend to do. They deliver the vehicle when they promise. These are *high-quality, differentiated responses*. That's because Toyota constantly monitors their service through direct appeals to the customer, and will reward or punish its dealers commensurately. There is a direct feedback loop and consequences right down the line.

If you want to experience one of the finest examples of focused, no-nonsense customer service, simply send your priority parcels by FedEx. You can call their 800 line, use the Internet, or use software they'll provide for your computer and modem. They will pick up at your door and deliver to your door. The couriers will provide you with shortcuts and even rewrite the air bill if it's not completed correctly. You can track any package, any time, anywhere.

I was speaking once at the Woodlands Resort in Houston, when the client informed me that my books, which were to be a gift for every participant, had not arrived. The hotel meetings manager loftily assured me that my boxes had not been received

---

2. Researchers are astounded every time they confirm that a huge portion of existing savings are in relatively low-yield, old-fashioned savings accounts. Trust and loyalty often overcome pure economic reason.

from FedEx, and that she had personally "exhaustively searched" for them. I called FedEx, at 8 A.M. on a Sunday morning, and found within sixty seconds that the books had, indeed, been delivered the day prior, and who had signed for them. Confronted with this instant information, the meetings manager sheepishly retrieved the books from an assistant's locked office, where she obviously had not bothered to "exhaustively" search.

THE PRACTICAL BUSINESS VALUE OF EXPLICIT STANDARDS: ABSOLUTELY GUARANTEED TO GET THERE THE NEXT DAY, USUALLY

I've cited FedEx as one of my favorite examples of an organization that despises mediocrity. Like all outstanding organizations, they're not that good because they're always perfect, but because they recognize their own deviations from standards when they occur.

I was called one evening by a FedEx manager who apologized for the fact that my letter had missed their plane because it had been inadvertently left in the van and only discovered in a later check. "We have two options," she explained, "we can send it on the first flight tomorrow, meaning it will get there a day late, and we'll only charge you for second-day service, or we can put it on a commercial jet tonight at extra expense, which we'll absorb. Which do you prefer?"

"I'm sorry," I said, "but don't you talk somewhere about absolutely, guaranteed, positively, get there the next . . ."

She cut me off. "Of course. We'll send it out tonight on the commercial flight. Thanks for your business."

FedEx people are rewarded for getting packages where they're supposed to go within the time frames established for getting them there. They brook no interference with getting this accomplished. Airborne Express constantly leaves my packages at a neighbor's house a quarter mile away. FedEx never misses putting them on the same spot on my doorstep.

One of the great (perhaps apocryphal, but perception is reality within organizations) stories from FedEx's earlier years is that of one of their 727 cargo jets suffering a flamed-out engine en route to the Memphis hub (the 727 has three engines, so there was no imminent danger). The three-person crew had every right to land the plane immediately and get the engine repaired. But they carried only packages, no passengers, and they were quickly able to restart the engine in flight, arriving on schedule in Memphis without further incident. Asked why they hadn't made an emergency landing, the captain's response was: "Our job was to get the packages to Memphis. So that's what we did."

In still another famous FedEx story, a truck driver arrived at one of the company's pick-up boxes, only to find that he had been give the wrong key and couldn't open the box to get at the parcels. He could have skipped that stop, or called his supervisor and made it into someone else's problem (almost ensuring that the packages would not be delivered the next day), but instead he focused on the organization's credo and acted within its value system. Somehow, he pried the entire delivery box off its base and loaded it into his truck.

When he arrived back at his distribution station, a team of employees, alerted to the problem by phone, immediately fell upon the box with levers and hammers. They had it opened shortly thereafter, and every package made its intended flight. The driver became a local hero.

I told that FedEx story during a speech I was making to executives in the service industry. During a break, a few of them gathered nearby to discuss my story. They concluded that, had that situation occurred involving the U.S. mails, there would be no way that the postal service driver would have done anything other than skip that stop and report the problem later.

"But what if, somehow, the FedEx driver, with his value system, his innovation, and his determination, were the guy in the mail truck? What would be the outcome then?" asked one of the group.

After a few seconds, another responded, "He would have gotten back to his post office at which time he would have been hauled before the postmaster for destroying government property. He probably would have been suspended, and his union would have to defend him."

"I'm betting," said another, "that even his colleagues would not have been sympathetic. There's no value in 'going the extra nine yards' at the post office."

The final word came from the other member of the group. "He probably would have been investigated by the postal inspectors and prosecuted for a felony." Everyone nodded their heads and went off to get coffee.

The exemplar mentality is carried over to a company's public image, its "tag lines" in advertising, its self-proclaimed distinguishing characteristics. For years and years Mercedes advertised itself as "engineered like no other car in the world." A mechanical problem was treated by Mercedes technicians as a personal affront to their integrity. DuraCell promoted their batteries as durable and powerful. When some of their batteries literally decomposed on my shelf in storage, two of their research people communicated with me about the problem. This was serious business to them. The etiology of excellence or lack thereof is found in both individual and organizational exemplars, be it personal actions or company pride. We've all heard about the legendary Frito-Lay route salesman who abandoned his disabled truck to continue his rural deliveries on a bicycle, so that no store would be without the product. Excellence and mediocrity are antipodal.

> Only the Mediocre Are
> Always at Their Best

That observation was made by Jean Giraudoux. I find it to be unassailable. If we were raising mediocrity to new heights, at least we'd be making some progress. But we've managed to give even mediocrity a bad name. For example:

▲ Sometime past midnight on the day that most of the nation adjusts to daylight saving time, every Amtrak train underway in the nation stops, dead on the tracks, for one hour. This is Amtrak's way of adjusting its route schedules, since if the trains merely proceeded as if nothing were happening, they would all arrive an hour early.[3] Amtrak can't deal with a train that's an hour early, despite the fact it can easily handle trains that are six hours late. So management's answer is to just suspend time for a while, and the trains, like stunned reptiles caught out in the cold, hug the rails until they're warmed by the rising sun. The airlines,

---

3. Bear in mind here that the only reason the country adopted a common time with discrete zones in the first place was to accommodate the railroad schedules of the mid-1800s.

of course, operate tens of thousands of flights across international time zones every day of the year, and have no such problem. (Of course, they could always circle for that hour, or land at some remote airfield, which will probably happen if Amtrak executives ever get their hands on Delta or United.)

In a country that can put men on the moon, explore the ocean depths, and invent hair-in-a-can, how is it that we have a railroad system of a magnitude inferior to Albania's? We haven't chosen to apply tough standards, have become inured to the existing poor ones, and sit home and wonder why so many people commute by pollution-spewing automobiles. Meanwhile, Amtrak will digest more of its hundreds of millions in taxpayer subsidies as you read this page.

▲ Called by a senior vice president to investigate what he claimed were falsified expense reports in his human resources group, I was asked to determine what cultural factors were responsible for such wide-scale cheating. After a morning's interviewing, I had the answer. The senior vice president was known to take his first-class air tickets—a perquisite that was appropriate for his level in that company—and cash them in, keeping the difference while he actually flew coach. That difference can be huge. His people, taking his lead, would turn in expense reports for lunches with each other claiming entertainment of a customer, include receipts for materials which were really for private use, and generally abuse the system, albeit at far lesser amounts than his own scam.

When I told my client that the problem was remedial and highly personal—the standard he was setting was merely being tightly embraced—he ended our relationship. It was far easier to throw me out than to change the standard, since the standard was a considerable source of extra income for him.

▲ Adelphi University is a Long Island institution of some 4,300 students. Its former president, Dr. Peter Diamandopoulos, received a salary and benefits package of $837,000 in 1994–1995 and he lived in a Manhattan apartment valued at well over a million dollars, provided by the largesse of the Adelphi Board of Trustees. At this writing, Adelphi has been through more than a year of turmoil and chaos, focusing on Dr. Diamandopoulos's autocratic style, his cozy relationship with the trustees, an enrollment drop of 40 percent since his arrival, the second largest tuition on Long Island, and plummeting rankings in Barron's and other college guides.[4]

The trajectory of the school has not exactly been vertical. In an unprecedented move for a university of this size, the New York Board of Regents invoked its power to remove trustees and sacked eighteen of the nineteen Adelphi trustees (one was brand new to the job and deemed faultless). The Board of Regents had found that at least two of the trustees had been doing private business with the school that directly profited them and their businesses. The fired trustees immediately hired a lawyer and sued for reinstatement, but within days dropped their plans, formally resigned, and went about other business.[5]

The trustees had been acolytes, carrying the trailing robes of the president and attending to his needs, rather than representing the best interests of the institution and its customers—the students. The Regent's attention was captured by a combination of student and faculty protest that finally reached a level that was impossible to ignore. Those two interested groups had had it with poor service and scant responsiveness. To quote Peter Finch in his tour de force in the movie *Network*, "I'm mad as hell, and I'm not going to take it anymore!" Let that be our marching cry.

Of course, that marching cry isn't always heard by the power elites. In December of 1998, Dr. Diamandopoulos was hired at an undisclosed salary to be a special assistant to John Silber, president of Boston University. Dr. Diamandopoulos will work on "special projects" directly for the president. Historical footnote: Dr. Silber was one the trustees cashiered by the New York regents, and had served as the head of the compensation committee at Adelphi. During that tenure he rigorously defended the salary the trustees were lavishing on Dr. Diamandopoulos. Another historical footnote: Drs. Silber and Diamandopoulos had an informal rivalry going as to who would be the highest paid university president. Both of their base salaries were well above $500,000, and it's obvious that the higher the level is raised overall, the better bargaining position any one president is in.

---

4. See Bruce Lambert, "State Regents Oust 18 Adelphi U. Trustees," *New York Times,* 11 February 1997, A14.

5. Bruce Lambert, "18 Adelphi Trustees Resign, Abandoning Their Court Fight," *New York Times,* 14 February 1997, A19.

The press has long commented on "interlocking" director-ships, in which two CEOs are actually allowed to serve as chairs on each other's compensation committees, but we rarely can view so egregious an exercise of that abuse as in this lovely case from academe, even though only one served officially in that role. At the time of the announcement, no one raised any concerns about Silber's role in his long-time friend Diamandopoulos's riches, his being fired by the Regents of the State of New York, and his ac-quiring his friend's talents for his current school. Alas, it's now something for the students, faculty, and alumni of BU to worry about.

Like the students and faculty at Adelphi, we have to make our unhappiness manifest in some way that causes pain to those who can change the system. A reservations agent might not care if you berate him or her for constantly putting you on lengthy phone holds, but the supervisor might if such complaints must be recorded, and I guarantee you that the general manager will if that person's time is consumed with such elementary service problems. Enduring poor service is no different from providing wine for an alcoholic—we're enablers to destructive behavior. De-stroying one's liver and poisoning the internal organs of an orga-nization are analogous pursuits. Both are the detritus of apathy.

▲ A few years ago, the Digital Equipment Company lost $2.1 billion. That's not easy to do, even if you're trying, which Digital clearly wasn't. During that same period, the DEC board granted pay increases of 70 percent to its five top officers. (Imagine what they might've earned if they had *made* money?) Where was the board? What were they thinking? Were they sentient?

▲ In San Francisco, the symphony voted during 1997 to re-turn to work for the current season with a salary structure begin-ning at $75,920 and rising to $83,200 before overtime pay. They have bargained down to a maximum of four performances and four rehearsals a week, with ten weeks vacation. The union barely ratified the terms, 54 to 41. At the current trend of productivity for the symphony, the *Wall Street Journal* has concluded that mim-ing rather than actually playing an instrument can't be consid-ered too remote a union demand.[6]

6. Editorial, "Asides: Symphonic Suicide?" *Wall Street Journal,* 14 February 1997, A14.

EMPOWERING EMPLOYEES DOES NOT MEAN DISEMPOWERING MANAGEMENT—THIS IS NOT A ZERO-SUM GAME

The *absence* of money is a demotivator. People will focus on perceived injustices—often over relatively trivial amounts—at the expense of their work and accountabilities. But the converse is not true, in that the *presence* of money is not a motivator. Even more importantly, the *addition* of money is not a sufficient mechanism to overcome unhappiness about other aspects of the job. If financial enhancement were such an alchemist's stone for morale, no one would be upset by unsafe working conditions, sexual harassment, excessive travel, poor leadership, management vacillation, or downsizing. But, the last time I asked, they certainly were.

That's why the values and leadership behind those goals at Ritz-Carlton in the example cited above are so important. If you walk into an employee-only area at any Ritz-Carlton around the world, you'll find the organization's vision and values prominently displayed for every employee to see. Somewhere it will state, "We are ladies and gentlemen serving ladies and gentlemen." That's a tough and lofty goal in a day when one can observe guests with T-shirts and torn shorts sitting in the lounge of the Ritz concierge floor in downtown Atlanta. Yet it's a goal that the organization successfully meets every day. I've never encountered a Ritz employee who could not or would not help me with a problem, and have found only one rude Ritz employee in close to a hundred visits. I'd gladly accept that success rate in every business I patronize.

In most organizations, however, employees are powerless and the organization conspires to keep them that way. If Ritz-Carlton can educate their staff and reinforce the required behaviors, why can't every organization? It's because of a disdain for excellence, caused by a fear that employee empowerment requires management *dis*empowerment. Power, some think, is a zero-sum game; if I give any to you, then I'll lose some of mine. Welcome back to the schoolyard, but that's where management often is today, trying to keep control of the only ball in the place.

Traditionally, American management has derived its power from the control of two resources: people and information. Thus, "head count" and exclusive meetings were key purveyors of power. The more people I control and the more I am uniquely able to disperse information—and withhold it—the more I am needed and the more I am heeded. That's why we once had the proliferation of management layers, with each strata formed in an attempt to create its own corral of people and its own maze of hidden information. Ironically, that's also why a training industry in "delegation skills," management "grids," and "situational leadership" elements sprouted. It was as if managers were simply dying to share power with subordinates, but just didn't have the tools! In fact, they didn't have any *intention* of sharing power, so they gladly took the courses offered up by an out-of-touch human resources department and then went right back to hoarding their secret decoder rings.[7] It wasn't that managers didn't know how to delegate, but that their power base was derived specifically from *not* delegating. As in most human development, skill sets are usually a secondary consideration to behavioral reinforcers.

Two events finally ended that reign. The advent of the computer created instant access to information for most of the organization[8] and the frenzied search for profit in corporate downsizing meant that smaller staffs were better staffs. With neither people nor information proprietarily theirs, managers found themselves dangerously exposed. The modern manager serves as a team leader, leveraging the results of the team, working through others, and ensuring that resources are optimally distributed and shared. Yet those are skills never required or developed in the previous dynamic of fiefdoms and secrecy. Some managers had the tools (and/or the help) to make the leap. Most remain on the wrong side of the chasm.

Reluctance to empower people creates a closed loop system in which management is overwhelmed with working *not* to empower people and consumed with resultant tasks. No one else gets developed in this system, so job satisfaction, job expansion, careers, and aspirations can't be advanced. This results in at best

---

7. See Chapter 3 for more on the "touchie-feelie" approach to management development.

8. Take an airplane trip today and you can ticket yourself electronically, avoid any kind of paper ticket if you prefer, and hand your bags to a sky cap whose computer prints out your baggage claim tags, provides the gate and tells you if the plane is on time. You can go from your home to your seat on the plane having dealt with exactly one United sky cap who receives a minimum wage and makes a living on tips.

diffident and at worst apathetic employees who perform poorly. Such employees are the last people in the world whom management would want to empower, so the circle is complete. "How can we empower people who are clearly not interested in the work? It would be a calamity. These people simply want a paycheck and to be left alone." Ah, and who created them?

People who tell you "It's not my job" are stuck in this closed loop system. Why should I go to extra lengths when there is no gratification, there is no support, and there is great risk?

When my son was being graduated from the University of Miami, I arrived at the airport in Providence in the morning with my wife, daughter, mother-in-law, and tickets, well in advance of our flight. We were scheduled to arrive in Florida at 3 P.M., comfortably prior to his 7 P.M. commencement. We checked in at USAirways, waited near the gate, and rested in the calm that good planning provides. At boarding time, we were informed that a mechanical malfunction had cancelled the flight altogether. All passengers were directed back to the lobby ticket counter for re-booking. I could foresee the madhouse there and, in looking through my *Official Airline Guide*, I could also see that there were no other combinations of USAirways flights that could get us to Miami on time for the graduation ceremony.

I approached the gate agent who had made the cancellation announcement, and explained the predicament. In a few minutes she verified on her computer that I was right about the lack of remaining connections. Then she said something that bought USAirways all the benefit of the doubt it will ever need for the rest of my airborne days.

"I can get you there on a nonstop American flight out of Boston, if you're willing to drive up there," she explained.

"But these are free USAirways tickets from your frequent flyer program," I pointed out.

"No problem," she said, reaching for forms, "we'll simply buy the seats on American."

And she did. She directed us to the American desk on the way out to get the new tickets, we dashed to Boston, and reached the site of the graduation ceremony thirty minutes prior to its start. That gate agent didn't direct us back to the ticket counter, didn't tell us that free tickets had lowest priority, and didn't try to pass us off to someone else. She created a sterling moment for her company because:

▲ She knew she was responsible for passenger satisfaction—an *outcome*—and not merely boarding aircraft—a *task*.

▲ She had the ability and initiative to recognize a customer need and to provide an innovative solution.

▲ She had the tools at her disposal to take action.

▲ She had the absolute support of management for her judgment and actions within her sphere of accountability.

REQUISITES FOR ACCOUNTABILITY: I COULD, I WOULD, I SHOULD, *BUT* WILL I?

The need in any organization to create accountability and empowerment throughout the enterprise requires the dynamic seen in Figure 2-1.

First, every employee requires an *awareness* of the environment. How many times have you waited while two salespeople finished a conversation between the two of them, or been delayed while an employee finished a personal phone call? In restaurants, I've offered to buy a stunned manager a drink on the assumption that the gesture might at least bring a waiter to the table to take the order. That awareness has to include the nature of the probable help that customers will require.

Second, the *values* of the enterprise must be clear to everyone. One component of values is the raison d'être. The organization has a purpose (to provide travel comfort, to provide the best food flavorings, to provide family entertainment, etc.). Organizations do not exist simply to make money, although that is almost always a mandatory outcome. But if the bottom line ruled supreme, then any enterprise would enter any field, so long as there were money to be made. Sony would buy a profitable ice-cream venture, and American Airlines would have a profitable landscaping subsidiary. Such diversification is rarely the reality, and is almost never successful.[9] Those values are best expressed as outcomes,

---

9. Only the old conglomerates managed this: ITT under Harold Geneen, TransAmerica, Gulf & Western. United Airlines' venture into a broader travel strategy (rental car, hotel) was a disaster. The best of what's left is represented by GE, which conducts the likes of broadcasting, aerospace, and financial businesses within a large, encompassing strategy (and a requirement that each one be first or second in its respective marketplace).

Figure 2-1. Ethical actions dynamic.

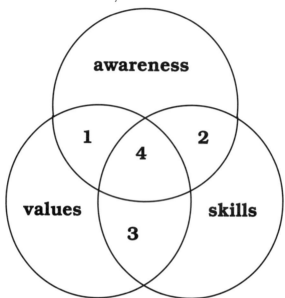

1. Should do

2. Could do

3. Would do

4. Will do

such as improved health, comfort, financial return, security, reliability, and the like.

Another aspect of the infrastructure values provides for the constant reinforcement of desired actions (application of the skills). Employees have to believe that they will be supported when they make an error, try a new course of action, and engage in prudent risk. They also have to be free from retribution and repercussion if they venture new ideas, identify poor practices, and criticize inappropriate decisions.

Third, *skills* are required to enable employees to take necessary actions. I can't perform without the tools, no matter how much I may see the need and feel the urge. I can't repair an engine without a tool kit, and I can't resolve a customer complaint without interpersonal skills.

The combination of these three elements creates the behavioral attributes required to do the right thing every time. The absence of any one is fatal.

At position 1 in the graphic, I know what I'm supposed to do and I see the need to do it. But I lack the skills. Call this the "should do" position. I'd do it if I knew how.

At position 2 we have the "could do" circumstance. I have an awareness of a particular incident (an inferior meal was served, we caused a customer to miss a flight, the product failed far short of its expected lifetime) and I have the skills to do something about it (provide a refund, offer a substitute, reduce the price), but the value system has not been compromised. Either I don't feel that the situation is sufficiently out of the ordinary, or I know that the organization won't support any remedial action I attempt. Therefore, while I understand your issue (the car was supposed to be ready today) and I have the ability to ameliorate the situation (provide a loaner for a day), I either don't believe it's a serious transgression (we're always a day or two late, and we've been told to fend people off) or I know there will be a price to pay (if I provide a loaner the paperwork will take forty-five minutes of my time and they'll charge the cost against my department's expenses). No matter which cause, the effect on the customer is the same: TNMJ. ("I'm sorry the car isn't ready. You'll just have to check with someone here tomorrow.")

Position 3 is "would do," in that I have the correct value system in place and the skills to take appropriate action. But I don't know that anything is wrong. Either no one has told me, or I'm blissfully unaware of the surroundings. I may be effectively isolated by my staff ("Sorry, but Ms. Martin does not receive direct calls from customers. Call our toll-free hot-line."), or I may simply not notice (the maitre d' studiously ignores the patron complaining to the waiter about an incorrect entree). In any case, nothing is done.

Only position 4 constitutes "will do." I'm equipped, I'm confident of organizational support, I'm aware, and I know what's right and what's wrong. Those don't seem like complex requirements. They're not, but they're quite rare. Telling someone why something can't be done has become a neologism for service. "I know you were expecting the computer to be repaired by today, and I can empathize with your frustration. But we're severely backed up because of the recall, and you're not alone in experiencing the problem."[10]

Thanks, I feel much better, and I'll be sure not to buy your product and patronize your store again. Empathize with that.

REAL POWER AS A POSITIVE ATTRIBUTE, ARTIFICIAL POWER AS ANATHEMA

There is a grand myth extant in organizational life that "power corrupts," a vestige of an overzealous reading of Edmund Burke 200 years ago. Actually, the opposite position is true in business: powerlessness corrupts.

When employees are truly powerless—that is, they cannot make decisions that influence the outcome of their work—they will create artificial power. Psychologically, most people can't remain healthy if they are engaged in a job which they routinely cannot influence. This is a sometimes desperate and always encumbering attempt to control their environment and bring some influence to their work lives. What we encounter as customers are ridiculous policies, rude comments, harsh treatment, and deliberate sabotage. That's because employees who feel powerless create artificial power, which we generally refer to as "bureaucracy." Bureaucracy is the triumph of means over ends. The application of immediate, albeit false, power is more gratifying to the employee than the outcome of the job and the customer's well-being. I discussed earlier the importance of job gratification to employee morale and performance. In the case of powerlessness, employees create their own gratification that is contrary to the actual job output desired by both the organization and the customer.

Several years ago I had taken a commuter airline out of Boston to Quebec late one February night. There were only two passengers aboard the nineteen-seat aircraft. When we arrived at about 11 P.M. in Quebec, the airport was deserted, and it was

---

10. This was the verbatim conversation with my local retailer after Apple recalled its 5300 series PowerBooks. This was a $6,000 item (not counting prior computer business) that the company had to recall, and then compounded the problem by missing its return deadlines.

freezing, inside and out. The commuter plane agent told us to wait at a desk for the immigration agent.

After about ten minutes of waiting in the cold, we were greeted by the immigration agent, who carefully placed his books, stampers, pens, and forms on the table. Then he turned to me and said, "Next!" He took a moment, stamped my customs declaration, then turned to the other passenger (and the only other person in line with me) and said, "Next!"

After the other passenger's customs forms were duly stamped, the woman from the airline escorted us about thirty-five feet to another station, and said, "Wait here for the customs agent." In about five minutes (Who can make this stuff up?) the exact same guy walks out, but now he's the customs agent. And he turns to me and says, "Next!"

I asked him if we were in a Fellini movie. I told him that, since I had seen him only minutes before, he could have stamped and kept my forms, preventing an even longer wait in a freezing airport. He raised a finger into the air and intoned, "This is the procedure!" (The other passenger told him that he had left his forms with the first guy . . .)

If people do not have real power, they will make it up. The process of empowerment merely serves to ensure that people focus on real power and its subsequent productivity, not artificial power and its natural bureaucratic morass. Empowered people are healthier as well, because there is less stress in their work and lives.

There are two conditions that can create high stress levels at work. One is the uncertainty surrounding what might happen the next day. The other is an inability to do anything about one's work.

Where do we see such behaviors? I believe you can probably relate to the following:

▲ Airline ticket counters during bad weather or cancellations
▲ The Department of Motor Vehicles with long lines and surly clerks
▲ Organizations in which senior management is under fire (Exxon, Texaco, Apple, TWA, Digital Equipment)
▲ Immigration and passport offices
▲ Luggage service supervisors at airports
▲ Toll collectors on roadways

- ▲ Organizations prone to downsize to resolve financial problems (AT&T, GE's Aircraft Engine Division, Sunbeam, Scott Paper)
- ▲ Utility customer service operators
- ▲ Organizations that bring in "turnaround specialists" known for radical cost cutting (such as Al Dunlop)
- ▲ Post office employees, especially those working inside
- ▲ Stockbrokers, traders, and attendant financial industry employees

It's no accident that some of these people are in government jobs and/or in what once were regulated environments. When the emphasis is on following orders and not on personal accountability, we find artificial power. The Department of Motor Vehicles in most states has a surfeit of people who do not see their jobs as trying to help the customer. They aren't rewarded for it, aren't evaluated by it, and don't have role models supporting it. Hence, the telephone contacts, hours of operation, forms to be completed, and all the other customer interventions are designed for the benefit of staff, not the customer.[11]

Ironically, utility customer service line response becomes *worse* when there is a major problem such as storm damage or lines down, because operators are besieged with identical calls and have no alternatives but to take down information and make vague promises about service. Travel the New Jersey Turnpike and you will find some of the rudest working people in the world collecting tolls. Not only will you rarely hear a "thank you," but give someone a ten dollar bill for a sixty-five cent toll and they'll actually abuse you, as if you're part of a plot to make them miserable. (Actually you are, but not of your making.) Many years ago, the toll collectors successfully lobbied to ban pennies from motorists, ostensibly because they caused too many problems but actually because the customers found them a quite effective means of retaliation against the rude behavior. (If you don't like to make change for ten dollars, think about counting sixty-five pennies.)

---

11. By the way, no matter what type of business, when someone tells you that a request normally takes two weeks (or four or six or whatever) to fulfill, what they're really indicating is that your request will sit on someone's desk for 90 percent of that period. With the advent of computers, it simply doesn't take more than a day to process any request, and even the postal service can deliver something within a week (usually).

The nastiest, vilest public behavior I've seen in visiting fifty countries and traveling over 2.5 million air miles, is at U.S. immigration and naturalization sites. People who speak little or no English arriving from other lands are treated, by and large, with contempt and suspicion. An American traveling overseas can almost always find someone who speaks some English—and usually will encounter fluent English—but in the United States there are rarely officials who speak any other language at all. These employees are trapped in a deadly dull, hierarchical control system with no recourse other than self-abasement or humiliation of the public, so they choose the latter.

An insurance company called The Hartford made an effective marketing offer to me not long ago, trying to solicit my auto insurance business. My family owns four relatively new cars and has a positive claims history, so I imagine I'm an attractive potential customer. I responded to the solicitation, completed an application, and submitted it by mail.

Two weeks later I received a phone call from a woman who was as disempowered as they come. She might as well have been rowing a Roman trireme to the beat of a drum. Here's the conversation:

"Dr. Weiss, I have to go over the information on this application. First, please give me the correct spelling of your name."

(After I did so . . .) "Please verify your address."

"Wait a minute. That form was six pages long. Are you going to ask me to give you every piece of information all over again on the phone?"

"Yes. It takes about fifteen minutes."

"Why do you need this?"

"It's our procedure."

"I don't understand why you have to hear everything I recorded, then confirmed with my signature."

"Because we must do this."

"What if I don't choose to? Would your claim service involve the same bureaucracy?"

"Sir, this is what I have to do."

"I'll tell you what. Let me speak to your manager."

"That's impossible. There are no managers at this location."

"How do I reach the vice president whose name was on the original letter to me, Cynthia Thomas?"

"Ms. Thomas does not talk to customers."
"Where can I reach her?"
"We never reveal an individual's location."

A call to the corporate switchboard in Hartford got me Ms. Thomas's address, phone number, and mail drop. I wrote her to explain how her innovative marketing effort went for naught in the actual acquisition of a customer. Unsurprisingly, she never wrote back. If my phone companion's manner was tolerated by the organization, then leadership is always to blame.

There is only one answer to "Who's in charge here?" It's the people making the big bucks in the large offices with the covered parking spaces. They are the ones responsible for high standards and low, empowerment and disempowerment, action and bureaucracy. And contrary to what the protectors and screeners, the gatekeepers and filters would have you believe, you can always find out where they live within the organization.

All of this, of course, is a miserable failure in leadership. The modern, powerless organization is led poorly, and in a manner contrary to what we know about productivity and performance today. Modern leadership is solipsist, creating its own artificial reality. If you don't view the organization from the customer's vantage point, you never really know how it functions.

The failure is in the leaders, not the led. As managers vie for power using old standards of head count and information, or as they blunder around aimlessly in front of teams they don't know how to lead, employees are left to their own devices. In those organizations that deny them power, they will create their own, and the latter is invariably toxic to the customer and the ultimate goals of the business (selling a product or providing a service, and retaining customers).[12] In the case of government functions, the customers generally have no opportunity to take their business elsewhere,

---

12. In a remarkable example of ignoring standards of performance from contemporary business, in 1998 Textron hired away the president of NYNEX in Rhode Island to become its senior vice president of human resources. NYNEX was generally acknowledged to have the worst service of any of the regional phone companies, and Rhode Island may have had the worst of the NYNEX service: antiquated equipment, high rates, service calls that are never fulfilled, and so on. Why should Textron have looked anywhere else to obtain an executive to head their human resources?

so the bureaucracy intensifies. In regulated industries that was also true, but with deregulation in full bloom, there is ongoing trauma. Electric, gas, and telephone utilities suddenly find themselves in a competitive environment that is the equivalent of having been deposited on Neptune with an hour's worth of survival gear. Hospitals and the health care industry are in the same situation.

It's amazing what competition can do to moribund leadership. Once upon a time, AT&T had no marketing department and the customer gratefully grasped whatever phone service was provided. Today, that customer has a plethora of services, with payment plans and equipment choices that continue to proliferate. You can fly from Providence to Miami on Southwest Air for about $150 currently, and while Northeast Utilities can't get out from under its own mismanagement of its nuclear operation, other New England utilities are about to offer competitive services across state lines.

LEADERSHIP AT EVERY LEVEL

Raising the bar of performance, standards, and results requires everyone to play a leadership role. There are at least five different aspects of leadership power. Note that these are not "personality profiles" or "quadrants" that befit personality types. These are objective organizational positions and dynamics from which leadership leverage can be exerted.

1. The Power to Reward

Rewards are not purely financial. While the absence of money is, indeed, a demotivator, its presence is not necessarily a motivator. Nonetheless, the ability to give both financial and nonfinancial benefits are one of the keys to power and leadership. Nonfinancial rewards can include the following:

- ▲ Recognition by respected sources
- ▲ Ability to take greater latitude of action (empowerment)
- ▲ Discretionary time off
- ▲ Increased interaction with customers
- ▲ Participation in higher level decision making or strategy
- ▲ Management of other people

▲ Project management
▲ Collaboration with vendors
▲ Management and coordination of consultants
▲ Hiring responsibility
▲ Team leadership
▲ Public spokesperson for the organization
▲ Serving nonprofit or community organizations on behalf of the company
▲ Internal education and development
▲ External education and development
▲ Varied job assignments
▲ Overseas work
▲ Increased (or decreased) travel
▲ Budgeting accountability
▲ Self-evaluation of performance
▲ Paid time on personal projects[13]
▲ Sabbaticals
▲ Job sharing
▲ Telecommuting and work at home

If you examine the above list, which could easily be two or three times longer, you can see that even first-line supervisors possess some discretionary power in many of these areas. Simple *inclusion* is often a very powerful leadership technique, and this can be accomplished at virtually any level. Asking people their opinion has always had a salutary effect on their feelings of worth and involvement.

2. The Power to Punish

This is the natural converse of item 1 above. Punishment, or providing penalties, is one of the most tangible and feared positions of leadership power (yes, fear is a motivator). However, this power base is best used with a soft glove if the end objective is to help people to become more productive and to respect their leadership.

---

13. 3M routinely provides 10 percent of researchers' work time to pursue anything they want, company-related or not. Don't forget that this is the company that derives 25 percent of its revenues from products that didn't exist five years prior.

If John has been attending one of Mary's meetings every Friday at 9 A.M. for six months on time, and suddenly arrives twenty minutes late for three Fridays in a row, Mary has two basic options.

Option One:

"John, I've now watched you walk in here 20 minutes late for three weeks running and I'm fed up with it. You're not a team player. You have a lousy attitude, and you clearly don't respect me or the other team members. Now plan to get here on time next week or else, and don't think that I won't take this into account during your performance review."

"Mary, how dare you speak to me that way. I'm the one who volunteers first when you need overtime. I'm the one who leads the United Way campaign in this department. I personally helped you with the Scott report over a weekend when no one else was willing to do it. You're the one with the lousy attitude if you can't take the time to even ask me about the lateness—which only occurred twice for maybe ten minutes of a boring meeting anyway!"

Option Two:

"John, it seems to me that you've been late now for three weeks to our meeting. That's not like you. Am I right about that?"

"Yes, unfortunately, I've been a little late recently."

"Why is that?"

"It's the traffic."

"But the traffic hasn't changed, and you've never been late before. Has something else changed?"

"Well, my wife has changed jobs, and now on Fridays I have to deliver my kids to child care. It's an extra fifteen minutes, and I get there as soon as the doors open, but it's the best I can do. My wife has to be at work early on Fridays."

"All right. Why don't you think over our options, talk to some of your colleagues who have dealt with similar situations, and get back to me on how we can resolve this, okay?"

Mary's power to punish is no less real in option two, but her outcome will be qualitatively much higher because she:

▲ Focused on observed behavior and didn't make emotional leaps
▲ Obtained agreement from the performer about the problem
▲ Found the cause (not the blame)
▲ Involved the performer in developing a solution
▲ Made it clear the issue had to be resolved

The power to punish is best used lightly, tangentially, and infrequently. In those cases, it's highly effective. But if you're whacking everyone every day, after a while people get used to the pain and figure that they might as well get away with something significant if they're going to get whacked anyway.

3. The Power of Position

Hierarchical position has traditionally been the most important source of power, and is increasingly becoming the least important, although it is still not to be ignored. As people in the military are fond of saying when they salute an officer they believe to be incompetent, "I'm saluting to show my respect for the office, not my respect for the person."

Hierarchies have been flattened. Cost considerations have finally eliminated the rank upon rank of managers whose sole duty is to manage other managers. Executives have been urged to get closer to the customer and the work itself. A more informal office environment, replete with "dress-down days" and casual atmosphere, along with a movement away from offices to cubicles for all ranks, and a first-name preference for everyone, regardless of status, has reduced the cachet of many high level positions. In addition, many titles are essentially meaningless, having either been created as a sop in lieu of promotion (in banks, *everyone* is at least an assistant vice president) or as a concession to political correctness ("vice president of new ideas" is a nice touch, but what the hell does it mean operationally?).

Nevertheless, a clearly perceived executive vice president, general manager, or comptroller is going to strike fear in the hearts of the laggard and the slothful. The advantage of hierarchical or positional power is that it is constant: You know where those leaders live, how to reach them, and what to expect.

Positional power can be hollow, however. At one southern New Jersey power company project, I heard my escort say, "Now we're going to be delayed." When I asked what caused his conclusion, he pointed to a group of people studying an excavation.

"The people with the white hard hats are the site workers," he explained, "and the ones with the yellow hard hats are the site supervisors. The orange hard hats are from home office management. But the two guys without any hard hats at all, well, they have to be corporate executives and they inevitably ball everything up." I'm from the home office, and I'm here to help you . . .

Lack of credibility undermines positional power. In these cynical days, merely arriving at a certain position does not vest one with credibility or power as it did years ago. Too many workers have watched the conservative, non-risk taking, "don't rock the boat," type of individuals who play office politics inexplicably ascend the corporate ladder. The new title doesn't change their perception in the eyes of colleagues. People who depend solely on positional power are seldom effective leaders.[14]

4. The Power of Expertise

There are many who derive power from their intelligence, experience, knowledge, or some combination thereof. This is independent of their official corporate position. On plant floors, it's not uncommon to hear "get George" when a given piece of equipment is down and no amount of reading of the manual or trial and error will get it going again. However, George knows what to listen for, or was there when it happened in the past, or can quickly diagnose what's a likely cause and what's not.

Similarly, even in service environments, we now hear, "This is a tough meeting. Get Joyce to facilitate it." Joyce may or may not be normally included in this group, may or may not be of their level. But what she is as a facilitator is the only quality that's important. This kind of demand creates an informal leadership

---

14. Note that these power sources are not mutually exclusive. Most positions carry the ability to reward and punish, for example. Some leaders may, potentially, possess all five dynamics. The questions are to what degree, and how well, are they employed.

power, because people will defer to that expertise and will be hesitant to move forward without it.

The power of expertise is an ideal vehicle for people who do not possess the other dynamics listed to influence organizational life far beyond what is possible for coworkers. People at all levels seek them out. Decisions are often delayed until their input is secured. They are named as unofficial advisors or as formalized task force leaders. Other leaders seek them out for their "team." They can often write their own ticket in terms of the recognition factors noted above.

The trouble with the power of expertise is that it is normally relegated to one perceived area, meaning that as much as the bearer is in demand in that area, they go unthought of in other areas. Expertise is limited. I once consulted at a poultry hatchery owned by the animal health division of Merck. Having listened to a focus group that morning, I remarked to the afternoon's focus group that their concerns were very similar to their colleagues' earlier in the day. The afternoon group was outraged.

"Our concerns are of an entirely different nature," stressed one of the supervisors.

"But the morning group talked about egg fertilization problems, and so are you," I pointed out.

"Yes," he said, "but those were *chicken* people, and we are *turkey* people. There is a world of difference."

Apparently so.

The power of expertise is earned, not readily claimed, and is inherently rather narrowly focused. However, it is one of the truly informal dynamics of leadership in any organization. The other powerful informal leadership is the final type.

5. Referent Leadership

This is the most powerful of all the leadership types, because it is the most natural to follow effortlessly. Referent leaders are those to whom others look because they *believe in them.* It may be charismatic. It may simply be someone who has never lied and faithfully held up his or her end of the bargain every time. It might be someone who is known for accepting failure personally but sharing victories with the staff.

Referent leaders can be at any level, in any job. They can be CEOs—I would think that there are quite a few of them in successful companies—and they can be rank and file workers. More normally, they are spread throughout the ranks of middle management.

These are the true exemplars, the people whom followers will unabashedly tell you that they would like to emulate. Referent leaders get that way over time. They demonstrate their values, perform consistently, and develop a reputation. Their characteristics usually include:

- ▲ Support of subordinates
- ▲ Intolerance for poor quality
- ▲ Lack of political orientation
- ▲ High regard for competence
- ▲ Admission of error and failure
- ▲ Standing up for values and beliefs
- ▲ Outspokenness and candor
- ▲ High ethics and integrity
- ▲ Calm and effective in crises
- ▲ Shared victories and a sense of fair play

Here is how the five types of leadership power sources compare against some standard variables:

Power Source	Commitment	Compliance	Resistance
Reward	possible	likely	possible
Punishment	unlikely	likely	possible
Positional	unlikely	possible	likely
Expert	likely	likely	possible
Referent	likely	likely	unlikely

As you can see, referent power is the most likely to consistently achieve commitment and avoid resistance. Many leaders state that they would prefer to have referent power, yet they continue to adjust their behaviors to punishment or position.

SOLUTIONS: LEADERSHIP THAT PROVIDES REAL POWER AND REWARDS ITS USE

Many of our organizations, public and private, are simply dead from the neck up. Their constituent parts are left to fend for themselves without common leadership, and they create their own rules, often at odds with each other. "That's not my job" becomes the corporate mantra until, ultimately, no one can determine whose job it is. But there are explicit and clear approaches to creating leadership accountability.

1. Create the Playing Field

Empowerment is not abdication. In fact, effective empowerment requires that the boundaries be established and agreed upon. The playing field could be six-sided or eight-sided, as large as a football field or as small as a tennis court. If the boundaries aren't established (or if they're only the size of a postage stamp) then empowerment isn't possible. Only by knowing my limits can I have complete freedom within them. And only by establishing limits can leadership indicate that, while I can call my own "plays" (make my own decisions) on the field, if any of those plays come close to being out of bounds, then I have to inform leadership first.

Conversely, the employee is able to open negotiations to enlarge a boundary (I need an increase in my grant-of-authority to successfully resolve these customer issues) and to engage in an objective discussions with leadership only when boundaries are clear to begin with. It's far better to continually debate the boundary locations than to have them abrogated daily because of their ambiguity. Imagine the hostilities in a football game if no one were sure which lines represented the out-of-bounds or the scoring areas.

2. Provide the Skills

Empowerment doesn't result from a kneel and a sword's touch to the shoulder. I have to possess the skills to do the job required. This is the "can do" aspect of the work.

Performance expert Bob Mager has long asked an endearing question: "Could he do it if his life depended on it?" If the answer is "no," then, presumably you have a skill problem. If the answer is "yes," then you have an attitude problem.[15]

---

15. For fabulous reading of one of my favorite people in the field, see Robert F. Mager and Peter Pipe, *Analyzing Performance Problems or Your Really Oughta Wanna,* 2d ed. (Belmont, CA: Pitman Learning, 1984.)

If you are empowering me in a customer service job, I will probably require skills in asking questions, resolving conflicts, managing time, and negotiating compromises, among other things. If you are empowering me as a team leader, I might require skills in delegating, running meetings, making presentations, and writing reports. If you empower me without providing the requisite skills you are merely giving me a car without the keys.

There is a terrific organization called Strive that provides intensive training to the chronically unemployed. Unlike so many approaches that deal with "soft" skills, such as attitude and confidence, Strive's tremendous success rate[16] is largely based upon specific skill transfer, right down to how to shake hands, how to smile during a job interview, how to fill out an application, and so forth. In the private sector, Motorola has popularized the internal "university" that provides continually updated skills and competencies to employees at all levels.

At Avon, each employee in the information systems department receives sixteen to twenty days of development per year at a cost of $15,000 per person. Its training budget increased by 20 percent in 1996 over the prior year, and each computer staffer in the company has an individualized development plan.[17]

3. Reinforce the Proper Behaviors

Not everyone can be or wants to be empowered. Even with the proper skill set, I need to *sustain* the required behaviors. This is the "want to do" aspect of the work.

In the customer service work mentioned above, I'll need patience, calmness, attention to detail, and low assertiveness (with the customer). In the team leader position, I'll probably require higher assertiveness, high persuasiveness, an urgency for results, and strong attention to detail. In the ideal world, you can choose someone with those behavioral sets for the position. In the real world, you'll have to make compromises and provide feedback and reinforcement to modify behaviors.

Behaviors are modifiable only within finite limits. It's un-

---

16. About two-thirds of graduates still have jobs two years later.

17. Wendy Webb, "Top Techie Trainers," *Training Magazine*, August 1997, 14.

likely that a person who is low in assertiveness, low in persuasiveness, and low in urgency for action will perform well in a highly pressurized sales job. Similarly, it's unlikely that a highly aggressive, highly interactive, low patience individual will perform well in a counseling job. The behaviors should be within shouting distance of the job requirements if empowerment is to be effective. (This is why blindly promoting the best salesperson to the sales manager position is the height of folly. Think about it: Virtually none of the great sports coaches and managers were star players themselves. That's no accident. The behavioral demands on the field and on the sidelines are quite different.)[18]

If you don't attend to the appropriate behaviors, you've given someone a car and the means to drive it without an understanding of the rules of the road.

4. Provide for Structural Support

Finally, empowerment requires that the systems, procedures, and culture of the organization support it. If I'm "empowered," but need four approvals, three days, and two follow-ups to produce a desired result, then the empowerment is a sham. Even worse, if I'm negotiating internally with a person at a higher level, we reach agreement, and that person says, "Fine I'll just check with your boss," I'm not empowered.

The provision of laptop computers, cellular phones, 24-hour voice mail, and other technological aids represents structural support for greater empowerment and independence. Ingram is a book wholesaler. Any person you get on the line can help you with even the most complex of transactions and ordering procedures. Amica Insurance, one of the top-rated organizations of its kind in the country, operates without so much as a single agent. Any Amica representative can handle virtually any kind of inquiry or need in his or her specialty. They have access to the information required, the support to make use of it intelligently, and the equipment and resources to make rapid, intelligent decisions for customers. Such support removes expense from the operation, as well.

---

18. For detailed descriptions of the key behavioral factors and how to modify them, see my book *Managing for Peak Performance: A Guide to the Power (and Pitfalls) of Personal Style* (E. Greenwich, RI: Las Brisas Research Press, 1994).

Ironically, leadership sometimes goes to great lengths to provide a car, driving instructions, and thorough aptitude testing, but then leaves roadblocks in the highway.

I was walking through a multibillion dollar division with an executive vice president. He pointed to a department head sitting in a corner office.

"His work has been disappointing for months, and it's time we did something about it."

"Are you going to confront him right now?" I asked.

"Confront him? Hell, no. We're on our way to see his boss. If anyone in my operation isn't performing, it's the fault of the direct superior. A poor performer has to be developed, moved to other work, or let go. If one of those three options isn't being successfully undertaken, the boss is failing.

"It's never the poor performer who's the real cause of the problem. It's always poor leadership."

You can't solve a problem until you find its cause. When people are lost, it's the leader who got them there.

Challenge Three

Reestablish
Common Sense
The Erosive Nature of the
Touchie-Feelie Brigade

Not long ago, a client asked me to check out a new approach to employee involvement called "open meetings." It had been described in the "B" section of the *Wall Street Journal*, which is often reserved for the off-beat and bizarre. I had seen the piece and had dismissed it immediately as still another crackpot scheme from the Neverneverland School of Management. But my client was hopeful, and I, as the organization development consultant during whose watch this had developed, was now responsible for investigating.

"Why is this attractive?" I queried.

"Our surveys keep telling us that employees want more communication. This seems like maximum involvement."

"Jeff, *every* survey ever undertaken indicates that employees want more communication. Roman legionnaires wanted more communication before marching off into Gaul, and NASA astronauts wanted more communication built into the early capsules. But the test has to be whether more communication is really what's needed, and if it helps or hinders productivity."

"Look, just make my day, OK? You can tell me it's a bad idea and I won't do it, but I want your opinion based upon the facts."

Here, then, a brief survey of open meetings.

The article described "open meetings" as an approach to employee involvement that was basically without leadership. Employees would assemble—by the hundreds, if necessary—and begin to chat about current issues as they wandered around a room. Eventually, groups of common interest would form, and they would congregate around flip charts, listing their common issues. In this way, the meeting would ultimately produce six, or ten, or thirty groups who were naturally interested in the topics they chose.

The teams would then attack the issues, without common methodologies or experience bases, and decide such things as who would lead the discussion, what process would be employed, and what the next steps were to be once they left the room. There was little if any formal tracking and, for all senior management knew, the teams might be working at cross-purposes, duplicating their efforts, focusing on low-priority issues for the business, and/or creating more problems than they were resolving.

I had actually seen an "open meeting," run by someone who claimed to have studied the process. A group of 150 people arrived in the cafeteria of a financial services firm, milling around uncertainly, viewing the scattered easels as though each were the giant, preternaturally intelligent slab in *2001: A Space Odyssey*. The facilitator tried to get people moving toward common issues, but without facilitating too much, which would have undermined the process. A couple of easels drew groups interested in better food, not a completely unlikely topic to come up while in the cafeteria. Another couple of easels attracted some heated discussions about compensation, but the only consensus developing seemed to be around the phrase "more of it."

Finally, the vice-presidential equivalent of "senior officer on deck" asked the facilitator what could be done to get things moving, to which the latter replied, "We have to let it take its own course." After another hour of searching for the course, everyone went back to work and the company was poorer in productivity by about eight work weeks (150 people times two hours). I estimated that about $25,000 was effectively blown away, as well as a great deal of credibility for whatever the company's next initiative might be.

Since my client wanted facts and I wanted to be fair, I pursued the source and found the open meetings guru in Maine. I asked him about the history of the process, its evolution, references, re-connections to corporate objectives, and other rather mundane matters. I guess that he and I must have needed an open meeting, because there wasn't much communication, even after I told him that a major client was interested and I could arrange a mutually convenient meeting to explore the application of his work. Apparently, the entire approach was a casual idea that somehow had been picked up by the media and embraced by some human resources people. The state of his methodology reminded me of the days when, new to sales, a group of us used to meet for drinks and plan our next day's "strategy" on the cocktail napkins.

The clincher came when I asked him about the downside of the process, since I've never met a management technique that didn't have to be concerned about Murphy's Law.

"There are none," he informed me.

"Come on, there are always risks. What about some people using the meetings to force support of private interests, or not having access to information that might change one's view of an issue, or gaining commitment as you cross disciplinary lines? Surely . . ."

"Nope," he cut me off. "If you do it under my instruction and you're serious about your commitment to the integrity of employees, it won't fail. It hasn't yet."

Right, and employees believe every banner that's hung in the cafeteria. Even Little Red Riding Hood finally got suspicious when she noticed that her grandmother had developed fangs.

QUALITY IS A LEVEL OF PERFORMANCE, NOT A PROGRAM

For decades, management has been influenced, persuaded, cajoled, fooled, tricked and scammed by an assortment of gurus and snake oil sales people, the likes of whom make Professor Howard Hill's Music Man seem legitimate and sincere. There is trouble in River City, but it's not at the local pool hall; it's in the local human resources department.

Any organization has only 100 percent of its peoples' energies and talents to utilize. "Give me 110 percent" and "Do more with less" are empty aphorisms that mean nothing. In fact, most firms have a surfeit of talent, but they don't apply it well. The goal should be to focus 90 percent of that talent and energy on the external business outcomes—the customer, product, service, and relationship (see Figure 3-1). The final 10 percent can be eroded away by internal focus on compensation systems, gossip, seeking better positions, envy, lust, sloth, and greed. Some degree of that internal preoccupation can never be completely eradicated, and may even be healthy. But in most organizations, the numbers are terribly skewed, with 50 percent or even 75 percent focused on internal, personal concerns, and only the remainder leaking out toward the customer and business goals.

The secret of enhanced productivity isn't in throwing people out on the street and thereafter "doing more with less," whatever that means. Instead, its in refocusing attention from the inside of the circle to the outside. A shift from 50 percent internal/50 percent external to 30 percent internal/70 percent external represents a huge productivity improvement without spending an extra dime.

Guess what happens when organizations launch their latest "let's all feel better about ourselves" management strategies? The internal focus percentage goes through the roof. As one of my

Figure 3-1. Distribution of organizational energy.

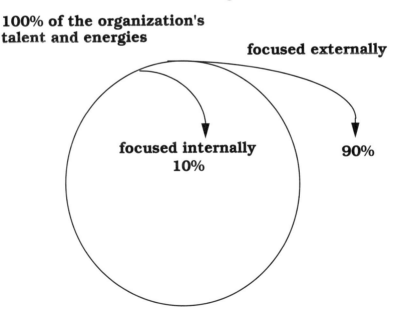

Where Are The Resources Going??

100% of the organization's talent and energies

focused externally

**focused internally
10%**

90%

disillusioned colleagues from the quality movement noted, "If the customer doesn't feel it, and feel it continually, it ain't worth doing." In other words, no amount of internal razzmatazz is worth the investment unless there is a demonstrable and continuing effect outside the circle. Organizations don't exist in order to help people find spirituality, regain lost self-esteem, find their inner beings, or determine why their parents let them down. They exist to serve customers and, in so doing, provide a return on the shareholders' investment.

Why do otherwise coherent senior managers endorse and support some of the peculiar interventions that we've seen over the last decade or so? The approaches have no indication of enhanced business outcomes, heightened productivity, or improved service. For example:

▲ In a host of surveys taken by independent sources, two-thirds of executives who funded "total quality management" projects report that they did not realize the cost savings or performance improvements they had expected.[1]

▲ A new CEO at Florida Power & Light immediately dismantled the infrastructure that had resulted in the organization winning the esteemed Baldrige Award the prior year. His reason: The structure existed solely to win the award, not to improve results or serve the customer.

▲ We can see complete cycles of dubious approaches rise and fall. Consider just a few, from the early days of the fads up to the present: transactional analysis, left brain/right brain thinking, quality circles, process improvement, total quality management, reengineering, customer focus, and on, and on.

▲ One of the most famous of the management metaphors, Maslow's hierarchy of needs,[2] has absolutely no supportive literature indicating that it is of applicability in the modern workplace.

---

1. For example, see Barbara Presley Noble, "Questioning Productivity Beliefs," *New York Times*, 10 July 1994, 21.
2. Abraham Maslow postulated that people have levels of needs, each of which had to be met before ensuing levels could be addressed. The needs begin with basic security and safety, and culminate in what he termed "self-actualization," which is the ability to impress oneself on the society and environment through the application of interests and talents.

Yet it is frequently cited to explain behaviors, despite the absence of any research that suggests that people actually conform to its tenets. It may be useful to trained psychologists; it is utterly useless to line managers.

▲ Organizations are spending millions in training funds to put employees through experiences that most sane people would find deplorable. The least offensive are the "outdoor" experiences, in which rappelling down mountains or coursing through rapids with one's business colleagues is supposed to improve teamwork and trust. There are neither empirical data nor longitudinal studies that demonstrate that this is so and, in fact, the very groups providing these junkets would be the last to want to support such research. There's nothing wrong with managers enjoying themselves, but it does get questionable when they do so with company funds under the rubric of "team building." The worst of these boondoggles, perhaps, is represented in a report by the former Inspector General of the FAA, Mary Schiavo, who tells of a six-figure program in which trainers asked participants to sit in their underwear while the trainers sniffed their discarded clothes in order to determine participants' "essences."[3]

Current business management is largely composed of people whose formative years were in the 1950s and 1960s. Despite the roaring social revolution of the late 1960s, managers are still predominantly white men who have little, if any, experience in high technology, instantaneous communications, media scrutiny, diverse work forces, global competition, diverse customer bases, educated and demanding consumers, and all the other accoutrements of our business environment. The best of them learn and change, often with judicious help from internal and external resources. The worst of them engage in corporate insanity, which is doing the same thing over and over but expecting different results each time.

In the middle are the majority, who recognize the need for help, but want it only on the condition that they, personally, don't have to be involved and that a sufficient amount of dollars will make the problem go away. This is called the "put your head back under the blanket and we'll call you when it's over" school of leadership.

---

3. As reported in an interview by Morley Safer, *60 Minutes*, CBS, 23 March 1997.

MANAGEMENT FADS ARE MORE HARMFUL THAN WE THINK:
P.T. BARNUM AS MODERN CONSULTANT

"There's a sucker promoted into management every minute" might be the great impresario's current version of his famous motto. Visit the conventions and conferences, the book signings and talk radio shows, and you find a host of slick-talking smoothies, all espousing the technique to make you the best salesperson, manager, leader, customer service agent, and/or entrepreneur in the world. By comparison, the goofiest product of the 1990s, the Thighmaster, is downright pragmatic.

But let's be reasonable. Is it really so bad to expand people's minds, provide them with some techniques, suggest other options? Won't some good come of that for everyone, even if it's in varied amounts? What can possibly be objectionable about developing people's abilities? A lot.

These programs are far beyond silly. They risk the organization's credibility and reputation, which means that other, truly valuable initiatives down the road will be received with cynicism and rejection based upon prior experience with the outlandish. They eat up profits, both in terms of direct costs (consultant's fees), indirect costs (salary and benefits), and lost productivity. Finally, they create stressful cognitive dissonance, in that they express values and theoretical rewards that the organization seldom truly supports. For example, an airline may tell reservations agents that customer satisfaction is the top priority, supporting that message with training sessions and fancy catch-phrases. But when the airline then rewards and punishes those same agents based upon numbers of calls processed per hour, it creates highly stressful dislocations. Similarly, announcing to employees that they are empowered (or that quality is uppermost, or customer focus the driving factor, or self-initiative and risk taking are key), and then demanding that all decisions be approved by two levels of management is worse than having never told them anything at all. Trusting one's colleagues or supervisors in a white-water raft is one thing, but having no such trust back on the job is another. I was in a distribution operation whose managers had all gone mountain hiking together for a week. Back on the job, the boss was still *Mr.* Lewis.

The problem is that we all pay for the foolishness as shareholders, consumers, employees, managers and, often as not, suckers. The faddists are not a harmless or inexpensive casual diversion. They are hustlers and sharpies. They are costing us money, productivity, and morale, all of which are in short supply.

The major incursions of the touchie-feelie brand of consulting began about a decade or so ago. Consider, if you will, the strange case (even for this genre) of an organization known as Pacific Bell, a subsidiary of the Pacific Telesis Group in the late 1980s. Senior management, egged on by the human resources folks, decided to transform the corporate culture, which is a viral problem that seems to surface seasonally. They hired a star guru of the hour, one Charles Krone, a self-styled trainer in the art of problem solving. The philosophy behind what became known as "Kroning" was to de-emotionalize issues so that they could be objectively resolved. The methodology employed was to actually alter normal language.

For instance, a manager might say, "The problem is that we never get much done at meetings," a common-enough complaint. The facilitator would "translate" this into something like, "There is an inability for participating parties to reach mutually harmonious relatedness over job-specific end-products." (I kid you not, this is all a matter of public record.[4])

Here's a quote from Pac Bell's statement of principles at the time:

> We define "interaction" as the continuous ability to engage with the connectedness and relatedness that exists and potentially exists, which is essential for the creations necessary to maintain and enhance viability of ourselves and the organization of which we are a part.

Kroning was variously denounced by employees as brainwashing, forced spirituality, and a violation of their religious beliefs (because Kroning urged a common set of values about treating one's colleagues that many found in conflict with their religious teachings). The California Public Utilities Commission found that *$40 million* of the customers' money had been spent

---

4. See my article "Let the Manager Beware: The Dangers of Mystical Management Advice," *Success Magazine*, October 1988, 96.

on this twaddle, a sum that could have gone toward improved service, newer equipment, lowered rates, and pay for top performers. The PUC said that $25 million needed to be charged to the poor shareholders, not to the poor customers. The president, Theodore Saenger, took early retirement, and his heir apparent, Lee Cox—a Kroning devotee—was placed in charge of a much smaller subsidiary.

I ask you: Who could make this stuff up? And who says there's no harm done?

Even the good organizations aren't immune to the insipid and ridiculous. GE, at this writing, has launched a quality initiative that includes, as in karate, green and black belts. The belt holders, various degrees of "quality masters," use lingo and acronyms ("Six Sigma" is a particular favorite) to demonstrate their "in" status. There are fraternity-like initiations into each successive degree of quality martial art. I can't help thinking that there's a consultant somewhere laughing his rear end off at what he was able to get away with while being paid half a million bucks for this program.

During early 1997, a consultant by the name of Martin Rutte began "chicken soup" groups within companies (sparked by a runaway bestseller, *Chicken Soup for the Soul,* by Jack Canfield and Mark Victor Hansen, which is a compilation of "uplifting" anecdotes), at which he sits and reads stories of "courage, compassion, and creativity in the workplace." He asks $10,000 for this adult sandbox session, and some companies have actually hired him, albeit with very mixed results according to a story in the *Wall Street Journal.*[5]

Would you like to hear what that $10,000 would do in the form of 100 on-the-spot employee performance awards of $100 each? I stood next to the CEO of Allianz Insurance, Lowell Anderson, while he announced over the headquarters public address system that there was an envelope awaiting each employee who was not in the company's incentive plan, as a token of the company's appreciation of their contribution to outstanding business results. He directed all employees who qualified to pick up their envelopes in the human resources department "whenever convenient."

---

5. Timothy D. Schellhardt, "Feeling Dispirited? Have Someone Read This Story to You," *Wall Street Journal,* 10 February 1997, 1.

Before he clicked off the microphone, the doors to the human resources department flew open and a steady stream of smiling people beat their way to their envelopes. It was apparently very convenient to do so right at that moment. Lowell and I watched in gratification as smiling employees trooped past. Each envelope held a $100 bill, and Lowell had approved 370 of them—one for everyone not covered by the senior level incentive plan. His total cost was $37,000. Of course, he could have had four sessions with Mr. Rutte instead, but fortunately neither one of us knew about him at the time. (This is not a contradiction of the point that money doesn't motivate. The $100 was not making anyone rich. It was the symbolism that was so powerful: An unheard of—at that level immediate monetary award to share the organization's good fortune with those responsible.)

There is no management skill that involves walking over hot coals. There is tremendous harm done—reported occasionally in psychological journals—where people who have trod hot coals (or performed some other dramatic feat) aren't able to transfer that feeling of accomplishment back to the job. That creates feelings of frustration, loss of self-esteem, and hopelessness. There is no leadership trait enhanced by rappelling down mountains. (On the Internet one day I received a request from a consultant I never heard of. He specializes in "outdoor experiences" but one of his clients didn't want to risk the top team on some mountain. So he was inquiring if any of us had experience "gaining the outdoor benefits on an indoor basis." After a while, you just need a stiff drink.) Yet Tony Robbins far outsells Peter Drucker. The "self-help" and guru industry does have one quite tangible result to provide for the skeptic: a constantly growing, very good-looking bottom line.

PERSONALITY AND MEDIA ATTENTION OVERWHELM VALIDITY AND RESULTS

There are two types of management movements that grow into menaces that threaten to consume, blob-like, the nearest sentient beings. (Picture the pods from *Invasion of the Body Snatchers* being stacked by the janitorial staff in the spare conference room.)

First, some legitimate techniques are allowed to run amok and become ends in themselves, and, second, some techniques are pure hucksterism. Transactional analysis is an early example of the former.[6] It is still a valid intervention technique utilized by eclectic therapists. But in the dynamics of the workplace, it's impossible to pragmatically apply a full-fledged training program on transactional analysis. It is, however, useful, to realize that the conflict you are engaged in is caused by a parent/child relationship with a colleague, and that you might be able to break that impasse by phrasing your request in a different manner. You don't need two days of a seminar, three books, a facilitator, and $400 per person to impart that skill. You need about two hours and a good facilitator leading a discussion.

Right brain/left brain thinking is another modest idea that became an industry.[7] Essentially, the point is that people learn in different ways. Some of us prefer visual cues, some of us sequential explanations, and some of us are comfortable with both. The "left/right" split—right side of the brain controlling creativity and inspiration, the left side controlling logic and analysis—has been debunked by researchers at least as often as it's been promulgated by the supporters. But who cares? People do learn in different ways, and we need to ensure that learning is offered in a wide variety of formats.

However, this doesn't necessitate retreats, classes, development of your right brain (ostensibly through artistic exercise), or a $150,000 outlay from the corporate coffers. I've actually sat in rooms with "experts" who have led the group through breathing exercises using alternate inhaling and exhaling through each nostril, claiming this somehow developed brain functionality. It clearly does create lightheadedness, which explains why no one walked out and demanded their money back. These facilitators generally have few credentials beyond being prepared to facilitate the program.

How do these things come to pass? Is it the result of some vast research organization investing billions to discover, experi-

---

6. Transactional analysis was created by Dr. Eric Berne and popularized in Thomas A. Harris, M.D., *I'm OK, You're OK: A Practical Guide to Transactional Analysis* (New York: Harper & Row, 1967). The approach suggests that our communications with others are based upon roles of adult, parent, and child, and that certain combinations are more conducive to honesty and effectiveness than others.
7. Popularized by Ned Hermann and described further below.

ment with, and validate the next great breakthrough in management science? Well, it's not quite so grand as all that.

Ned Hermann is the creator of the Hermann Brain Dominance Instrument, and one of the leading gurus in the "brain dominance" field. I met him in 1972 at GE, when he was in charge of their management training center. Ned's job was to evaluate and purchase training courses for the thousands of GE employees cycled through the management institute. He was quite an artistic guy, never tired of telling you of his near-death experience, and had risen to the rank of four-star curmudgeon. Also, he apparently had a lot of time on his hands.

In his latter years with GE, he received permission to investigate brain dominance theory and, upon retirement, to take his research with him. As a retired GE employee, he launched his company, selling instruments to measure brain dominance, conducting workshops on using the approach within companies, and making speeches at every major conference and convention that attracts the gurus. When he was asked at one of these conferences to respond to the current academic research that seemed to indicate that people use both the left and right sides of their brains situationally, and are not dominated by either hemisphere, he responded, "Well, it was only a metaphor." Now that's flexibility. When I asked him once what someone should do with the talent that was described on his own instrument as "double dominant," Hermann replied, "Use it."

"Brain dominance," transactional analysis, the management "grid," situational leadership, total quality management, reengineering, continuous improvement efforts, and a myriad of other "programs du jour" have kernels of truth and germs of applicability. But they are too often the panacea of the month, desperately employed by management to still employee discontent, resolve issues they don't care to understand, and keep their own human resources "experts" off the streets.

PLEASE WALK THIS WAY TO CONFORM TO MY BELIEFS: THE FALLACY OF BEHAVIOR PREDICTIONS

Human behavior is very difficult to predict, which is why we've spawned a highly suspect industry that tries to predict it, replete with charts, graphs, quadrants, formulas, and typologies. The trouble with all that is that our behavior is actually based on these quite complicated combinations:

1. One's heredity creates the biochemistry streaming through our system. We inherit a range of physical and physiological factors that influence our behavior.

2. Nurturing plays the greatest role in early learned behavior. Our environments and our early influencers create baggage that can last for all our days ("You'll never be able to throw a ball well," "You have wonderful musical ability.").

3. Environment strongly influences behaviors. Many people act profoundly differently in family, work, civic, recreational, and social situations. This is why people who know someone in only one of those spheres react so strongly when they're told of radically different behavior in another sphere ("You must be mistaken—that's not the person I know.").

4. Perceived success and failures reinforce behaviors. We tend to try to repeat those that resulted in gratifying conditions, and we tend to try to eliminate those that resulted in punishing conditions. This dynamic often prevails despite the fact that factors other than our behaviors might have had most influence over the outcomes (i.e., another candidate was simply better qualified for the job, our spouse was having a bad day and was going to take it out on us no matter what we said or did).

5. Finally, the *other* performer's behavior strongly influences our own. You may be highly assertive normally, but someone else in a meeting who is assertive to the point of belligerence may force you into a much more malleable, much less aggressive set of behaviors ("Wow, John made you look mild in comparison.").

Because of these complex combinations, all of which come into play for all of us, blanket motivational programs and generic approaches to improve morale or influence others seldom work. There are only two rules that you can effectively rely upon to try to anticipate people's behavior at work:

Rule #1: People believe what they see, not what they read or what they hear. The role of the exemplar is paramount in shaping behavior on the job.
Rule #2: When people are told something or given litera-

ture in an attempt to influence their behavior, they will immediately resort to Rule #1.

Once of the primary reasons for excellence being so elusive is that we are sending out a profusion of messages every day that it's just as effective to lower standards as it is to raise performance. Once people notice that lowering the standards not only gains them equivalent rewards, but is also much easier than raising performance, so they tend to flock to the path of least resistance. What's so strange about that?

If you hang signs on the wall announcing that respect for employees is a key organizational value, but then you allow managers to ruthlessly berate employees in front of the signs while still rewarding those managers for meeting their goals, what do employees believe, the signs of the walls or the berating in the halls? They will quickly understand that the organization values meeting the numbers at any cost, including mercilessly abusing employees. Since it's far easier to treat people harshly than to develop the skills to lead them effectively, that's the path of least resistance—all reward and no punishment for the manager.

Show me a reward system and I'll show you a value system. Organizations reward what they truly value.

THE HORRIBLE LABELS AND ABUSIVE EFFECTS OF THE PERSONALITY PROFILERS, OR WHAT DO YOU EXPECT FROM A "LOW C"?

By far some of the worst harm being done is the insistence on evaluating your colleague (or neighbor or spouse) based upon their "type." In the 1950s, someone wrote a book called *The Mind Masters*, debunking the burgeoning postwar psychological assessment craze. It caused a furor at the time, with its implications of brainwashing, unfair practices, and hidden evaluations. Maybe we should dust it off.

In the Providence Gas Company years ago I found employees with coffee mugs that bore patterns such as in Figure 3-2. I was amazed to find that these were graphic representations of the "personality assessment" of the cup's owner, printed there so that others could readily identify the owner's personality type and make necessary adjustments.

Figure 3-2. "Personality assessment."

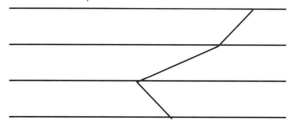

"You mean, this is how someone acts all the time, consistent with this profile?" I asked. "What if someone is having a difficult day? What if I've just received good news? What if I'm using someone else's cup?!"

My questions went unanswered, since I was not their consultant, but only a customer trying to straighten out an incorrect gas bill. Presumably, the bill got fouled up while everyone was deciphering the coffee hieroglyphics.

This is dangerous stuff.

In organizational America, we are being asked not to understand each other, but to label each other.[8] If personality and/or behavioral assessments are conducted to better appreciate how someone will respond to reward, how to better communicate, and how to establish a motivating environment, that makes sense. But we're asked instead to use the labels to explain away behavior.

The Carlson Companies, a diverse billion dollar, privately held organization headquartered in Minneapolis, markets an instrument with a trade name of Performax, and commonly referred to by devotees as the "disc" system. It uses four behavioral traits and their relationships to assess one's "style." Consequently, one can be referred to as a "high d" if one's assertiveness is high, or a "low c" if one's attention to detail is low. These tests have come in self-scoring versions, wherein the participant simply looks up the scores to his or her responses, and then reads preprinted interpretive paragraphs in the back of the instrument.

---

8. This is not an American private preserve. The French, to this day, place such an emphasis on handwriting analysis—grandly called graphology—that companies will not seriously consider typed résumés, because they can't be analyzed. Some applicants choose "ringers" with presumably more positively regarded writing to substitute their own cursive. I know, this is a country that has deified Jerry Lewis, but still . . .

In one version, there was a great line to this effect: If this description doesn't completely describe you, or there are aspects with which you don't agree, focus on those that are most accurate and use them for your development. In other words, here's a fortune cookie, folks, see how well its message fits.

The "disc" instruments come in a wide variety of versions and types, include training and workshops, books and tapes, and represent huge sales. At one point, a bank president I encountered was using them for his hiring assessments. "How much do they cost?" I asked. "We get them from the local salesperson for $12 each." (I'm figuring that means they're probably $5 wholesale to the salesperson.)

"Ted, just how much validity are you willing to place in a $12 investment in terms of a person's career and potential impact on your business?"

"Well, it's just a tool that helps our human resources people in their judgment."

No, it's become the judgment, and all too often these tests are wielded by a bevy of "consultants" who are really speakers or trainers or passersby who have no other skills, no psychological training, no education in behavior, and precious little experience. And they're showing up everywhere. These and other tests are aggressively promoted commercially (just take a look at the ads in the back of training magazines) as a legitimizing tool for people who want to appear as knowledgeable consultants. They are used on a vast scale and they are very dangerous.

At this writing, I have never seen any concurrent validity studies of the "disc" system, nor read any articles in refereed, scientific journals indicating that there is any validity to the approach whatsoever. Perhaps there is. But wouldn't it help to prove it, before the acolytes brand someone as highly assertive or not very persuasive? There is tremendous danger in using nonvalidated instruments—which are almost always in nonprofessional hands—to make assessments about one's behavioral style, chances of success, job suitability, and job candidacy. Aside from the very real legal potential of being sued, there is the ethical issue of making judgments based on what amounts to amateur psychology, and the pragmatic problem of hiring, promoting, and developing the wrong people, based upon the wrong interpretation of the wrong instrument.

Several years ago I was working with Marine Midland Bank. The bank had become enamored with the Myers-Briggs Type Indicator (MBTI), one of the more respected and validated instruments in the assessment field. Most psychologists and counselors will tell you it's an important tool if used wisely, interpreted carefully, and applied with discretion.

However, the bank had certified Myers-Briggs analysts on staff and, like total quality team leaders or the licensed instructors of most training programs, their focus was on justifying and using their technology, not on organizational business goals. One in particular—I'll call him Rob—saw evaluating and interpreting the MBTI as the exclusive mission in his life at the bank. He was causing his manager a colossal headache, but she was powerless because he had become a guru to the senior management team.

One day I found Rob providing an executive vice president with an interesting bit of feedback. Rob was asking the executive the questions on the MBTI (normally completed in writing—it's a multiple choice instrument) and the executive was responding *with the answers he believed his dead mother would have given*. When I inquired about the objective, I was told that the executive was trying to "type" his mother, which would help him to understand some of his problems with her as he grew up. A year later, both the executive and the analyst were gone. But at what price in the meantime?

Peter Block is a bright, articulate, and lovely guy whom I first met in 1982. He was a principal of Block-Petrella-Weisbord, and he's written highly popular books such as *Flawless Consulting, The Empowered Manager,* and *Stewardship.* Pete has shown tremendous insights into the role of human resources. He has become the darling of many in the human resources community because he focuses almost exclusively on soft, touchie-feelie, esoteric issues, which allows practitioners to think they are involved with the company's well-being without once getting dirty in the soil of tomorrow's business plans. In *The Empowered Manager,* for example, he talks about:[9]

▲ Dependency versus autonomy
▲ Claiming our autonomy by creating a vision

---

9. Peter Block, *The Empowered Manager* (San Francisco: Jossey-Bass, 1987).

▲ Finding peace with the boss
▲ Authentic statement in the face of disapproval
▲ Moving toward tension

Even with the most liberal interpretation, there is little in the book about empowered managers being accountable for results, aligning business objectives with their subordinates' objectives, and managing scant resources to meet changing needs. You can make the case that the book isn't about those issues, but that *is* my case. Too many people are reading Peter Block without also reading Peter Drucker.

Peter's colleague, Marv Weisbord, has recently propagated a strange new system called "future search." This is a planning process during which participants must reveal their most salient recollections about their early lives, influences on them, and other personal issues before beginning the planning. The planning process itself is like nothing I've ever seen. Here's what happened when I sat through such a session with one of my clients—a division of a Fortune 500 firm—that was led by an internal consultant qualified to facilitate the process and another facilitator experienced in group dynamics.

After two days of exhaustive meetings with a group of forty people, who were asked to report on those personal connections and future musings, a humongous document was created detailing everyone's inputs. It read as though the construction crew from the Tower of Babel had recorded their methods. The group itself was apoplectic, in that they felt they had accomplished nothing and didn't know how to use the output, and this included the COO of the division. Instead of calling things a bust and launching a legitimate planning process with the few people actually needed, they called *another* two-day meeting to sort out the first one and make sense of it. Call it *Future Search: The Return.*

The second two days were marked by dynamics we've all experienced in the absence of leadership. There were side talks in the halls, murmuring in the meetings, and great confusion as assignments were completed with little enthusiasm and less understanding. The facilitators began to openly argue with each other. It was the Marx Brothers in management. Finally, people began standing up to openly challenge the process and the facilitator. The session bumped along to a close, but with another round of genuine unhappiness, loss of credibility for leadership, and total expenditure inside the circle I depicted at the outset of this chapter.

In fact, the average salary in that room was $100,000. Four ten-hour days of forty people represent 1,600 person/hours. The company had spent about $640,000 before fringes, and without counting the preparation, interim, and follow-up time required of facilitators and participants alike. Call it three-quarters of a million dollars, conservatively, and for what? For an exercise in the ethereal and surreal. This organization's future landscape was je-june, because its planning process was a child's game raised to management respectability by designers with no experience running companies or leading others.

No Guru Is Ever Held Responsible for Results—Managers Are

A final example of the ability of even top executives to pretend to see the emperor's clothes, even when he tells everyone that he's really naked.

Michael Hammer is the Harvard professor who launched a consulting firm and untold riches for himself by creating "reengineering" in a business bestseller by the same name, a process by which organizations change their basic processes and, essentially, "reinvent" themselves. As surely as the sun rises, there ensued consulting firms, specialists, internal departments, publications, learned articles, and academic euphoria over reengineering. Shades of the quality movement.

And, apropos of the quality movement, it hasn't really worked.

Reengineering has too often been an excuse to throw people into the streets, which itself is euphemistically called "downsizing." This alarmed even Hammer's crusty soul, so he wrote a second book *to explain why he wasn't right in the first book* and why so many firms were not reaping the benefits of his thinking. One of his key omissions, it seems, was that people were not sufficiently taken into consideration the first time around. It was time to rectify this oversight.

Hammer appears at executive conferences for $50,000 to explain—often in terms described by attendees as "barnyard"—what they ought to do next. Only in America would senior executives pay $50,000 to hear someone who's never run a company use barnyard expletives to explain why the money they spent on his "original" thinking was wasted because he neglected to consider the people who worked for them. My dog has more common sense, and he doesn't ask for stock options.[10]

I used to know a guy who got thoroughly drunk at business meetings, and when confronted with his poor performance always replied, "I didn't walk in here and I'm not leaving." That Mad Hatter logic seemed to take care of any challenges to his credibility. When someone figures out how to downsize the self-appointed, vainglorious, irrelevant gurus, we'll finally have found some management wisdom. Until then, we'll just have to keep searching for excellence.

LET US NOT FORGET THE MOTIVATIONAL SPEAKERS, FOR THEY SHALL INHERIT THE WEALTH

Only in America could motivational speaking become an industry. It generates billions of dollars in seminar attendance, book sales, motivational tapes, T-shirts, coffee mugs, and a variety of other goods and services for those who need to be extensively and exhaustively uplifted. And it is almost pure hokum.

The only people getting wealthy from books on how to grow rich and speeches on how to make a million dollars are the people doing the writing and speaking. After all, if their advice was really valid and pragmatic, everyone buying and listening would soon become rich and the advice would no longer be needed. And why, exactly, would any individual have to attend more than one such seminar, listen to more than one such tape, or read more than one such book? Because it's almost pure hokum, and hokum sells.

Since the days of Barnum, people have been willing to be suckered and admit to it. The difference today is that entire corporations have endorsed the hucksters. Corporate meetings are highlighted by people who are espousing that we be our own best friends, ring our own bells, bounce back from adversity, and become winners. The trouble is, while the presenters can cry precisely on cue at twenty-seven minutes into their presentations, can laugh at stories that they've told thousands of times as if

10. See "Re-Engineering Gurus," *Wall Street Journal*, 26 November 1996, 1.

they've never heard them before, and can involve the audience in ludicrous activities such as rubbing each others' shoulders and telling colleagues how good they are, they never get around to explaining *how* to accomplish the transcendence, improvement, or change. Instead they tell us stories.

Generals Colin Powell and Norman Schwartzkopf are two of the stars of the motivational circuit in the late 1990s, and they are both quite good. They share practical advice on leadership, are self-effacing, use humor effectively, and give the audience the opportunity to see and hear two heroes. Each of them commands $75,000 for an hour's appearance. (At one conference, Schwartzkopf made his entrance from a mock Cobra attack helicopter with a platoon of heavily armed soldiers escorting him.) At the other end of this scale are the $2,500 speakers who have little training or expertise, but an abundance of platform skills, and who provide the audience with simply dreadful advice. They throw in some quotes from philosophers they've never read, cite incorrect research, use some standard exercises from trade publications such as *Games Trainers Play*, and they're off to the races.

One example: Many motivational speakers are fond of citing a study by Albert Mehrabian that found that "only 14 percent" of what influences people is from the words they hear. The rest of the influence comes from nonverbal gestures and movements. They conclude, therefore, that in meetings, things like eye contact, smiles, hand gestures, and body language are more important in influencing colleagues than the actual content of the presentation, words chosen, or reasoning. They cite no other research, just that one study. Yet Mehrabian never conducted such a study. What he researched was the dynamics of people in social situations and their reaction to being interrupted or asked a favor, and the requester's success in being cordial (smiling) or uncordial (not smiling). He did this with waiting lines in the post office, for example, not in the workplace and not in meetings.[11]

This is an example of the pseudoscience and psychobabble that poorly educated, borderline-incompetent speakers and trainers are engaged in. It was bad enough when it was an individually focused effort, in which people paid to hear this nonsense, and

---

11. See Albert Mehrabian and J.A. Russell, *An Approach to Environmental Psychology* (Cambridge, MA: MIT Press, 1974).

often subjected themselves to the bizarre conditions of est[12] years ago, or to the mumbo jumbo, trod-over-hot-coals of a Tony Robbins today. But when it's introduced into the organizational environment by corporate meeting planners and event managers, then legions of people are forced to digest the pap.

Then there is the "rally" business, the leading exponent of which is Peter Loew. Loew runs dozens of these a year around the country, drawing 10,000 people or more to the events. His typical exhortations are questions such as, "Do you want to be more successful?!" and "Are you ready to be more successful?!" each bringing resounding cheers from the audience. Loew's rallies are interesting cultural events for two reasons. First, they combine the individual with the corporate, in that people may sign up themselves, but many corporations underwrite their employees' attendance. This makes all kinds of corporate sense, since it's a modest investment (typically a couple of hundred dollars per person plus travel costs), it pumps up the employees, however briefly, and it passes very well, thank you, as employee development.

The second peculiarity is that Loew has managed to draw a host of celebrities, from former President George Bush, to Muhammad Ali, to Colin Powell, to Elizabeth Dole, to Christopher Reeve, to serve as guest speakers. They are the "draw," while the only slightly lesser known but highly effective fulltime motivational speakers, such as Zig Zigler and Brian Tracy, spend almost all of their platform time hawking their books and tapes. Those sales are shared with Mr. Loew, of course.[13]

Why would "big name" successful people share the stage with the likes of Peter Loew? Perhaps because he is the consummate impresario. Perhaps because they believe in positive mental attitude and uplift. Perhaps because they relish the opportunity to remain in the spotlight in front of a safe audience. And perhaps because they're being paid an awfully large pile of money. Mr. Loew won't disclose the fee arrangement, but all of those cited

---

12. Earhart Seminar Training, all the "new age" rage in the 1970s and early 1980s.

13. Zig Zigler is actually captured on tape (see the following footnote) telling the audience that, if there were a choice between sending his daughter to college for one year, and listening to his motivational tapes, it would be an easy decision. She'd listen to his tapes and skip college. How's that for an out-of-world experience? Yet he says it with a straight face. Thanks, but I'll pay the tuition.

above command premium fees on the circuit. And, in case you haven't done the math, 10,000 attendees times $200 a person is $2 million.[14]

As I said, those who are speaking and writing about making millions are the ones most likely to actually be doing it.

Motivation is an intrinsic event. It can only come from within the individual, which accounts for its self-perpetuating nature. I can't motivate you, and you can't motivate people who work for you. What we can do is to attempt to establish environments that are conducive to motivation occurring. Typically, those environments:

- ▲ Reward performance
- ▲ Are nonpoliticized
- ▲ Provide empowerment
- ▲ Provide ongoing feedback to the performer
- ▲ Allow for innovation
- ▲ Tolerate prudent risk taking and setbacks
- ▲ Utilize referent power sources

Moreover, the way in which people best motivate themselves is through the dynamic shown in Figure 3-3. People must acquire specific, tangible skills that have the potential to improve their performance, personally and/or professionally. An example would be the skill set that allows one to negotiate successfully by separating out the "musts," which can't be lost and are non-negotiable, from the "wants," which are desires and can be compromised or sacrificed for the greater goal.

Once the skills have been learned, they must be applied. This is the failure of most classroom approaches, in that the skills remain eternally theoretical, because they've only been discussed or practiced on artificial case exercises, or they atrophy altogether. Once applied on the job, they may be unsuccessful, requiring more learning, or they may be successful, creating confidence from that success. When successful with a set of skills, the indi-

---

14. Many of these details are from my appearance on CNN's and Fortune's *Newstand,* 9 September 1998, which aired a critical review of the Peter Loew's seminars including interviews with Mr. Loew and footage from the events.

Figure 3-3. The success cycle.

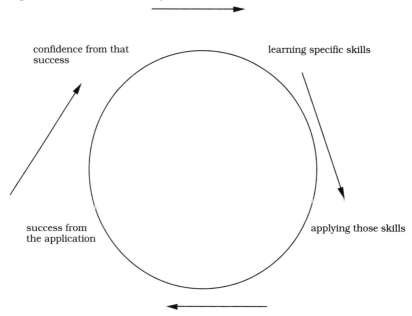

vidual is prompted to use them more—we all engage in behaviors that have historically produced desired ends in our self-interest—which creates mastery from the repetition. The confidence that results from the mastery encourages us to continue to learn new skills that will have similar, positive outcomes for us.

Hence, the cycle of motivation is based on successes from learned skills, not abstract beliefs in our own beauty, perfection, competence, or fortitude. Walking across hot coals is not a skill set that is repeatable in one's normal professional or personal world, and there is not one scintilla of evidence suggesting that the "skill" (which is merely walking rapidly—whether you get burned has nothing to do with your beliefs or self-worth) has any transferability or sustainability in the workplace.

We can help others (or ourselves) become motivated, but not through pop psychology and glorious yet empty phrases. We do it through acquiring skills that can be rapidly put to use to meet our objectives on a repeated basis.

Isn't it odd how the most successful people always seem to be so motivated? It ranks right up there with another peculiarity I've noticed: The harder I work, the luckier I get.

Let's Ignore the Numbers, and Just Sell to Each Other

Before we leave the subject of the touchie-feelies and the charlatans, a few words are due about one of the greatest business self-delusions of our times: the euphemistic "multilevel marketing." (If we pursue the etiology, we go back through "network marketing," to "pyramid marketing," to "Ponzi scheme." Somehow, each succeeding strata of sediment has gained more verbal respectability.)

What's now obscurely referred to as "MLM" is a purported business in selling a product that is really a business in selling entry to the club. Whether it's floor wax, cosmetics, telephone services, or driveway sealant, the product is relatively unimportant. What is important is selling the distributorships, because the seller then continues to move up the hierarchy while getting paid commission not only on the fee that the new distributor paid for entry, but on every new distributor they recruit, and the recruits recruit, and so on, forever.

Well, not quite forever. You see, if we start with a small number of people, those arriving early do very well on the recruiting. If 10 of us have to generate 6 recruits each, that's only a total of 60 people. If one person in 20 agrees to join (a high ratio), then we need a pool of 1,200 people to draw from. But now those 60 new recruits, each responsible for 6 newer recruits, will have to find a pool of 3,600 people. And those 1,200 third-tier recruits will need 144,000 people, which is greater than the population of Providence, Rhode Island. The fourth tier recruits, now 7,200 strong theoretically, would need a pool of 864,000 people to produce their 6 recruits each. That figure is greater than the population of all but a half-dozen of our greatest cities. The next tier produces a number greater than the population of several states.

The people who start these schemes do well, which is why they show up at the recruiting meetings in the stereotypical Cadillac and wearing the diamond pinkie ring. It's why they can afford infomercials. They're making money from *every* recruit at *every* level, no matter how unsuccessful those down the hierarchy may be individually. Sooner or later, the numbers collapse the system. Amway, which has been doing a version of this longer than anyone else, is a fine example. Although apparently successful as a corporate entity (numbers are not released), the average Amway distributor, according to documents obtained by *60 Minutes*, earns about $88 a month. Not exactly enough to quit your day job for.

I have encountered hundreds of fine, well-meaning, wouldn't-hurt-a-fly people in my work who are engaged in MLM. When I ask why on earth they would do that, they tell me that they are looking for independence, trying to help others, and have seen evidence of the industry's effectiveness. And they're right. The network marketing/MLM/Ponzi folks have managed to gain respectability. There are MLM conferences (an absolute bonanza for the motivational speakers noted above) and books, and the name has been transmogrified into respectability (if, for no other reason, you can't figure out what MLM means).

The industry has tapped into the entrepreneurial fire that has been lit by mass layoffs and downsizing, the American myth that overnight riches are not dependent upon talent, hard work, and luck, but rather on finding the "quick hit" and following the pied piper in the luxury car. It has shown that you can "help others" by helping them into the recruiting process.

In the American junk culture of the late 1990s, it has become a artifact.

The guy who plasters my walls, Murray, is a superb plasterer and a great guy. He's been doing the work for years. He's obsessive about quality, and very reasonably priced.

One day, out of the blue, he asked if he could give me a cassette to listen to. "It's a business opportunity," he said. "Maybe you can give me some feedback."

The tape was for a pyramid opportunity involving long-distance telephone service. The idea was to quickly sign up your family and friends for the services, and maybe generate some recruits in the bargain. When I explained to Murray the craziness of it, he then produced a video, which he respectfully asked me to watch. Out of friendship, I did.

Both the video and prior audio were filled with two claims: The first was that the technology was revolutionary, and this was the leading edge of long-distance call rates. The second was that the two people on both tapes, executives with this company, were getting richer and richer, as you were watching them. They were unabating in their appeals to independence, wealth beyond your dreams, helping your neighbors, and, well, wealth beyond your dreams. At no point, in the two hours of both tapes, were the details of *how* the wealth was to be generated shared.

Murray finally asked if he could bring along the regional executive, who was his mentor. This was too good to turn down, so I said "sure." Murray brought him to my house, and we talked for over an hour.

At the conclusion, after tap-dancing all over the room, when he couldn't refute my pyramid numbers but rather danced around the issue because what they were really selling was "high technology," he said that he'd like me to come to one of their rallies and address the sales team, openly and honestly. "We have to hear from people like you," he piously intoned. "I'll be in touch later this week."

He left, and I've never heard another word. I just hope that Murray will still do my plastering.

SOLUTIONS: FORGET THE FADS AND ASK THE FOLKS

We need a test that will determine the legitimacy of management advice and consulting/training interventions. The test questions, I believe, are these:

1. Will the customer benefit?
2. Will our business goals be demonstrably better achieved?

While I can live with one being answered in the affirmative and the other subject to circumstances, I believe that both have to be clear, unqualified positives. We don't want to *feel* good, we want to *do* good. (And it's amazing how achieving the latter aids the former, anyway.)

Here, then, are three pieces of advice on how to achieve excellence through the avoidance of the touchie-feelie brigade and the focus on the external, pragmatic business goals:

1. Anyone Who Recommends a Major Initiative Based on Someone's Popular Book Should Be Thrown Out the Door

Here are two quick examples, from very good books.

Margaret Wheatley has written a very interesting work, called *Leadership and the New Science*.[15] She raises two quite promis-

---

15. Margaret J. Wheatley, *Leadership and the New Science: Learning About Organization from an Orderly Universe* (San Francisco: Berret-Koehler, 1994).

ing issues for organizational life and productivity. One is that consciousness is a function of the processing of information and, consequently, dogs have more consciousness than snails. That may mean that people have varied levels of consciousness within organizations, and that some work on information exchange and processing may dramatically heighten productivity, customer response time, etc. The second point is that even chaos has boundaries, and if you can define the boundaries you can control the chaos, or at least manage it. That has fascinating implications for agility, response to new market conditions, anticipating disruptions, and so on.

If these ideas (or whichever other ones suited the reader) were studied and applied, organizations could benefit outside the circle cited earlier in this chapter, focusing externally, not internally. Instead, Ms. Wheatley has been called to the lecture circuit (no fault of hers), seminars are created, and touchie-feelie types are heard uttering words like "fractal" from her book in the course of meetings. A good idea does not a movement make.

For example, it is one thing to adapt the Wheatley message to customers and their various levels of knowledge about the company. Their "consciousness" might vary considerably, and a variety of educational messages may be called for to raise consumer consciousness about the benefits of the organization's products and services. Such an initiative has clear profit potential. However, examining chaos theory in the organization, another concept from the same book, is most likely a high-cost initiative that will be embedded in the human resources department (or with outside consultants) and will achieve nothing other than significantly raise costs.

Another insightful book is called *The Knowledge-Creating Company*.[16] While a lot of it is dry description of Japanese organizational successes, the authors make a superb case about taking what they call tacit knowledge—the stuff in our heads that guides our actions—and turning it into explicit knowledge—the commonly known, documented information that colleagues can use. They then reverse it, and explain how documented material must be translated into internalized knowledge, the explicit to the

---

16. Ikujiro Nonaka and Hirotaka Takeuchi, *The Knowledge-Creating Company: How Japanese Companies Create the Dynamics of Innovation* (New York: Oxford Press, 1995).

tacit. Among other implications is the ability of an organization to stimulate productivity by eliminating "failure work" caused by people without access to the best techniques, or who constantly must reinvent their own wheels.

The authors' approach is far more tangible and immediately applicable than the esoteric "learning organization" that we're constantly reminded we ought to be a part of. I haven't heard their work or their names elsewhere, however, probably because their salient points don't make for an interesting seminar series or their academic approach isn't conducive to the speaking circuit.

2. All Training Ought to Be Commercialized, Just Like R&D

Excellent companies don't make R&D investments without a careful assessment of their commercial potential. (Unsuccessful ones do all the time, but that's another story.) Similarly, organizations shouldn't embark upon any developmental initiative without a similar investigation. No one is arguing that we shouldn't make an investment in people. The question is, what should that investment be?

Are people really performing better because they know their personality types and the styles of those around them, or are they performing better because someone has taught them the use of key questions at a crucial point in the sale? Do organizations meet business objectives better when legions of people are included in cumbersome planning processes for "ownership," or when each individual receives clear, honest, and frequent communication about corporate progress and his or her role in it? Is the customer better served because the service team went off on an outdoor adventure, or because the staff was cross-trained so that any employee can answer any phone? Do people go the extra yard because they can mindlessly cite the requirements of a learning organization, or because they've seen evidence of the company rewarding that extra effort, in the form of personal days and family time?

Allowing the people who propose major cultural interventions to justify them in terms of who wrote which book, what the seminar circuit is promulgating, or what their brethren in other companies are doing is like asking a lemming for directions. You might as well just follow the crowd.

Senior management has to demand specific returns on training, development, education, reorganizations, reengineering, quality programs and any other device that comes down the pike with bells and whistles in its wake. How will we be better off on the bottom line? How will the customer be better served? How will business goals be achieved faster?

And here's a good question to ask the perpetrators: Would you bet your job on it?

3. Ask

In twenty-five years of consulting I am never less than astonished at what happens when I simply ask people what they need in order to do their jobs better, and report their responses back to senior management. I am treated with the respect that's usually accorded the supernaturally insightful.

"These are excellent ideas. It pays to get someone from outside the organization, who isn't tainted by it."

"Thank you. That will be $50,000."

People doing the work know what they need to do it better, and what ought to be removed that is impeding them now. They can smell out a silly program or lunatic approach from half-a-mile away or more, and can puncture an empty phrase without thinking hard. The problem is, no one asks them.

Convene a small group of people from different areas in an informal setting. Tell them you want their opinion. Here's a program the company is considering. Here are the presumed benefits. Here are the anticipated downsides. What do you think?

If the question is honest, the inquirer is trusted, and the potential program understood, you'll find out quickly enough whether or not the effort will pay off. These are not people impressed by gurus, paid to attend workshops, or intrigued by the arcane. They are people who have to do the work every day, who understand the current standards, how well they're met, and what the standards might actually be. They are a superb resource, a virtual consulting mother lode. Yet no one wants to enter the mine.

Venture into that territory. Bring a light. Don't be afraid of going deep down into the organizational shafts. Take a canary—like the coal miners of old did to test the air—if it helps. (If the canary croaked, so would they.) Don't worry about getting dirty. These are fine, hard-working people who know what the work is all about. Ask them about your plans to determine if they're realistic.

Just don't do it in an "open meeting."

> I was visiting a prospect who, intelligently, asked me to spend some time with the existing consultants working on various projects to ascertain if our approaches would be complementary. One of them was implementing a nebulous piece of froth called "self-authenticity."
>
> "What's this all about?" I asked.
>
> "It's putting people in touch with their own greatness. It allows them to be real no matter what the conditions."
>
> "What the hell does that mean? It sounds like warmed-over est from the 70s."
>
> "It's a spiritual, inner-focused movement that's based on work done by new age psychologists and counselors."
>
> "How do you know it works? How do you know it's what's needed here?"
>
> "This client meets my primary criterion for implementation, that's how I know."
>
> "And what's that, purchase of crystals?"
>
> "Their credit is good and their check cleared the bank."

Challenge Four

Create a Corporate Vision—The Ability to See Well

Consultants Aren't Always Competent Consultants, and Are Never Good Optometrists

In the history of organizational life there has probably never been a period with as much emphasis on "vision" and strategy formulation as is represented by the last decade or so. And no other stretch of time has seen more corporate failures reflected in bankruptcies, more bad judgment reflected in market share loss to international competition, and more desperate measures reflected in downsizings, reengineerings and outright panics.

In the face of an academic wave of books on strategy, vision, mission, and values, amidst an army of consultants earning their daily bread on the guidance of directionless companies, how does an organization manage to fail to clearly see its alternative future paths, let alone the natural extrapolation of its current one?

Is anyone else disturbed by the irony? Businesses are taking it on the chin, with the likes of Kodak, IBM, AT&T, Sears, GM, Polaroid, TWA, Digital Equipment, Apple, and tens of thousands of other organization whose names aren't that familiar struggling to "reinvent" themselves, cut dividends, and fire hundreds of thousands of productive people. But their consultants and advisors (such as McKinsey), their corporate recruiters (such as Ward Howell), and their reengineers (such as Ernst & Young) are having banner years. What bizarre math produces several years of cut dividends, reduced staffing, and loss of market share alongside increases in executive pay and millions paid to external consultants?

After all, how can you see the future down the road if you can't even see the balance sheet at the end of your nose? The cause of the distorted vision is found in the peculiar alliance between organizational leadership and external consultants.

FORTUNE TELLERS REQUIRE MORE CERTIFICATION THAN CONSULTANTS

I can tell you about the weakness in the consulting profession because I have been a practicing member for over a quarter century. The weaknesses apply to the giant consulting consortium and the lone wolf consultant, to the veteran and the neophyte, to the Fortune 500 strategist and the mom and pop small business coach.

In March of 1997, the firm of Towers Perrin[1] was "outed" in the media for a practice that is hardly unique to it and that many of us were aware of for some time. Towers would undertake a diversity audit of an organization, conducting management interviews, employee samplings, analysis of promotions, and the like, and then issue a report with a template for whatever corrective actions were necessary, which the firm could also help implement. Its charge for the diagnosis aspect alone was in excess of $100,000. Implementation would often cost several times as much.

The problem was that Towers turned in *virtually the identical report no matter who the client was or what the audit reflected.* The analysis was not only stunningly identical, but the recommendations echoed the "findings," and those recommendations were incredibly simplistic. (Some examples include such insights as to "build diversity into the performance evaluation plans," and "provide training about dealing with others in orientation pro-

---

1. Formerly known as TPF&C. Towers is a former human resource compensation and benefits firm that, like so many of its brethren, transmogrified into a full-service consulting operation. That transition was often imperfect, sort of like what happened to David Heddison when he tried to transport himself across the room in the movie *The Fly.* Neither human nor insect emerged intact.

grams.") A high school honors graduate could tell you the same thing never having seen your company, never having attended college, and never having taken over a hundred grand out of your pocket.

Towers' lame response was that it was—get this—"common practice" in the industry to provide similar findings when it was known that the same interventions would work. Excuse me, but that's the Suzuki response to the *Consumer Reports'* evaluation that their four-wheel drive vehicle flipped over too easily: "It only flips over if it's driven in a manner that allows it to," said Suzuki. Oh.

Shortly after being appointed, a new COO and heir apparent at AT&T had ruled that any consultants hired in any division for the purposes of strategy formulation had to be approved at the corporate level by him, personally. Why? Because he discovered that the corporation was spending *over a billion dollars annually* on strategy consultants, and it occurred to him that he also had a billion dollars of executives presumably charged with developing strategies for their units. The shareholders don't need both, and for the moment he decided to give senior management the opportunity to earn their keep. That's why he makes the big bucks, right? Afraid not; he was fired less than a year into the job for those kinds of insights and the threat they posed to then-CEO Robert Allen's way of operating.

The shelves, storerooms, computer disks, and filing cabinets of organizational America have become the repository of consulting reports, audits, interventions, strategies and schemes. The trouble is that, in my non-scientific but highly experiential observation, about 50 percent of all consulting firms, large and small, don't really know what they're doing, and about 90 percent of all those buying consulting services, at all levels, don't know how to detect that fact.[2]

It takes more work, application, legal conformance, and certification to become a palm reader on the boardwalk of Atlantic City than it does to become a consultant. Anyone, anywhere, at

---

2. I once sat in a meeting of executives of a Fortune 25 firm and its "Big 6" reengineering consultants. The client asked the consultants how they intended to help people with the transitions necessitated by the past year of reengineering work. The consultants took out templates and attempted to explain how the process was no different with people than it had been with the hardware and the systems. The client was appalled, and was also a couple of million dollars poorer.

any time can hang out a figurative shingle that advises the unsuspecting public that a consultant works there. A prospective lawyer
can't do that, because he or she has to attend to certain trivialities,
such as three years at an accredited law school and successful
completion of the bar exam in every state in which he or she
would like to work. The same holds true for doctors, certified public accountants, masseuses, manicurists, barbers, taxi drivers, volunteer firefighters, school teachers, day-care providers, funeral
directors, and bartenders. But not consultants. (My wife recently
presented me with a Dilbert cartoon T-shirt proclaiming, "I'm not
unemployed, I'm a consultant.")

There is a legion of "accrediting" bodies in consulting, 98
percent of which merely cash a check and send you their initials,
e.g., The American Association of Consultants and Window
Dressers, and "allow" you to use the initials ASCWD after your
name. If you're lucky, you might also get a quarterly newsletter,
and if the client's lucky you won't do too much harm. (If the
physician's oath, "First, do no harm," were seriously adhered to
by consultants, the profession could also qualify for endangered
species protection.)

The only accrediting group that I know of that goes so far as
to demand evidence of work performed, testimonials from clients,
continuing education requirements, and a sitting exam on ethics
is the Institute of Management Consultants (IMC), headquartered in New York. It grants the "CMC" (Certified Management
Consultant) designation to those who meet the criteria. It's better
than nothing, but it's still not tough to join.

Moreover, the IMC, like so many professional trade associations, is caught up in its own self-importance. The title CMC,
which means almost nothing to anyone who hires consultants in
the United States,[3] is based on evidence provided by the applicant.
Although client testimonials are required, those are easy to
gather, and for candidates applying who have been in the business for an extended time, the rules are relaxed even further. The
IMC makes no attempt at an exhaustive investigation as to
whether the applicant's work is of high quality according to the
clients, or if those clients even exist. The sitting exam on ethical

---

3. There is more heft behind the designation in Canada, where
that governing body has made it tougher to receive it and has created
significant public awareness as to its merit.

standards is based on a simple handbook that the candidate receives prior to it, not unlike the motor vehicle exam, where the issues are both common sense and can be absorbed by being studied just minutes before.

A "board" of existing CMCs interviews potential candidates, but the boards are chosen by whomever is available, and members receive no special training in interviewing, behavioral questioning, or fact checking. Finally, recertification, inaugurated in the past year, requiring that CMCs requalify every five years, demands no proof whatsoever of any consulting results, only an honor system response that the CMC has engaged in educational activities. (Similarly, the National Speakers Association recertifies their Certified Speaking Professionals every five years through a series of questions about the individuals attending the trade association's own functions. There is no requirement that a Certified Speaking Professional has had to deliver even one speech in the prior five years!)

Can you imagine a state bar association failing to check whether an individual has actually been graduated from law school, or providing the answers to the current year's bar exam just prior to its actual administration? Could a board-certified physician receive that rating if he or she hadn't touched a patient in the last five years? Let's hope not.

The larger firms, such as McKinsey, Boston Consulting Group, Bain, Towers Perrin, and another twenty-five or so like them, might or might not belong to consulting industry trade associations. But even if they do, it means less than nothing in terms of those firms' individual practitioners, whose competence and ethics might be all over the spectrum. In 1997, in a poll of MBAs reported by *Fortune*, the most desired company to work for was McKinsey & Co. Historically, that firm has also been among the very highest in salaries for new MBA recruits.

THE UNHOLY ALLIANCE OF BUSINESS AND CONSULTANTS (THE BLIND LEADING THE BLIND)

Eisenhower warned of the "military-industrial complex." Today, we're facing something much more pernicious: the "executive-consulting paradox." In organizations paying the world's largest sums[4] for executives' purported ability to guide and lead their businesses, those same wealthy executives are hiring the world's most expensive consultants to tell them what to do. (The tendency of McKinsey consultants, for example, to sell multimillion dollar deals, go on to become executives in client companies, and then bring in former colleagues for more multimillion dollar deals in their new environment is legendary in the industry.) Perhaps nowhere in America has excellence suffered as much as in the executive suite, where the following bizarre gnostic wisdom holds forth:

- ▲ If the company does well, I deserve a fortune. (Eisner at Disney)
- ▲ If the company doesn't do well, I deserve a fortune for preventing it from having fared even more poorly. (Brennan at Sears)
- ▲ If I'm going to foster success, or at least avert failure, I must be able to hire consulting help to guide us. (Everybody)
- ▲ If the consultants' advice does well for us, it's because I had the wisdom to hire them. (Everybody)
- ▲ If the consultant's advice does poorly for us, it's because the consultants misled us, I've been able to determine this and prevent more damage, and I'll make sure the consultants are replaced. (Figee International suing Boston Consulting Group)
- ▲ If all of this fails, through no fault of mine, but you insist on blaming me, then I will utilize my golden parachute, designed by consultants, and expect you to buy out my contract. (Bill Agee at nearly everyplace he's been)

I've met very few consultants who can tell a senior executive, much less the CEO, that the trouble has been located and it's in the room with the two of them. Yet, not surprisingly, that's often the case. It's the CEO (or division general manager, or departmental vice president, or sector executive) who has chosen the top team, who sets the example, who has approved the strategy and/or who agrees to the reward system. Consultants generally can't offer such insightful help because:

4. See Challenge 7 for the problems with executive compensation.

▲ They've come as mendicants to the company, begging for food, and received an invitation to dine at the table. They are not about to insult the host when he or she serves rancid food or sour wine.

▲ The relationship has begun with a high-powered, peer-level, insightful principal from the consulting firm, but the actual work is conducted by junior partners and associates whose billable days represent much greater profit to the firm while the original rainmaker is off seducing another client.

▲ Consultants place an obsessive emphasis on compulsive data gathering, which automatically increases the time before recommendations can be made and inevitably turns up peripheral issues that deflect from the original thrust. Coincidentally, both of these developments tend to increase project length and fees.

▲ Consultants overwhelmingly bill by the hour. This is one of the biggest contributors, ironically, to both poor profitability among smaller consulting firms and client inability to extract quick responses to clear challenges. (I once had two proposals from rival bookkeepers. One charged by the hour and also informed me that she did not use a computer, preferring to make manual entries. I pointed out that she expected her clients to pay for her own laborious inefficiency and technological ignorance. She didn't see the point. She also didn't get the job.) Although this is the subject of another book in and of itself,[5] suffice it to point out that this is like paying a house painter by the hour. Why rush to finish and go on to the next job if you can make the same amount sitting here on the current one? If I bill by the hour, I'm going to look for opportunities to create more inquiry, not to achieve resolution. I have arrived to study a problem, and may stay to become part of it.

▲ Consultants are often working both sides of the street. They are the ones helping the executive formulate his or her golden parachute, compensation package, or stock options. Even in real estate transactions, in which an agent is often perceived to represent both buyer and seller, it's clear that the agent is being paid by the seller out of the proceeds of the transaction. However, consultants are often simultaneously working to improve organi-

---

5. See Alan Weiss, *Million Dollar Consulting: A Professional's Guide to Growing a Practice,* 2nd ed. (New York: McGraw-Hill, 1998).

zational results while also assisting executives in their escape plans if those results don't materialize. It's no wonder that golden parachutes are so well designed, in that they are conceptualized with a very clear idea of what the likely failures may be. Corporate vision should only be so clear. *The buyer may be an executive, but the client is almost always the organization.*

▲ Finally, high-level buyers are often high-powered, intimidating people. Consultants are simply afraid of them, even though they've been specifically retained as impartial, objective outsiders whose judgment shouldn't be tainted by their retirement plans, job security, salary grade levels, or political correctness. Many consultants fold under the perceived pressure, and simply become as spineless as the "yes people" down the hall, or as out-of-the-loop as the blissfully ignorant employees chowing down in the cafeteria, buttressed against those executive dining room doors. In most cases, companies hire consultants but merely get the equivalent of employees who aren't on the benefit plan.

The truly honest, shocking, and mordant feedback flows from the client to the consultant ("Why haven't you provided the findings and recommendations we had agreed upon as planned last month?") rather than from the consultant to the client ("The problem is that you want to improve productivity while you downsize, which is stupid and irresponsible. Either invest in your people or reduce the size of the business, but don't ask us to pretend you're doing both successfully.").

In 1996, Jay Leno, the comedian and *Tonight Show* host, wrote a rather poorly received autobiography called *Leading With My Chin*. In it, he related an embarrassing story about an appearance he made on the old *Dinah Shore Show*. But *U. S. News & World Report* verified that it never happened to Leno but rather to another comedian by the name of Jeff Altman.[6] Leno paid Altman $1,000 to "meld" his story into something similar that Leno claims actually happened to him. Consultants often do the same kind of "melding."

Consultants who may be ill equipped to provide useful feedback anyway—because they're young, new, or simply incompetent—are rarely going to provide painful feedback to the

---

6. John Leo, "This column is mostly true," *U.S. News & World Report*, 16 December 1996, 17.

executive whose hand will approve the payment of their company's monthly bill. And so we can see an interesting dynamic taking shape: Executives lie to the consultants about the real problems so as to shift focus from themselves, and consultants lie to the executives about the real causes of even the distorted problems so as to shift culpability from the executives. It's no wonder that the employees sit around and—*rightfully*—pontificate that what's gone wrong is as obvious as a ham sandwich, but management and the consulting firm will spend a kibillion dollars to ensure that it becomes as complicated as possible.

Several years ago, the CEO of Calgon asked me during the course of a project I was conducting if I'd sit in on the compensation meetings taking place, run by another consulting firm. These meetings occurred weekly with the consultant and Calgon's top vice presidents, in search of a compensation and incentive plan that was agreeable to all parties. So far, the process had taken three months, with no clear progress in sight.

"But I'm not a compensation consultant," I explained, "and I shouldn't really enter the process at this point, anyway. It won't be helpful."

"I just want you to observe one meeting," said the CEO. "Tell me what's going on. I promised not to interfere, and if I even merely attend and observe, everyone will act deferentially instead of honestly. Surely you can give me feedback on the process, right?"

Right. Off I went to attend the meeting. I found the consultant, a woman in her mid-twenties, to be open, honest, and quite sincere. She also knew nothing about how to conduct a meeting with so many conflicting interests represented, would not confront or challenge, knew precious little about Calgon's history and its current strategy, and wasn't even all that sharp on compensation.

The vice presidents, who were accustomed to seeing me wandering around and were comfortable with me, acted as they had every meeting: They argued incessantly about protecting their respective operations, rejected compromise, and tried to hold out for the best possible package for themselves.

Two hours later I reported to the CEO.

"Let me make a wild guess," I said, "that the person who sold you on this project was a managing partner from that comp firm."

"Right," said the CEO.

"And after the contract was signed, you haven't seen him again."

"Right."

"Well, you're paying a lot of money to help educate one of their high potential people to learn both their business and yours, and you're setting back your team-building efforts every time your direct reports get together with her. Other than that, it was a great decision."

The CEO dismissed the compensation consultants, told his direct reports that they had two weeks to devise an incentive plan that they all bought into or the CEO would impose one, and got on with business. One week later, the new compensation system was ready to roll.

In business, we have to provide the truth. That veracity is mandatory for executives, employees, and consultants. Ironically, the employees, often the most maligned by the other two groups, are often the most honest, at least in the surveys and samplings that my firm conducts. It's the unholy alliance of the other two that must be reconfigured. Jay Leno must come up with his own, personalized humor, or he shouldn't be making the money that he does. Organizations need to look in the mirror and see rationality, not hear a voice telling them that they are "the fairest of them all."

TRUTH BE TOLD, AND YET IT ISN'T: WHY CORPORATE VISION IS BLIND

Why can't organizations operate within the bounds of their own expertise? Why are external resources needed to help create what should be a very intimate and unique approach to the organization's own future? When organizations make decisions, one would assume that facts and figures would at least hold their own. While there's always room for emotion, intuition, and the visceral tendencies that excellent leaders often pursue, most of the time businesses can't be run by the seat of the pants. If it were otherwise, why do we pay the top people so much to run them? We certainly don't need to pay seven figures to find someone who simply wants to guess about strategy, or to hire an expensive consulting operation to guess about strategy.

Yet "guess" is often exactly what transpires. Never before in my memory have organizations paid so much attention to vision, mission, and values, and never before have they been so misguided, so unfocused, and so morally corrupt. The current emphasis on corporate vision is a good example.

"Vision" says Webster, can be the "act or power of seeing," presumably, for organizations, their own future. However, most of Webster's column inches devoted to "vision" define its mystical connotations: "the supernatural . . . an apparition . . . dream, trance or ecstasy . . . mystical awareness"—well, you get the idea. My observation is that most organizations that pursue a corporate "vision" are doing so in the metaphysical sense, not the bottom-line, pragmatic one.

Here's a vision statement, drawn at random, from the myriad examples provided in business publications every day. This is from a company called AquaGuard, which waterproofs basements.[7] AquaGuard states that it is "dedicated to excellence in everything we do."

Mission:	To achieve unrivaled customer satisfaction and "peace of mind" by providing the highest quality, most innovative waterproofing services.
Vision:	To consistently exceed our customers' expectations and become the standard by which all waterproofing companies are measured.
Core values:	▲ Uncompromising integrity and price in everything we do
	▲ A commitment to helping all team members strive to be the best that they can be
	▲ An obsession to provide high quality workmanship and value
	▲ An intense desire for continuous improvement and growth
	▲ A resolution to create a friendly and fun atmosphere where participation and creativity are valued

---

7. As cited in Wolfe J. Rinke, Ph.D., *Winning Management* (Clarksville, MD: Achievement Publishers, 1997).

Critical success factors: ▲ Anticipate and constantly improve customer satisfaction
▲ Continually improve employee satisfaction
▲ Increase sales and profits

AquaGuard's statements contain a total of 120 words; simply remove the word "waterproofing" from the mission and vision statements, and the remaining 118 words can apply to almost any organization. Only 1.6 percent of AquaGuard's verbiage about mission, vision, and values applies distinctly to it, and the remaining 98.4 percent could apply to almost anybody. *This is the norm in these statements, not the exception.* Yet this level of near-total, generic abstraction is what many organizations proudly release after expensive consulting help, retreats into the woods,[8] six months or more of executive time, and assorted other obfuscation and footwork. Apparently, AquaGuard did have the benefit of a consultant's help to develop their material.

AquaGuard may be the finest waterproofing company in existence for all I know, and I mean them no disrespect for the quality of their work. But it is this kind of exercise in semantics, feel-good, "impress the stockholders," "throw a sop to the employees," and "everybody's doing it" that makes corporate vision so hilariously out of focus so much of the time.

How often do you suppose companies review their vision and mission to test current decision making? How many meetings have you participated in where someone said, "I don't think this meets our vision of the future," or "Is this action really consistent with our values?" Certainly no one was asking that rhetorical question when companies that valued "respect for our employees" and "mutual support for all team members" downsized people by the tens of thousands.

Executives don't seem to realize the irony, because they're discussing the plans in the executive dining rooms while the unsuspecting "valued" employees are eating several floors away in the cafeteria. It might sound like a *Saturday Night Live* skit, but who could make this stuff up?

Corporate vision is not founded in reality. It is the indoor

---

8. See Challenge 3 for the "touchie-feelie" approaches to executive development.

equivalent of trodding hot coals and shooting the rapids. There is no evidence or hard examples to prove that it makes a difference. How could it, when they all sound like AquaGuard's? If every company pursued the same vision, had the same mission, and shared the same values, the probability is enormous that they would all be mediocre, by definition.

LEADERS SEEK CORRECTIVE GLASSES, BUT THEY ONLY NEED TO OPEN THEIR EYES

There are some firms that, fortunately, provide exceptions to the blindness rule. For example, years ago Toyota had a mission state ment that was the equivalent of "Beat Benz." Komatsu, the heavy equipment manufacturer, had one that basically said, "Eat Cat" (meaning their arch-rival, Caterpillar Tractor). That both these firms are Japanese and highly effective global competitors is more than coincidence.

In both cases, those organizations were able to rally the entire workforce to specific business objectives that were unique to their competitive positions. Toyota wanted to create a quality perceived to be as good as Mercedes' near-legendary lead in that area, which they certainly achieved with the Lexus introduction. Komatsu wanted to gain market share from their giant rival, which they accomplished to Cat's utter stupefaction when Komatsu obtained significant business not only globally, but also in the United States. The fact that Mercedes and Caterpillar have since strongly recovered—albeit with some pain and great expense—in no way blunts the power of what Toyota and Komatsu accomplished.

Vision and mission don't have to be cute or concise, but it certainly helps. Unless employees can retain the purpose and direction of the organization *in their minds every day on the job*, the odds are that they won't be using them to guide decisions and take actions. If vision, mission, and values don't influence decisions and actions, then what good are they? Four things prevent vision, mission, and values from becoming a daily template for the workplace:

1. They are ignored regularly by senior management.
2. They are so long and convoluted as to be unmemorable.

3. They are so bland as to be uninspiring.
4. They are irrelevant.

In the case of Toyota, every designer, assembler, salesperson, technician, financial analyst, and receptionist knew what it meant to "Beat Benz." If a windshield were installed with just a tiny imperfection—unlikely to be noticed by all but the most scrupulous customer—the quality inspector merely had to ask, "Would this beat Benz?" No, it wouldn't, so the expense of replacing the windshield is justified. When potential customers approached Komatsu representatives with requests for discounts or additional services, the template for the decision was, "Will this enable us to eat Cat?" It's simple. It usually is.

Vision statements don't have to be cute, don't have to focus on clobbering the competition, and don't have to be only a few words. I've simply chosen some brilliant examples that have rallied organizations. But whatever they are, they require thought, dissemination, and unqualified senior executive support. Without these elements, the words are meaningless.

Yet setting vision in an organization is overwhelmingly an exercise that the senior team sees as a "necessary evil" or something that "some consultant sold to the CEO." It's rarely seen as a pragmatic management tool to help set standards for the daily behavior of employees, which is what determines whether or not strategic business goals are met and quarterly profits are made. Vision shouldn't be esoteric or generic, yet it usually emerges as cosmic and catholic. Establishing an organization's future[9] is a vital, rational act, not cause for an arcane, emotional retreat in the woods.

PRAGMATIC VALUES VERSUS HYPOCRISY AS AN ART FORM

In 1998, at a unit of Levi Strauss, over 50 percent of the employees signed the cards indicating that a union had achieved the right to try to organize that unit and hold an election to seek certification. Levi's management considered the situation and made an exem-

---

9. I've done this with Fortune 500 giants and local, volunteer non-profits. Size, nature of the business, and almost any other factors are irrelevant.

plary decision. They said that the response at that point was good enough, *and they recognized the union on the spot as the legitimate bargaining entity.* The union officials—I suspect once they were picked up off the floor—complimented Levi's management on its proworker attitude. This rational attitude toward people is not extant because of a twelve-month consulting audit on values. It exists because leadership—the exemplars—believes that it is the proper way to invest in the company's future.

Sit in a car in the parking lot of any major Hewlett-Packard facility. Over the course of the morning ingress, you are likely to see people of every color, size, shape, and dimension; you will likely see people in wheelchairs, and some assisted by aid dogs, which are welcome at the facility. Sit in a meeting at HP, and you might find yourself in a group of eight people, seven of whom are female. Visit the cafeteria at lunch and you might find a Native American art exhibit, a performance by the local school for the hearing impaired, or a lecture on alternative lifestyles. These conditions do not prevail because HP has a vision statement that mandates them. They prevail because HP believes in embracing all people, its criteria for success centers around talent and contribution, and its senior people exemplify those ideals. That's the "HP Way." Why can't it be everyone's?

Values aren't something written in memos, extolled in the annual report, hung on banners in the cafeteria, or trumpeted in releases sent to the press. Values are *lived;* they should be manifest and exemplified in behaviors every day. Organizations reward those values that they really hold dear, which is why so many reward hitting the numbers at any cost.

I often walk through client organizations and randomly ask an employee questions in this vein: What do you do in the absence of policy, precedent, or procedure? What criteria do you use to make decisions in areas of high ambiguity? The responses I get fall into two general categories:

1. "I do what's right for the customer" or "I do what I think is correct and fair." These are practical, operating decisions that clearly use the company's value system to guide them.
2. "I make my numbers" or "I make sure that we can't be blamed for the problem." These, too, are practical, operat-

ing decisions that clearly use the company's value system to guide them.

Both sets of responses indicate adherence to what people see around them, and form *the employee's perceptions of what the direction, vision, and values of the company truly represent on an operating basis*, which is the only basis that counts.

Organizations embrace or abandon values through the actions of their leadership. Prudential Insurance was once able to convince people to own "a piece of the rock." It was a profitable, clear symbol of steadfast financial security. But that's long been lost in agents' disreputable and unethical behaviors, including such things as persuading policyholders to cash in valuable, older policies for riskier, less valuable new ones that heighten agents' commissions and pad the company's profits. Prudential management was clearly aware of this because the agents' training films advocated these practices and were produced and approved at senior levels.

Ben & Jerry's received plaudits for years because of its purported (and highly media-savvy) support for the environment and unremitting support of its employees. Yet it was divulged not long ago that some of the ingredients in their ice cream did not originate where suggested, that some business was being done with "exploiters" of the land, and that the company wasn't being run all that well. A widely publicized, public search for a new CEO to replace the founders was conducted in a presumably egalitarian atmosphere, with applications welcomed from anyone and screened impartially. The resultant choice was someone who didn't last much more than a year, left the company without improving its condition, and departed with a hell of a lot less fanfare than that with which he arrived. The CEO was chosen in 1998 through an old-fashioned search firm and isn't at all in the mold of the Ben & Jerry's tradition, in that he's a former consultant for the manufacturers of Winchester Rifles! Not many people know this because the company has severely cut back on its publicity machinery. But if you read the financial pages, you can find that, at this writing, Ben & Jerry's is having some severe profit problems. From a high of $32 in August 1992, its stock sank to $13 and is currently at $28, eight years later. Dividends have been nonexistent.[10]

---

10. For the profit damage done through their purportedly noble causes, see Alex Taylor III, "Yo, Ben! Yo, Jerry! It's Just Ice Cream!" *Fortune*, 28 April 1997, 374.

Organizations *are* unique. It's the ability to recognize one's uniqueness and translate it into the everyday operating realties that employees can rally around that creates true vision, mission and values. Merck takes the greatest scientific research it can muster to try to address human health care and suffering. FedEx delivers things with unequaled reliability the next day. Mercedes builds what is still the most technologically sophisticated mass-produced automobile. Southwest Airlines flies you to your destination on time most of the time for less money than you'd pay elsewhere all of the time.

We've become obsessed with the intangible and the ambiguous because there is less accountability (no "right" and "wrong") and, consequently, more safety. Our society would rather debate whether or not to allow prayer in the classroom than to debate how to remove crime from the streets. We're more concerned with creationism versus evolution than whether our children are learning to read. Our businesses prefer alchemy and guesswork, feel-good retreats and banal vision statements—all with the "credibility" provided by expensive consulting interventions—to customer surveys, tough market analysis, and unique, distinctive values.

STRATEGY THAT ADMITS PEOPLE

There are two aspects to an organization achieving its business goals: the business strategy, and the organizational culture that supports it. "Culture" is simply that set of beliefs which governs behavior. Employees' behavior must be in concert with the performance required to produce the intended business results. It's as simple as that. Figure 4-1 illustrates the relationship.

Organizations should begin organizing their futures around some purpose. Whether that is termed "vision" or "mission" or "corporate goals" is immaterial, although the strategists love to debate such esoteric notions. The point is whether the organization can generate some picture of the future into which it will evolve.

On the left side of the chart are the "routine" business decisions that flow from that future vision. "Strategy" should define the nature and direction of the business and the overarching goals to be attained. This is the "what" aspect of that future.

The "tactics" stage is the "how." Those are the means, alternatives, and options that will be employed. If the "what" were

Figure 4-1. Strategy that embraces culture.

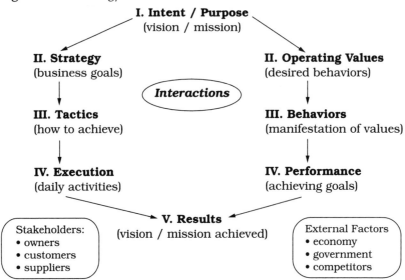

"Be the premier catalog retailer in the country," the "how" might include monthly mailings and Web sites. Mercedes-Benz and Chrysler had different strategies and differing tactics prior to their merger, even though they were both in the auto business (Mercedes' parent, Daimler-Benz, is in a great many businesses). Part of the appeal of the merger was that they each provided markets and products that the other didn't, while minimizing the overlap that both addressed.

"Execution" refers to those daily activities that implement the tactics. This is where organizations really make or lose money every day, not in strategy or tactics, but in mundane execution. The catalog company's tactics (and, hence, its strategy) will fail if catalogs are not sent out on time for the holidays, if customers' calls are not answered properly, and if insufficient inventory is available to meet demand. Daimler Chrysler will fail if their people do not cooperate in eliminating duplication, their dealers don't cooperate in promotions, and the management team refuses to share marketing information. This brings us to the cultural side of the house.

All organizations have "operating values." These are not the values boasted about in the corporate propaganda and annual reports, nor are they the beliefs plastered to the walls or provided on cards to be carried at all times. Operating values are those beliefs that actually determine employees' daily behavior, especially in discretionary decision making. They are most apparent when an employee is faced with an issue for which there is no policy, precedent, or procedure readily available. At those points, the employee relies most heavily of his or her operating values. Those values might encompass any of the following under conditions of uncertainty or stress:

- ▲ I do the right thing.
- ▲ I protect myself.
- ▲ I ask my boss.
- ▲ I protect our department.
- ▲ I ask a trusted colleague or friend.
- ▲ I blame accounting.
- ▲ I rely on my personal sense of right and wrong.
- ▲ I send it to someone else to become their problem.
- ▲ I research it.
- ▲ I make it disappear.

All of those possible reactions are verbatim responses from interviews I've conducted with employees in a wide variety of organizations. Their operating values will determine what actions they actually take, and "I do the right thing" has a much different outcome on execution and tactical success than does "I make it disappear," or "I protect my department." Every organization has operating values, *but they are not always consciously arrived at nor explicit.* The great organizations test these values continually, and arrange reward and feedback systems to promote those values that are commensurate with organizational strategy and intent.

For example, if an employee gets whacked by his or her immediate boss for airing an unhappy customer's complaint because it adversely reflects on that department, all employees receive a message about what to do with negative customer feedback. However, if that employee is lauded for the effort by the immediate supervisor, cause rather than blame is pursued, and a positive example is produced of the episode, other employees will be prone to step forward under similar conditions. Nordstrom's and other legendary service providers don't get that way by accident. They do so by managing the operating values. Similarly, the poor service provided by just about every software vendor is not an accident nor an inescapable factor of that industry. It is simply a reflection of a widespread value system that says, "The customer is an uninformed technological amoeba, and doesn't deserve anything more than the minimum we're willing to provide."

"Behaviors" constitute the observable, objective criteria that tell us what the operating values are. Poor managers say, "You have a lousy attitude." Good managers say, "I noted that you didn't pick up the ringing phone. Why is that?" The effective management of the cultural side of the equation demands that we focus on what we can see, not what we suspect; on what we experience, not what we expect. By focusing tightly on observed behavior, management can quickly and effectively evaluate whether the tactics of the business are being supported by the actions of the employees. "Outstanding customer service and responsiveness" as a tactic requires people picking up phones prior to the fourth ring in terms of behavior. "Absolute guarantees of our work" as a tactic demands employee behavior that deals with customer discontent immediately and doesn't pass it up the line to higher and higher levels of management.

"Performance" is that level of successful implementation that meets the executional requirements. On the most basic level, it means being there every day. On more sophisticated levels, it means being innovative, taking prudent risk with the solace that the company is supportive, dealing with mistakes and failures constructively, and meeting the expectations of supervisors. Individual performance is the sole criterion determining whether execution will be successful and, therefore, whether tactics will be implemented in support of the strategy.

Any strategic approach that ignores the cultural side of the equation is doomed. This is why strategy is always successful in formulation, but frequently fails in implementation, because on paper, at least, the cultural side is easy to ignore or gloss over. In reality, however, it's the much more difficult of the two tracks to effectively manage. Human behavior does not lend itself well to flow charts and templates.

True strategic management is involved with the management of the interactions between business strategy and culture. It is hard work. It is not for the unskilled. And it requires a comprehensive and sensitive appreciation of *both* the organization's strategic intent *and* its cultural nuts and bolts.

Figure 4-2 shows another way to view strategy as a motive force. The core values of the enterprise (as opposed to the operating values cited above) determine the organization's approach to business. "We bring the greatest capabilities in scientific research to bear on the greatest human health and suffering challenges." "We create information exchange opportunities that enable customers to share knowledge rapidly and accurately on a global basis."

From those core values—why the business exists—comes the strategy for its future. The formulation is the easy part. The implementation is the hard part. But the key is that the existing organization's people, systems, finances, rewards, operating values, research, image, and so on are managed in such a way that they

Figure 4-2. Strategic movement.

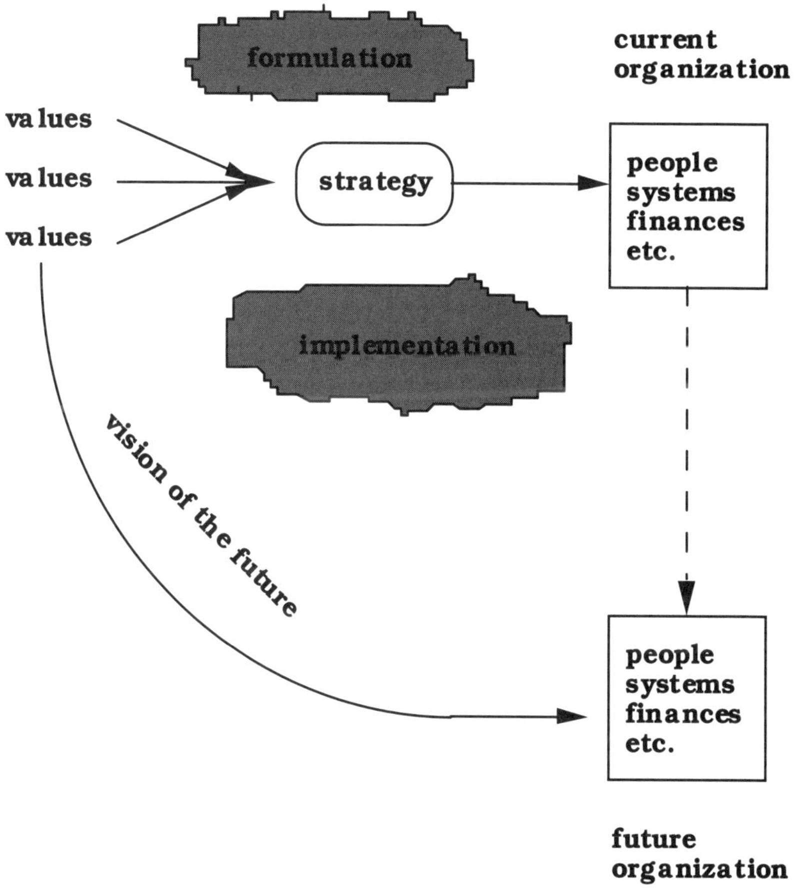

evolve into that picture of the future that the vision calls for. In the illustration, the existing organization becomes the future organization as described by the organization's vision. In reality, that future is always a moving target, since strategy and vision (and, sometimes, even core values) change. However, the intended meeting spot of the two must be consistent.

If the current organization is not managed in a manner consistent with the strategic vision, then it can "drift" right or left, up or down, or simply remain in place, fixed like a barnacle to a shipwreck. The comprehensive, sensitive management cited above is the crucial link to managing the cultural and business side of the strategic equation. However fine the intentions, organizations can otherwise drift. And when the operating values depart from the core values, execution will be unsuccessful.

When at one point I was working on a diversity audit for Merck—one of the finest organizations I've ever observed—I found that many minority employees felt uncomfortable and at a disadvantage. Respondents cited clear examples of the sources of their discomfort, from lack of minority people in key positions, to discriminatory statements about accented English, to ethnically insensitive comments made by managers in group meetings. White managers, especially males, often expressed frustration with what they perceived as the company's excessive efforts to diversify the employee base, and many felt threatened by careers with reduced opportunities due to preferential treatment of others. This is observed behavior, and reflects the operating values. The good news was that Merck people were candid and confident in reporting their observations and experiences, which denotes an overall healthy atmosphere and positive environment.

When I turned in my report and analysis, the chairman and CEO at the time, Roy Vagelos, was nearly apoplectic. "This is not my company!" he observed, rather strongly. What he meant is that it wasn't the company he talked about, wasn't the company he experienced, wasn't the company he envisioned. That's because some of the operating values on the cultural side of the business had not been managed well and had gone askew. In turn, the business side was affected because execution hinged on the performance of people who were discontent about their treatment, status, and prospects.

Today, Merck is consistently rated as one of the top companies for employees in general, and for minorities, women, and families. No matter how well it does in its research labs or sales to HMOs, Merck has to manage the cultural aspects of its business in support of its strategy.

No organization is successful merely by dint of creating strategy *or merely by attempting to implement it in a vacuum*, without consideration of what is a very real, very discernible, and very deterministic corporate culture.

SOLUTIONS: CREATING A VISION THAT PROVIDES LIGHT

"Values" exercises and "strategic retreats" to create statements of vision and mission are worthless unless they demonstrably affect the daily decisions made by management at all levels throughout the organization. A consultant's worth is never established by running a retreat or facilitating a strategy session and creating a report, document or, worse, "sense of teamwork." A consultant's value is in the *result*, which should be beliefs and principles that guide organizational behavior day-in and day-out. Here, then, some guidelines.

1. Values Should Be Seen and Not Only Heard

Values have to be manifest daily by senior management. The president of a billion dollar subsidiary of a $15 billion company told me that he didn't approve of the brutal behavior of one of his executive vice presidents, notorious for obscenely browbeating subordinates in public.

"I'm afraid you do approve, Peter," I explained, "because your failure to do anything about it tells people that Robert's behavior is the way to succeed around here. Not only that, but you're growing a host of 'miniature Roberts' at all levels, and losing talented people who don't see themselves comfortable in such a mold." I then provided employee samplings that supported my position. Everyone thought that Robert was merely conforming to Peter's own behavioral preferences. Robert was dismissed shortly thereafter, but it took almost a year to convert or terminate the "clones."

Organizations that have tremendous "bench strength" have

it because senior people continually reinforce those behaviors that are responsible for success and promotion.

2. Values Should Be Memorable

Values and vision have to be concise enough to be used as daily templates for decision making and planning. All businesses make or lose money daily as the result of decisions made by relatively low-level employees. In a single appliance store, the owner can control this fairly effectively. In a multisite appliance chain, it's much more difficult, and in General Motors it's impossible.

When I walked around Johnson & Johnson *before* the Tylenol crisis, and asked what people did in the absence of policy, precedent, and procedure, they said, "We do the right thing." The company placed strong emphasis on simple values: Do the right thing for the patient and the physician. Sometimes you'll be wrong, but usually you'll be right if you use that guide, and we'll support you in any case. Small wonder J&J reacted immediately and courageously, recalling the best-selling Tylenol, when product tampering by a sociopath endangered their customers.

At GE, people are encouraged to cross boundaries and act swiftly. Management is evaluated on helping them to do just that. When was the last time you saw an employee consult a convoluted, tabbed, three-ring binder to determine which values pertain to a decision about to be made? People make decisions on the fly, using their heads, which is where values should be stored.

3. Vision Is Useless if Behavior Doesn't Change

Vision must lead to demonstrable behaviors that, in turn, realize the organization's business objectives. The Los Angeles Dodgers, from the time they were the Brooklyn Dodgers right up to the present, have had a long-term vision of building championships through finding and investing in their own young talent (as opposed to trading for existing veterans, for example). The Dodger farm team system of developing young ballplayers became legendary, and Dodger coaches and scouts at all levels were rewarded for their successful pursuit and acquisition of young talent. Most recently, this is reflected in an unprecedented string of four consecutive "Rookie of the Year" awards to Dodger players. The team is usually in the postseason playoffs and its attendance figures are perennially at or near the top of organized baseball. That equates to a return for the fans and a return for the owners.

4. Vision Should Be Aligned With Individual Goals

The future must be relevant for the implementers. The CEO of a bank might be evaluated on improving shareholder value, for example, but that's not something the local branch managers or tellers can relate to everyday. Translating corporate goals into individual goals for relevance and passion are what energize organizations. Cutting expenses creates compliance; generating growth produces commitment.

5. A Little Consulting Goes a Long Way

Consultants can bring fresh, provocative, external views and techniques to turbocharge a company's culture. Or, they can arrive to study a problem and remain long enough to become an integral part of it. Remember, my experience tells me that as many as 50 percent of all consultants don't know what they're doing, *and as many as 90 percent of corporate purchasers of consulting help don't know how to tell the difference.* A consultant should have strong references, a track record of major projects in credible organizations, proper credentials, and the right personality and chemistry for the buyer and the culture. Show any consultant the door who:

- ▲ Talks more than listens.
- ▲ Disparages the client company and/or its people.
- ▲ Doesn't possess the vocabulary or intelligence that you do.
- ▲ Has no sense of humor.
- ▲ Is inflexible, and must do things his or her way only.
- ▲ Pushes off-the-shelf, ready-made solutions for a fixed fee.
- ▲ Doesn't make you feel confident and supportive.
- ▲ Can't provide you with immediate value during the very first meeting.

Hire a consultant as you would a key executive but knowing that the term of service will be much shorter.

6. Managers Manage, Consultants Consult

Strategy should be based upon market realities and competitive likelihoods. We don't need to pay tens of millions of dollars for organizations to be run 100 percent viscerally. I can find you people who can do that for a warm meal and a place to sleep. Consultants can be useful, but primarily as objective, third parties revealing a perspective that internal management has trouble appreciating because of a necessarily narrower frame of reference. But consultants don't run companies; senior management does. The most valuable consultants are those who can readily find and verbalize organizational blemishes and individual shortcomings. Boards of directors should approve any consultant funding of, say, $500,000 or more, and such projects should report to a board member (just as certain audit activities report to a board's finance committee). Otherwise, consultants often wind up working for the executives and not the shareholders, even though the latter are the ones footing the bill.

7. The Buck Stops at the Leader

Salespeople on the street, underwriters in the home office, and customer service people on the phones are held responsible for the amount of their sales, the return on their risk taking, and their satisfaction of the consumer. As we ascend the organizational hierarchy, measures should get tougher not easier, scrutiny should be tighter not looser, and safety nets should be under high wires not corporate jets. We must hold organizational leadership responsible for the establishment of the enterprise's future, the quality of the journey toward that goal, and the reasonable attainment of at least legitimate milestones along the way. The helmsman may technically steer the ship, but the captain sets the destination. Navigators simply recommend the best route. Consultants may be fine navigators or they may run you onto the shoals. The captain is responsible to the people who built the boat and to those who have decided to sail in it.

Senior people are, presumably, hired and paid to make tough, senior-level decisions, not to make decisions about which consulting firm to hire. If they're doing the latter often and the former rarely, keep the consultants and get rid of the senior people.

I was working with a large insurance organization that was struggling to set its vision and mission. The CEO had tackled it, a senior team had fooled with it, and now the vice president of human resources had been charged with the job of somehow getting it articulated. He came to me for help.

I pointed out that the company was in the midst of five consecutive years of record profits, working with the current, simple, clear vision and mission.

"What are you suggesting?" he asked.

"I'm suggesting that you all get back to work."

Challenge Five

End the Mindless Mantra of Litigation Threats

They're "Courts of Law," Not "Courts of Justice," for a Reason

The McDonald's coffee case has entered legal legend.[1] In the absence of an overarching moral code in society and business, we've resorted to the worst possible arbiter to determine right and wrong: the legal system. What is illegal is often ethical, and what is unethical is often legal. Any honest attorney will tell you that, and that's about all you need to know to determine that this alternative is not a very good one.

There are two basic reasons for ethics and morality being decided by default in the courts:

1. WE NO LONGER TRUST EACH OTHER

Believe it or not, this is partially an improvement, in that we used to trust each other implicitly because we all looked alike and came from the same background. The white, Anglo-Saxon male was

---

1. Unbelievably, McDonald's was sued by a woman who was burned by its coffee after she tried to open and drink it in a moving car. Her lawyer claimed that McDonald's was negligent in preparing its coffee exactly as it should be—very hot—and convinced still another mindless jury that the woman should have been warned. McDonald's lost the case, although an appeal reduced the award.

the predominant force in business and society, and the values, beliefs, common frames of reference, and mutual reliance created an implicit trust.

Today, we are blessed with a vibrant diversity in society and the workplace, including gender, religion, ethnicity, lifestyle, origin, and a dozen other elements of the American mosaic. From the 1950s to the 1990s we've seen societal and business change perhaps more dramatically than at any other time during the century. However, that evolution has created a workplace of strangers. The Texaco tapes[2] are but the tip of an iceberg I traverse daily, ranging from the genuinely mystified to the secretly malicious managers who now have to interact with women, minorities, physically challenged, homosexual, and other employees whose viewpoints they don't understand or whom they have never regarded as "equal" to them. In nearly every survey that our company conducts, we find members of these groups receive less mentoring and sponsorship by key managers because those managers are far more apt to choose to support people who look like they do: white males. Organizations are struggling to create a rapport where there has been little basis for one.[3]

Our school systems have equated their effectiveness with simply moving students through the grades, with some education injected into the experience. The infusion of values, or even their discussion, is beyond all but the most elite of school systems, and those elite systems seldom represent the diversity of the external world. Our traditional religious institutions have been shocked by scandals ranging from pedophilia to embezzlement, and new age institutions advocate a "feel good" spirituality that's more about self and narcissism than it is about contribution to one's human colleagues.

Every day we see evidence on the evening news of corruption in government (from local politicians to the President's office), business fraud (including charges against such giants as GE for

---

2. Recordings of Texaco executives purportedly expressing dismay at having to deal with cultural traditions unfamiliar to them, including Kwanza and even Hanukkah.

3. There are two equally noxious extremes today: The diversity industry, which employs thousands of consultants to help firms "manage diversity," which is actually not the point; and the "grievance" industry, which is on the alert to threaten suit for any perceived slight, which is definitely not the point.

price fixing or phony reporting on NBC, its network subsidiary), and suits against the clergy, high school coaches, and therapists for every imaginable sexual transgression. And all of it is pronounced in the calmest, most routine inflections of the network anchor, underscoring its abject banality. Deviations from the straight and narrow are commonplace. Ho, hum, what else is new?

Finally, the family dinner table has disappeared in the wake of divorce, two-income families, extracurricular activities, multifarious electronic entertainment, and, to paraphrase the prison guard in *Cool Hand Luke,* a general failure to communicate. Once upon a time a child could discuss the ramifications of other students stealing the math test answers, and of the prejudice being dished out to a minority student, as well as listen to a parent's quandary over whether to change jobs or hit the boss for a raise. That daily reality check has disappeared, replaced, perhaps, by today's talk radio or television talk show. The vestiges that haven't disappeared have been blunted by hypocrisy. How does a parent tell a child not to use drugs while commiserating with the spouse about marijuana in the dorm before the finals thirty years ago, or warn about liquor abuse when tossing down martinis?

The absence of endemic trust has driven us to find other means to work out our differences. "The benefit of the doubt" has given way to "don't let them screw you." This is caused by several relatively modern dynamics:

▲ Downsizing has eliminated the historic employee/employer bond, which stated that if you worked up to basic expectations you could expect lifelong employment and a comfortable retirement.

▲ The demographic change in the workplace has created moral "strangers" who can no longer rely on common culture and references.

▲ Many managers continue to view control of information and head count as the keys to their power base, even in times of reduced head count and a computer on everyone's desk and lap. They are ill equipped to lead cross-functional teams, for example, which is increasingly what they must do. They attempt to lead by power rather than influence.

▲ The "victimization" mentality has demonstrated that employees can, on occasion, make much more money through litigation than through performance, so every imaginable slight becomes a suit. I have seen legal action ensuing from an employee claiming that his chronic lateness for work was, in and of itself, a medical condition warranting protection as a disability, making his firing illegal.

▲ The legal profession has—through a surfeit of its own kind and a capacity to move to systemic vulnerabilities so swiftly as to embarrass a cheetah—created an equal and opposite reaction to burgeoning corporate legal staffs. It is contingency fees, and has resulted in the Faustian-like ads on television that advise people "who may be hurt in a car accident" or "who may be subject to harassment at work" or "who may feel their doctor has erred in their treatment" to call for free consultation. In the workplace, even after surrendering up to 40 percent of a monetary award to the attorney, a nonperformer can collect some big bucks for actual and even perceived slights.[4]

2. WE HAVE BECOME A NATION OF VICTIMS LOOKING FOR THE EASY WAY OUT

Not long after the McDonald's coffee victory, another suit was filed on behalf of a teenager who was riding his bike at night against traffic (which is illegal) without any lights on, although the bike was equipped with a functioning headlight. He hit an oncoming car and was injured. The driver was held as faultless. Who did his attorney sue?

If you guessed that it was the bike manufacturer, go to the head of the class and receive an honorary legal degree. The attorney successfully argued that the manufacturer should have had warning signs indicating that the light should be *turned on* when

---

4. As this is written, one of the most active attorneys in suing the breast implant manufacturers in class action law suits, Mark Quinn of Texas, is under both legal indictment and possible disbarment proceedings for allegedly using "runners" to solicit clients and share in their proceeds from victims' families after a USAirways plane crash a couple of years ago. These practices are both illegal and unethical under legal canons.

riding at night. Since the manufacturer did not have such signs on the assumption—acceptable for at least a hundred years—that a bike rider would have the brains of a wombat and know to turn on the light when it was dark outside. Not so, said still another oxygen-deprived jury, and an award was bestowed. (I'm anticipating that at birth doctors will soon tattoo on the back of our hands the message, "If it rains while you are outside, come in.")

We've become a nation of people looking for the easy win, through the lottery (unlikely but remotely possible) or through the courts (highly likely and distinctly possible). It certainly beats hard work. A police lieutenant in Providence recently sued the city because he wasn't promoted to captain. The facts were:

- ▲ There were two captain's vacancies.
- ▲ Two people finished higher than he on the captain's test (which he had taken twice before and had, both times, also finished last).
- ▲ The two people finishing higher than he were promoted, according to the law and the regulations.
- ▲ He is suing, has held up the appointments, and I'd lay even money on his chances.

It doesn't matter that you're not good enough or not competent, because we've entered a falsely egalitarian society, a grievance-mentality workplace, and a nadir of self-respect. The mere threat of legal action by potential "victims" influences policy and procedure with a subtlety that few of us realize. Many schools have abandoned their separate yearbook listings of the top ten or top twenty students, or even Merit Scholars, because of the fear of those left out feeling "inferior."[5] Well, they are inferior, at least in that objective assessment of ability. No matter. Let's not risk a lawsuit.

It is easier to be a victim than it is to be a hard worker. It's easier to cite perceived discrimination than it is to demonstrate talent. The limbo is far easier than the pole vault and requires no training.

As you've no doubt surmised, I'm as big a critic of poor customer service as you'll find. One time my wife was trying to find

---

5. For example, see Bethany Gendron, "Through false equality, we lose the best," *Providence Journal*, 7 April 1977, F1.

a letter I had written to Delta Airlines and I suggested she use the search word "complaint" on the computer. She shrieked with laughter as the screen filled with over forty entries, ranging from rental cars and theaters to parking garages and newspaper delivery. Call it healthy outrage.

However, the other side of the coin is that the customer always being right is a cute aphorism from an age when the local store dealt with a familiar and consistent clientele, manners were such that we called each other "Mr." and "Miss," and strange paper called "cash" was the medium of the day. Today the customer is often wrong, sometimes inadvertently and sometimes maliciously. The threat of lawsuits often prevents businesses from reacting too harshly except when, thanks to corporate legal staffs that now outnumber the sales force, they react like Attila the Hun on a bad day.

Ironically, because of the existence and large fixed costs of corporate law staffs, there is momentum to file suit and contest issues that otherwise might have been settled through negotiation and even conversation. On the one side we have the threat of litigation influencing actions, and on the other we have overzealous litigation. It's a pendulum that describes a circle's circumference and never traverses the diameter. "Tell it to the judge" has replaced dispassionate discourse.

One of my recent projects (and a sign of the times) was for a foreign-owned pharmaceutical manufacturer that asked me to counsel one of their few senior woman executives and broker a departure deal, if possible, that would prevent legal action while still meeting her needs. She had claimed harassment in the form of impolite conduct from two senior male colleagues, and felt she had been passed over for promotion and wasn't receiving the entitled perquisites of her position.

What I found was, indeed, some rude treatment from the two men she had cited, but not unlike the rude treatment that is encountered regardless of gender in a political, poorly led, mediocre organization. I found her to be a totally average performer, with minimum responsibilities and a very competitive pay package. She had claimed that various promises about promotion, title, and benefits made by a former (and dismissed) president were not being honored. One of the company's senior attorneys had asked me to intervene, fearing prolonged litigation if the issues got out of hand, and the woman had, indeed, already been seeing her own counsel.

The company was afraid that the woman's peripheral claims of harassment might become embroiled in some larger, serious legal difficulties it was encountering from other employees, and sought to prevent more fuel from being poured on that fire. A settlement was reached that was favorable to both sides—though not without demands from her attorney to become a part of the process, and not without outrageous demands from both sides being dampened—and the woman walked away with more than enough benefit to comfortably begin a new career elsewhere with no great hurry. The company considered itself lucky to perhaps have dodged a stray bullet.

I calculate that the total cost to the organization, over a thirty-day period—including the settlement, the salaries involved of those working on the negotiations, legal fees, the work not done while the issues consumed everyone, and my fee (which was the least of it)—was in excess of $250,000. Now multiply that times the frequency it occurs in this organization and others like it—and remember that the executives are considering this route of prevention to be far superior to the possibility of actual litigation—and you get an idea of the toll being exacted on productivity, performance, and energies. Moreover, we've created a self-fulfilling prophesy, in that the tendency to settle caused by the weak knees created every time a threatened lawsuit is fired across the bow *increases the likelihood of additional threats.*

After all, what do mediocre performers and contingency lawyers have to lose, except a few filing fees and stamps?

MINIMAL STRESS IS AS ORGANIZATIONALLY DYSFUNCTIONAL AS MAXIMUM STRESS

These workplace stressors—threats of lawsuits, uncertainty over what is actionable behavior, disenchanted employees seeking any redress possible—and the concomitant legal "remedies" are intertwined. When productivity and performance are so direly threatened, organizations seek legal protection, employees seek legal representation, and no one receives the benefit of the doubt. However, that's not to say that we should eliminate stress in the workplace, but rather that we should better manage it, another ability that most modern managers neither appreciate nor possess.

There is an age-old correlation of stress and productivity that takes the shape of a bell curve (see Figure 5-1). It's generally true that if stress increases uncontrollably, productivity suffers. But the converse isn't true, because if a stress-free environment is created, *productivity also suffers.* In truth, a moderate amount of stress is healthy if people are to work productively. Perhaps you've heard yourself as well as colleagues say at times, "I work best under pressure," "I'm most creative as the deadline nears," and "I enjoy the electricity of this organization." The opposite of *distress* is *eustress,* and psychologists will tell you that eustress is a

Figure 5-1. Relationship between productivity and stress.

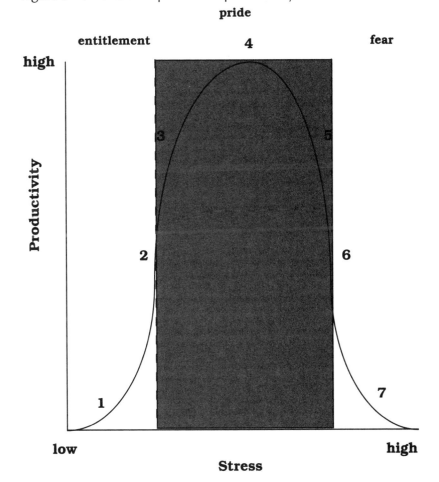

healthy state. We all need that adrenaline rush, that energy that results from the compunction to perform. However, the stress should be about meeting performance goals and objectives, not about potential legal action and commensurate remedies.

At point 1 in Figure 5-1, an employee's attitude is "You're lucky I'm here, don't expect anything else from me except the energy to pick up my check." It is the height of the entitlement attitude. Its incarnation is the government passport clerk who tells you that she'll get to you when she can and doesn't care that you only have an hour over lunchtime to get a new document, or the airline lost baggage functionary who puts your call on hold and leaves it there because your request will cause him too much work. At point 2 are those people who might make an extra effort if they're having a particularly good day, but that effort is usually at the expense of someone else's time and request.

A Northwest Airlines ticket agent once responded to my inquiry about whether there were phones on the departing flight with, "I don't know, you'll have to wait until you're on board." When I told him that Northwest treated its passengers as poorly as any airline in my memory, he informed me that, "Then I guess you shouldn't expect phones on our flights." In the past, letters to Northwest about their low service standards never generated a response, and these two events are linked: Management can easily be at the first two positions on the chart as well as employees, and when managers are there you can bet that employees are there, as well.

When employees are in the "entitlement" domain, you can be sure of the cause: poor management, which is incapable or afraid of creating more stressful working conditions. Why do some airline baggage handlers—at the same airport, using the same equipment—get the baggage to the carousel in ten minutes, while others take thirty minutes? It's not because of differing talents. It's because the management of one group has aligned their objectives with the corporate objectives (repeat customers are those who get their baggage quickly) and has provided penalties for failing to meet that goal, while the management of the other group has failed to achieve either alignment or penalty (and may even be an active abettor of the wrong behavior).

The "pride" domain, at its apogee in point 4, comprises people who say, "Let's go for it," "Let's try something new," "Let's take some risk." These are people whose pride in a job well done justifies innovation, risk taking, and initiative. It's the Air Canada captain who happened on me in the galley, and invited me into the cockpit of a 767 while at 38,000 feet (this is not illegal on that airline). It's the American Express travel service personnel who, on two occasions secured "unavailable" hotel space when I was stranded by weather in airports I originally had had no intention of visiting overnight. It's the postal employee—credit where credit is due—who used her own money to add some postage to my mailing, rather than have it returned and delayed.

Innovation, a bedrock of market leaders, can only occur when employees feel supported and comfortable, and when one failure or poor idea won't lead to dismissal. The cause of people being in the "pride" domain is superb management, or a job that they are so passionate about that poor management is irrelevant. The first condition is represented by 3M, where researchers are provided with company time and equipment to work on whatever pleases them while on the job. Another example is Home Depot, where employees are carefully selected and trained to meet customer needs, and often conduct sessions for customers on subjects such as laying floor tile or painting techniques. It's no accident that FedEx has consistently been able to rely on its employees to constantly "raise the bar," or that Home Depot has gained huge market share over rivals from its unprecedented—in their industry—customer service.

The second condition of pride is represented by unmitigated passion. Here is a conversation I had with a reporter from the *New York Times*:

NYT: This motivation stuff is absurd. People work because they're afraid not to.

AW: Why do you say that?

NYT: Look around here. The equipment is old and barely operable. The environment is filthy. The pay is below almost any other industry. Management hasn't a clue, and treats us like vermin.

AW: You're a talented guy. Why don't you leave and find something else?

NYT: Are you crazy?! I love this work!

The fact of the matter is that the *absence* of money is a demotivator, but the *presence* of money is not a motivator. Don't fall for the blague of inept managers that money motivates, and that a few more dollars will take care of the morale problems. If you have an employee unhappy about working conditions, a few more dollars in salary will not address the cause of the displeasure. You manage an organization through superb management, not through its compensation system.[6] When management relies solely on money as both "carrot" and "stick," employees will resort to legal remedies rather than dialogue, since litigation is viewed as the best route to corporate coffers.

As long as two conditions exist, legal and resultant monetary remedies will be sought in the place of rational discourse and negotiation:

1. Employees do not receive honest feedback from their managers because:
   ▲ Managers don't know how to provide it due to lack of skills.
   ▲ Managers are afraid to confront poor performance because of legal threats.
   ▲ Companies haven't been able to measure it because they are focused solely on short-term profitability for Wall Street.
2. Money is regarded as the sole metric of "wins and losses" because:
   ▲ Its acquisition is the only accomplishment recognized by the company and peers.
   ▲ There are no other reward systems extant (i.e., recognition, increased responsibility, promotion).
   ▲ It is the means of protection by exemplars (i.e., perquisites, golden parachutes).
   ▲ People have become accustomed to excessive stress and see money as the sole palliative, since organizations can't (or don't know how to) reduce stress to manageable levels.

---

6. I've sat through my share of meetings in which senior management debates and argues about next year's plan using the incentive system as the template. The market potential should be the template, otherwise you will always miss the true revenue growth potential, settling instead for the maximum amount that can be earned under the compensation system. This is another sign of horrible management.

We need moderate stress in our work. We need to know that failure will produce a penalty, and that various outcomes are not equally salutary. Otherwise, why bother, which might serve as the motto of the "entitlement" domain.

Finally, we have the realm of abject fear, which is caused by a surfeit of stress. This most commonly occurs in companies in which downsizing is underway or threatened, internal change is constant and uncontrolled, and/or management operates through intimidation, humiliation, and threat. In this environment, people keep their heads down. They figuratively disconnect the phone, take their names off the desk, and hide in the storage room. After all, if they can't find you, they can't embarrass or harass you, and they may even forget to fire you.

People in this domain are paralyzed by fear, and productivity plummets accordingly. No one will innovate or do anything to bring attention to their work. In position 7 the sentiment is "If they can't find me, I'm safe." The cause of this condition is, once again, horrible management.

A working definition of high stress on a job might entail just two components: I don't know what's going to happen tomorrow, and I don't have any control over it. Organizations that allow this kind of alienation produce a cadre of ill-informed, powerless people. Management claims of support and "the worst is over" are usually seen for the self-serving promises that they are. Ironically, sometimes management will find employees in the first domain (see Figure 5-1), and instill so much fear that they propel them directly to the third domain without so much as a pause in the middle. The resultant conclusion is that the employees are no good, since they aren't productive under any circumstances. In fact, management has merely provided two circumstances in which no one is very productive, but has failed to create the proper one, in which people can be productive.

People resort to legal means to retain their entitlements, often gaining union support or external support to do so. Companies use legal means to enforce fear, utilizing non-compete clauses, non-disclosure documents, and the threat of lawsuits to keep people in line. How else could Astra Pharmaceuticals have tolerated sexual harassment and abuse for so long from senior management in this day and age? They used threats of job actions, lawsuits, and other means to try to keep dissenters quiet. People at all levels were in fear, afraid to blow the whistle. Once

Figure 5-2. Classic view of ethical boundaries.

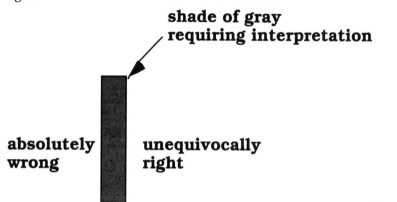

one person pressed her case, the entire structure of intimidation collapsed.

THERE IS NO "THEY": THE COURTS ARE ONLY ACCOUNTABLE WHEN MANAGERS AREN'T

I recently completed an ethics and compliance audit for a major financial services company. I demonstrated in the feedback to senior management that, while there might be some shades of gray requiring interpretation, there was also a line beyond which certain actions were just plain wrong.

I used the illustration in Figure 5-2 to make my point. There are clearly things that are absolutely wrong (i.e., stealing from the company), clearly things that are unequivocally right (i.e., satisfying the customer, making a profit), and a few shades of gray (i.e., we suspect that an alliance member's or partner's actions aren't up to our own—they apparently tolerate sexual harassment on the job—but we aren't certain, and don't feel it's proper to "meddle" in their conduct of their business). A division president, representing a good third of the entire company's profits, wasn't so sure, and offered the illustration in Figure 5-3. To him, the whole world was a shade of gray, and it was up to *him* to interpret it based upon prevailing business conditions.

This difference of outlook led to the following exchange:

AW: Wouldn't you agree, Dave, that there are areas to the left of the line that are clearly wrong, areas to the right that are clearly correct, and a relatively small gray area requiring judgment calls? There are ethical boundaries.

Dave: No. There are ethics and there are ethics. It depends upon who's doing the work. In fact, virtually everything is a judgment call in business. Has your study actually turned up actions that are clearly out of compliance?

AW: Here's an example. Your division is accepting applications from potential customers whose names are either not signed as required, or have been forged by the agent, which the agent has admitted. Isn't that wrong?

Dave: Well, there are instances where that's acceptable.

AW: Such as?

Dave: If the potential customers are incapable of signing their names.

AW: And you think that's the cause of the absences and forgeries in these amounts?

Dave: It could be. I'd have to see each one.

This kind of rationalization is occurring in business every day. Dave was simply candid enough to verbalize it, as his CEO squirmed in the back of the room. Moreover, of nearly two dozen other officers present, not one took Dave on or objected to the absurdity of such a defense. Dave wants a gray area as big as Wyoming, so that he can have the maximum opportunity to make his numbers and his bonus in any way possible. Doing it right takes a back seat to simply doing it.

Figure 5-3. Current, situational view of ethical boundaries.

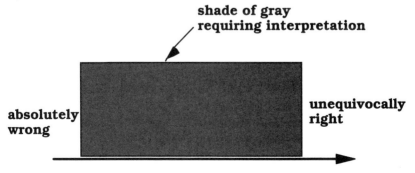

If the boundaries in Figure 5-3 prevail, and Dave can wiggle as much as he wants in the gray area, then virtually every business decision short of treason, arson, and sedition can be justified as "situationally appropriate." It seemed to me that forging a customer's name on an insurance application is just plain wrong, and that the company could safely make such an action result in a strict, subject-to-termination sanction.[7] But in Dave's case, he just might need that option some day to make the quarterly numbers, and it was easier for him to allow the door to stay open than to police the room to ensure that it stayed closed.

One of the reasons that we're engaged in so much expensive litigation today is that managers like Dave feel that they can continually blur the lines, knowing that the legal department is the ultimate backstop. Dave makes his numbers for the quarter, and his bonus, while the legal morass his kind of thinking creates costs the company (and, ultimately, its consumers) one hundred times as much as Dave's "profits." Managers need to do what's right the first time, every time.

There are shades of gray in business decision making. If there weren't, we wouldn't need managers. However, there is also clearly "right and wrong" in business decision making. If there weren't, we wouldn't need managers, either.

SOME POSITIVE EXAMPLES

At what was once Mallinckrodt's veterinary division, the CEO, Paul Cottone, had a general counsel named Tom who sat on the $600 million division's executive committee. That, in itself, wasn't unusual. What was unusual was that Tom was an active and passionate advocate for the business's growth by doing things the right way.

Here's an example of one interchange that also included Pete, the operations vice president:

Paul: Why are we getting the operations reports two days late and without including the European numbers?

---

7. While keynoting at an industry conference, I asked the CEO of Northwestern Life Insurance, seated next to me, what he would do in that situation. "Fire the agent who forged the name and everyone who knew about it and allowed it to pass," he replied, not missing a bite of his salad.

Pete: We've been having trouble with our new administrative supervisor. She doesn't get along with anyone, has been trying to install a new system, and has royally messed up the works.

Paul: Well, we can't tolerate the lateness and inaccuracies if we're going to make intelligent decisions. What are you going to do?

Pete: I'm going to fire her eventually. But for now, I want to keep her happy and here until I can find a replacement. The woman she replaced is on maternity leave and isn't available and, frankly, she wasn't all that great herself. I thought I'd take the opportunity to find someone really good to take over the job permanently.

Tom: Whoa! You can't fire the current woman unless you've put her on notice that she's not doing the job, and that conflicts with your strategy to "keep her happy." Also, you have to provide the same job, or a similar or better one to the woman returning from her maternity leave. I assume she had no negatives noted in her reviews?

Pete: Oh, for goodness sake! I'm trying to run a business here. I can't worry about all the niceties. That's why we have human resources, for whatever they're worth. I can't foul up my operation while I wait to see if people improve, or while I hold their hands so they don't get upset.

Tom: One of the reasons that human resources has a tough time here is that they inherit cases that have been mangled by line managers, and this is a disaster waiting to happen. I think your entire approach to evaluations and employee development ought to be examined. You're constantly in contingent actions, and they're not all legal, let alone ethical.

Paul: Pete, now that I think about it, you are chronically late with your performance evaluations, and they're all completed on a pro forma basis, with no real insights or recommendations. I agree with Tom. We have systems and procedures and our value system to uphold. Work with him and human resources to sort this particular problem out correctly, then take a broader view of your approach and bring it up to standard. In the

meantime, find someone in your operation who can get
these reports done correctly on a short-term basis.

Tom was constantly doing things like that. In plant shut-
downs he would advise what the legitimate options were in terms
of layoffs, decisions about severance, and union involvement. But
in plant openings, he would also take positions on "starting it
right" and creating policies that maximized management latitude
while also protecting the organization. He was one of the finest
general counsels I've ever seen in his ability to protect the company with assertive ideas for improvement, not merely conservatively protecting its assets.

Legal Structures That Actually Make Sense

The best examples of legal contribution I've seen occur when
the legal department is integrated into the business, and is not a
monastic operation shrouded in legal machinations on their own
floor. (When the legal department has more floors than some of
the operating units, you know you're in for trouble. I once worked
for a consulting firm that sued so many people for so many reasons, I suggested at a board meeting that we make the legal department a profit center. The owner didn't take kindly to the
recommendation.)

At State Street Bank, the general counsel dispersed the legal
team throughout the organization, with lawyers reporting to
business heads, just as proactive human resources operations and
management information systems often operate. The attorneys
reported to him on a dotted line basis, but their direct managers
were the business unit leaders. That created flexibility and accountability, not to mention much more rapid responsiveness.
Once or twice a year, the entire legal team (about two dozen attorneys) would meet to discuss common issues, share ideas, and
reinvigorate themselves professionally.

Another excellent model calls for legal and human resource
departments to work together closely. This approach can mitigate
the problems that occur when the ethics function is relegated to
the legal department, which is probably the worst possible place
for it. (Worth repeating: Some things that are legal are unethical,
and some things that are ethical are illegal in the corporate
world.) If the legal and human resources people can achieve a

true collaborative working partnership, the former tend to give some structure and direction to the latter, and the latter tend to provide some pragmatism and flexibility to the former. While any structure can work under enlightened leadership and mutual trust, the structure that I prefer is one in which a business head has his or her own legal, human resource, and MIS team reporting directly to him or her. This creates much more of an action orientation, and places a joint responsibility on the team to improve the business, not to defend their professional turf and lives.

In Figure 5-4 we see the traditional "commander-in-chief" approach, with support functions reporting to the chief operating officer, although it's not at all uncommon to find them reporting to the CEO at a higher level than the business heads. It's believed that this arrangement maximizes the use of support resources, avoids duplication, and prevents each business from having separate approaches to their legal, human resource, and informational needs.

However, just the opposite occurs in reality. The support functions are increasingly seen as divorced from the real businesses, and are virtually never proactively consulted. This means that the legal people must forever arrive too late to suggest preventive action, and forces them to play "bad cop," constantly pointing out problems, often with that particular lack of compas-

Figure 5-4. Traditional support function organization.

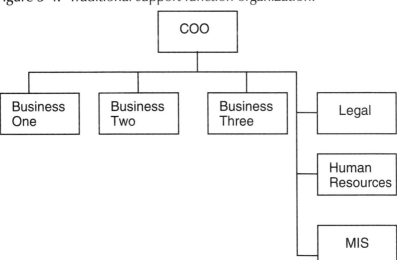

Figure 5-5. Integration of support function organization.

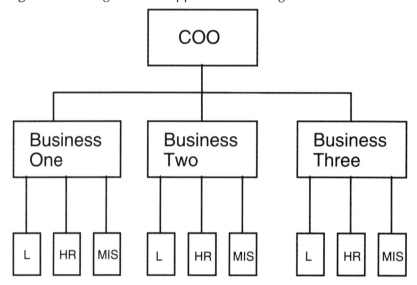

sion and empathy that lawyers can so masterfully muster. This increases the antipathy toward them among line management. Their very separateness reinforces their isolation.

Moreover, speed and resource utilization are not improved in centralized functions, because centralized functions, by definition, create their own bureaucracies, turf wars, policies, politics, procedures, and "lost corners." They actually maximize *inefficiency* by creating still another maze to negotiate. And that isolation is often perfect: I've been in scores or organizations in which lawyers can put in a forty-hour week without ever seeing a line manager within the business environment, and line managers never knowingly see an attorney.

At one client, someone forgot his identification card, with the result that the guard would not let him park in the reserved management lot adjacent to the building, but was forcing the man to park in a lot served by a jitney a half mile away. The man stormed at the guard.

"Do you know who I am!!??"

"It doesn't matter," wearily intoned the guard, "these are the rules."

"I am the assistant general counsel of this organization!" shouted the lawyer.

"Oh, that's different," smiled the guard.

"I thought it would be!" said the counsel.

"Sure, it was you guys who made these rules about no exceptions with no ID, so I don't have to explain it again to you, do I?"

In an integrated organization (Figure 5-5), legal, HR, and MIS are forced to respond rapidly to their immediate line boss. There is no separate bureaucracy, no separate hierarchy, no separate communications loop. Every day, these people are seen and are accountable to their colleagues to support them in their work. They often get to interact with the customers, suppliers, and alliance partners. The results of their efforts are quickly revealed in the success or failure of the unit's initiatives. They are in the game, not in the stands.

When you walk around companies you can actually tell which structure is in place by the differences in the pronouns. In the traditional structure, attorneys and line managers talks about what "they" are doing to "me," and how "I" have to protect "myself" from "them." In integrated organizations, the professionals simply talk about what "we" are going to do, what will happen to "us" as a result of a decision, and whether "we" lose or win a contract.

SOLUTIONS: THE LAW IS A SMALL PART OF OUR LIVES AND WORK, NOT VICE VERSA

We've replaced ethical vigilance, civility, and faith in one's peers with the most litigious social and business environment on the planet. Executives tell me regularly not to worry about ethics because it's in the hands of their legal department, and they're not kidding. The law, by default, has become the mechanism to compensate for personal lapses in accountability, folly, feelings of inadequacy, and the urge to grab whatever we can, irrespective of whether our talents earn it or not.

Societies and businesses can survive within the law, but I don't think they can really thrive or prosper without justice. When the accountants make the financial decisions, the lawyers make the legal decisions, and the consultants make the business decisions, senior management has become redundant. I've described how organizations are loath to confront poor performers due to legal worries ("Our legal department has told us not to" has become a mantra of mindless management, especially in human resources), yet are comfortable sending 20,000 people to the downsizing mill because they can defend it in the courts if they have to. Yet if you do regularly confront poor performers, there's seldom need to do the arbitrarily cut jobs in a frenzy of expense reduction.

We have to reacquire a moral compass, so that the law is used in its place and not as a substitute for ethical conduct, judgment, and civil behavior. We have to understand that "doing right" provides pragmatic, not just spiritual, reward.

Doing What's Right Creates Financial Return

Some of the finest organizations in the country have placed high premium on management and employee behavior, toward each other and toward the customer. Herman Miller, Merck, FedEx, 3M, Motorola, Microsoft, and scores of others have demonstrated that profits and appropriate behaviors are mutually reinforcing. Merck has lived by George Merck's admonition, "Do good and good will follow"; Motorola provides intense employee development and involvement; 3M provides on-the-job time for experimentation and has created an alternative promotional system to reward researchers who choose not to go into management; Herman Miller has practiced open communication and candor from the CEO on down, and invited customers into its plants to obtain their ideas; Microsoft has provided an atmosphere of innovation, experimentation, and fun, and rewarded people commensurately with their contributions at all levels.

I don't advocate doing right for it's own sake, divorced from the strategy of the enterprise. Ben & Jerry's and Stew Leonard's (once much-ballyhooed) Dairy are examples of organizations that claimed to be driven by lofty goals, but weren't totally candid and weren't well run. But neither is the converse appropriate—make the numbers, no matter what. For years, Burlington Industries was run by a CEO by the name of Bill Klopman who continually ran his meetings with lengthy strings of expletives, humiliating senior executives at his merest whim.[8] When they left the meet-

---

8. I was there and saw it, this is not hearsay. He had no compunction at all about embarrassing his people in front of outsiders, one time in my presence sending the corporate CFO fleeing from the room under a torrent of expletives to retrieve some balance sheet information.

ings, it wasn't hard to tell how they were going to treat their people. Klopman, for the most part, made his numbers, but left a company without a deep or impressive senior team (What self-respecting talent would have remained under those conditions?) and Burlington is not considered an innovative market leader today. Klopman's domain was "fear." His legacy is mediocrity.

I have never personally observed, in over 2,000 organizations I've visited, unhappy employees who were creating happy customers. It doesn't take a rocket scientist to understand the correlation. It only requires a decent manager. Senior executives have to set the example for what's right through their own actions and through the reward of the appropriate actions of others.

Understand That the Customer Isn't a Deity

I remember an American Airlines baggage supervisor taking a tirade of abuse from a passenger whose bags apparently didn't make the flight. He vented his unmitigated anger on her, citing everything from the weather delay to the lack of his special meal to the condition of the airport. When he was finished—or, perhaps, exhausted—the supervisor meticulously placed her glasses on her nose and quietly said, "You know, there are only two of us right now concerned about your lost luggage, and one of us in slowly losing interest." He stalked out, probably on the way to his attorney's office.

Self-confident, supported employees don't capitulate to the latest customer grievance. They analyze it and decide upon the appropriate response, which can range from a complete refund and profound apology to the polite observation that the customer is mistaken. That means that they neither default to legal opinion to deal with customer complaints, nor do they instigate litigious responses in customers who are made to feel that they have no other rational recourse. In one department store I heard a clerk innocently observe, "You must be mistaken about not wearing this dress, because those are deodorant stains under the arms." At an airline counter I heard an agent, with a smile on her face, point out that "We'd be happy to upgrade you if we had the space, but I'm sure you can understand that people paying full fare have to receive priority. It's simply good business." And at the local gas company I heard, "You've interpreted the contract incorrectly, and we don't provide this particular service for your water heater under that warranty. However, I can see how it might be confusing, and I am willing to refund the premium you paid for the insurance."

These are responses that successfully represent the company's best interests while maturely responding to a customer request (or even outrage). Legal action may result, but it will be less likely if employees don't view it as the logical repository for customer unhappiness and customers aren't made to feel that lawsuits are the equivalent of the two-by-fours necessary to get management's attention.

We're overwhelmed with books proclaiming that we should knock the customer's socks off, provide lifetime service, and delight, not satisfy, the customer. Fair enough, provided that there is some balance present, indicating that we should do that for most customers most of the time, but not all customers all of the time. The obnoxious, chronic complainers—whether usurping the server's time in a restaurant, tying up the service phones in a utility, or delaying the line at the motor vehicle registration office—need to be dealt with for what they are: self-centered, insatiable pests who are reducing the service to and satisfaction of other, valuable customers.

The customer service pendulum has swung too far. Let the madness stop. A stronger application of judgment, and support for employees' exercising it with customers, will actually result in less resort to legal claims and less vulnerability.

Anatole France observed that "The law, in its majestic equality, forbids the rich as well as the poor to sleep under bridges, to beg in the streets, and to steal bread." We can't rely on the law to set or enforce our standards of conduct. The law simply refers to the lowest common denominator, while our beliefs and behaviors should instead soar above the enterprise.

I was working with a CEO who had inherited a handful of dreadful performers in key positions. My advice was to terminate them, and stop throwing good money after bad.

She explained that their performance reviews had been equivocal, and that the corporate attorneys advised that firing them might well result in grounds for a suit. They advised keeping them on until at least six months or more of documented poor performance could be amassed.

"Why do you employ lawyers, Carol?" I asked.

"For legal advice, of course."

"And what legal advice is most effective *from their perspective?*"

"Advice that will prevent us from being sued and, heaven forbid, losing a suit."

"So you know they'll always advise against any danger of a suit. They've done that here. So what? What's worse, keeping these poor performers for another half year or more, with all the resources you'll have to invest in them and all the damage they'll cause in their operations, or running the risk of a suit? Give them a good severance, tell them to take it or leave it, tell the lawyers to get some backbone, and get on with your work as CEO. You're running the place, not the lawyers."

The poor performers were terminated that week, using severance packages drawn up by human resources and the legal department. Nobody sued.

The CEO had listened to advice from a lawyer and a consultant, and had made a decision. Too often, that progression never gets that far.

Challenge Six
Stop Trying to Grow by Reducing
Boards Act Like Houdini, but Disappearing Is Forever

Al Dunlap served as CEO of Scott Paper, a company whose brand and name were long associated with quality, household products you could trust. In less than two years, Dunlap fired one-third of Scott's total workforce (11,000 people), radically reduced the research investment, ended all charitable donations, prohibited managers from spending time on community affairs during business hours, and moved the headquarters of the 115-year-old company from Philadelphia to Boca Raton, where he just happened to have a $1.8 million home.

As planned, he sold what was left of the company to archcompetitor Kimberly-Clark, which cut 8,000 of the combined companies' workforce, and closed the Boca Raton headquarters. Dunlap departed with close to $100 million in combined personal compensation.

He then went on to do the same at Sunbeam, to the prospective glee of Sunbeam's directors. He was (and is) known popularly, as "Chainsaw Al," a nickname he seems to greatly enjoy. However, Sunbeam didn't improve after the inevitable bloodletting, and the board downsized the chainsaw in 1998. Dunlap feels he wasn't given enough time. He's right. In another year, he could have managed to fire everyone and simply sell off the equipment.

This is an example of one of the most unconscionable trends in the history of American business. It is a national tragedy, and it's called, euphemistically, "downsizing."

At its best, with the collusion of boards of directors such as those at Scott and Sunbeam, downsizing has boosted share price by focusing on short-term market value at the cost of virtually everything else. At its worst, it has been a brief palliative to buy ineffective executives time to try to think of something to save their jobs, with the board's grace, because they have neither been thinking nor doing their jobs for quite some time. In any case, downsizing is nothing more than mass firings by the morally and intellectually bereft and, as in the case of Dunlap and others, it can be downright malicious, with the egregiously obvious goal of redistributing wealth from the workers to the owners.

THE UNCONSCIONABLE ACT

Executives have been diligent in banging their heads against a well-beaten wall. That's because most of them rose to their current positions in times that were quite different from those that now prevail, as a result of:

- ▲ The emergence of a global economy
- ▲ The evolution of a diverse work force
- ▲ The increasingly diverse consumer base
- ▲ Deregulation and the loss of safety nets (e.g., in the airline and telecommunication industries)
- ▲ Increased regulation in the areas of worker safety and equal opportunity (i.e., OSHA, EEO)
- ▲ Instantaneous, mass communication via E-mail and fax
- ▲ Onslaught of information available on everyone's desktop computer
- ▲ Rapid technological obsolescence
- ▲ Program du jour and "guru of the month" initiatives
- ▲ Scrutiny by the media, both professionally and personally
- ▲ Consolidations and alliances creating size as a weapon
- ▲ Overzealous litigation of both real and perceived malfeasance
- ▲ Boards of directors unfamiliar with current dynamics
- ▲ Breakdown of employer/employee contract and bond
- ▲ Executive viewed with cynicism, not with innate respect

If you were reared in an organization of the old school, you kept your nose clean, supported the boss, avoided great risk or controversy, and worked your way up the corporate ladder. It was a clear, sequential process that required fortitude over talent, reticence over initiative, and a decision to "fit in" rather than "stand out." In the new corporate world, none of the old attributes amounts to a thing. All bets are off.

Some executives have learned new sets of behavior. They've ferociously pushed decision making downward, empowered subordinates, and surrounded themselves with strong performers, often from outside of the company. Some have shown an affinity for dealing with the variables presented above. They've changed focus and reset priorities. Others have demonstrated a impressive ability to learn and grow with the times. Gordon Bethune changed an entire culture at Continental Airlines, just as Herb Kelleher created a new one at Southwest. Jim Burke exemplified the highest ethical principals while leading Johnson & Johnson through unprecedented times. Jack Welch moved from "neutron Jack" to a positive force behind the integrity of people and principles while continuing to meet more and more challenging performance goals. But most CEOs and their boards have exemplified a solipsism that would make an ostrich proud.

Only the Good Die Young

Mass layoffs are heinous because they rarely cause pain among the group that should be held most responsible: upper management. If organizations have gotten "fat"—and surely many have—it's not because people slipped in the doors in the dead of night and finessed their way onto the company's books. It's because they were hired either in the embrace of strategic plans (blessed by executives and their board) that called for such expansion, or hired in the absence of any direction, which left such decisions to anyone who cared to make them. Either by commission or omission, corporate staffing grew because executives allowed it to occur. Sometimes those strategies and plans went awry, as they are wont to do, but the formulators, not the implementers, are the ones who should be burned.

A case in point. Robert Allen, former CEO of AT&T, announced that 40,000 employees would be terminated toward the end of his reign. He danced around the mechanism (euphemisms such as "they'll be asked to go into the schoolyard, and we'll then see who's invited back into the building" abounded), but the hard and cold fact was that tenure, ability, loyalty, past performance, and individual circumstances were not going to be high on the list of criteria that would determine who remained and who "wasn't invited back into the building." How did AT&T reach the point at which so many people had to be fired to ensure the company's prosperity?

Here's one major reason. Several years prior, CEO Allen had devised and overseen a disastrous foray into the computer business. It was a seriously flawed strategy implementation, reminiscent of "all the other kids are doing it, so why don't we," and it cost the shareholders over $300 million before AT&T finally extracted itself from the morass. Not only did Allen not get fired for his inappropriate dalliance in electronics, but he continued to be richly rewarded. In fact, at the very time of Allen's downsizing announcement, he steadfastly refused to take one dime's cut in his own lavish, multimillion dollar compensation package, while still other AT&T executives were getting raises and bonuses. Downsizing has become such an accepted crime that even attempts to soften the blow through symbolism (remember when Lee Iaccoca, certainly no pussycat himself, reduced his pay to $1 a year until Chrysler returned to profitability?) are deemed unnecessary.[1]

Allen is now gone (actually forced out early, but without suffering any financial consequence) with full honors and a retirement package that would make Secretariat blush. The 40,000 firings were ameliorated somewhat by an outraged public, but a large number of former AT&T people are no longer looking forward to retirement, but rather to finding some other job. Allen had also fired two consecutive COO heirs apparent, with the board's compliance and at great cost to the company coffers, before those distinguished overseers finally said, "Enough!" And they only said "enough" because profits were plunging, not because they were innately outraged by Allen's behavior.

Downsizing Doesn't Work; Otherwise, It's Great

The crime is magnified by the lack of evidence that mass firings pay off even for the shareholders. The American Manage-

---

1. When Fleet Bank, one of the dozen largest in the nation, announced its "Fleet Focus," which intended to reduce the staff by 25 percent, its board met *that same week* at The Breakers in Florida at over $600 per room per night.

ment Association (AMA) has found that only 30 percent of companies implementing job cuts since 1990 could report an increase
in worker productivity the following year, and only 40 percent
reported an increase in subsequent years.[2] While 45 percent of
downsizing firms reported an increase in operating profits, they
fared no better over the longer term than companies whose expenses rose over several years. In other words, a minor blip can
be accomplished through rapid expense reduction, but the longer
term effects are negligible on the bottom line, though devastating
on the talent line. That's supported by the AMA's findings that
firms that raised long-term training budgets were 75 percent
more likely to show increased earnings as those that didn't, and
were twice as likely to create increased worker productivity as
those that slashed training funds. Ironically—or, perhaps, logi-
cally—less than a third of organizations that aggressively cut jobs
also invest in the training and development of the survivors. After
all, if you don't believe in human capital, and people are merely
expenses, then mass firings and lack of training are natural ac-
companiments.

Nor is downsizing an event that has subsided. According to
Challenger, Gray and Christmas, an outplacement firm, about
43,500 cuts were announced in January 1997 alone. That's an increase of 12 percent from 1995 (1996 was an aberration because
of AT&T's massive cuts) and the second largest figure of the prior
twelve months.[3] From 1990 to 1995, the ten largest downsizers[4]
fired 850,000 employees. Multiply that times the small businesses
that depend upon those workers' patronage, the dependents of
those employees, the volunteer work that can no longer be accommodated, and other related issues, and it's likely that several
million people were adversely affected by the actions of those ten
firms alone.

The Longer-Term Fallout: Productivity

Executives usually try to justify downsizing on the basis of
productivity gains. In my own consulting work, I've found that

---

2. These and the following statistics from Gene Koretz, ". . . And
How It Is Paying Off," *Business Week*, 25 November 1996, 30.
3. For these statistics, see Gene Koretz, "Big Payoffs from Layoffs,"
Business Week, 24 February 1997, 30.
4. Digital Equipment, McDonnell Douglas, GE, K-Mart, GTE, IBM,
GM, General Dynamics, Boeing, and Sears.

arbitrary firings and layoffs—those divorced from performance issues and other causative factors—adversely affect productivity in the following three groups among the survivors:

1. *Those who feel guilty that colleagues were cut and they were not.* These employees become depressed, lose focus on their work, commiserate with both present and former colleagues, and suffer feelings of unworthiness. Both the quantity and quality of their work suffers commensurately. In interviews throughout organizational America, we've found that there is overwhelming empathy for even casual business colleagues who are summarily fired ("downsized") and perceptions of inadequacy among the survivors. One woman underwriter told me, "It was completely arbitrary. I can't think of any rational reason for the three people who were dismissed to have been selected ahead of me. I spend my days here wondering how long before they come for me." Every minute she is so engaged is a minute less of productivity.

2. *Those who fear they will be next.* These are the people who figuratively disconnect their phone and hide under their desk with the philosophy that "if they can't find me, they can't hurt me." Such employees spend most of their energy avoiding scrutiny and publicity, rather than producing work. Initiative, innovation, and risk taking are anathema. The key to survival is conservatism and disappearance. With voice mail and E-mail all-pervasive, there is no reason for an employee to be bound to his or her desk. Many "disappear" by running off to other areas under the guise of hustling to compensate for departed colleagues' workloads. Downsized companies have a complement of these "ghosts" roaming the halls.

3. *Legitimate talents and high-flyers who accept accountability for their own fate.* These are the people "cherry-picked" by the competition and search firms. They realize that it's now "every person for him- or herself," so they focus on creating a powerful résumé, choosing assignments for visibility to outsiders (not necessarily for internal impact) and network on company time. Those whose very talents are invaluable for moving a slimmed-down company forward are instead applying those abilities toward their individual fates, which are no longer deemed tightly associated with the present employer. Search firm principals tell me that there is no better time to find top-flight talent than in the aftermath of a

downsizing announcement at a major organization. "People who would never before return your calls are suddenly faxing you their résumés," said one partner.

Mass firings throw huge quantities of talent out the door but, more pernicious, they also derail the resident talents that should then provide the ballast to right the ship. The major difference is that those who were fired are gone, and their salaries have ended; but those who remain are no longer thinking very hard about the business at hand and are still getting paid. That's why organizations that downsize *and then refuse to invest in the development of the survivors*—fully two-thirds of the total as cited above—are like the service sign in the greasy spoon: "We may be sloppy, but we're also slow."

Failing to Grow the Top Line, or the Bankruptcy of Ideas

Much of my consulting work has been on behalf of organizations seeking to improve profitability. These organizations traditionally put caps on hiring, freezes on benefits, controls on expense accounts, limits on travel, reductions on training, and, overall, try to operate on something akin to "starvation rations." They exude aphorisms, such as "pull in the belt," "do more with less," and "lean and mean." Employees become defocused as more and more of their time is occupied by grousing and complaining, creating still more productivity loss and more need for cutbacks. It's the most vicious of cycles.

I was working with a $650 million division of a huge parent company. The CEO was shaking his head over the further cuts recommended by his direct reports that would follow on already vastly unpopular cuts made during the prior six months.

"I don't see any alternative," he said reluctantly, "but we have to protect our bottom line."

"It seems to me, Jim," I suggested, "that you've become locked into a defensive mindset: Let's defend the bottom line we promised the parent, no matter what."

"Well, isn't that prudent?"

"It might be prudently impossible. You've already cut so deeply that you're beginning to experience dysfunctional expenses in overtime, disability claims, absenteeism, and poor performance. It's time to take the offensive."

"Which is?"

"Grow the *top line*. Wouldn't every single one of your problems, not to mention your own stress level, be alleviated by increased business, above current forecasts?"

"Of course, but my people say they're going all out now."

"If they applied as much initiative to growing the business as they are to shrinking it, you'd have a banner year. Set them straight. No bonuses or incentive compensation for any profits that aren't due to top-line growth. Let them make additional investments if it will help them grow the business short term. You can't grow by reducing, and you're giving them incentive to reduce."

"What if, after all that, we can't grow the business and we miss the profit line?"

"Then you've got the wrong people."

A report from the Center for Economic Studies at the Census Bureau, covering 140,000 plants over ten years, revealed that operations that increased investment and employment created as much productivity increase as those that decreased and reduced.[5] Growth of the top line and investment in the business are key.

Increasing the top line is directly related to "raising the bar" and performance. Cutting expenses to preserve the bottom line is like doing the limbo. Some organizations have cut so far that they're crawling along the ground. They're happy that they haven't displaced the bar, but they're dirty and moving quite slowly.

Here are the characteristics necessary to continually grow the revenue line, obviating the need for draconian measures to try to preserve the profit line:

How to Grow the Top Line

▲ Incentive compensation must be paid only for real growth, not growth that results from cutbacks. It is unethical and poor business to pay anyone incentive for firing people or for padding their pockets at the expense of others' jobs.

---

5. Barbara Presley Noble, "Questioning Productivity Beliefs," *New York Times*, 10 July 1994, 21.

▲ Sales estimates should not be "bottom up," based upon estimates of the field force, which will have an endemic need to downplay the potential of the market. Revenue estimates should be created through a strategic view of the market involving cross-disciplinary teams of executives, and provided to the sales force.

▲ Under no circumstances should forecasts or plans be reworked or revised downward *without significant penalty to the executive accountable.* It would shock the average shareholder to know how common it is for the results of months of market planning to be undone in a twenty-minute conversation, during which a vice president whines that the original number was unrealistic (read: he or she has been unable to lead the troops toward the objective). I have seen plans reduced by as much as 30 percent only a month into the new fiscal year. Inevitably, the revised, lower plan, if met, will provide full incentive for all involved, so the margin takes a double hit.

▲ Implement real strategic planning. Abandon the vision, mission, and similar mush statements, and embark upon a cogent exploration of short- and long-term potential. Plan now for results desired in three years. Leave room for the flexibility required by the unexpected and the opportunistic.

▲ Demand a tight, comprehensive commercialization of research and development, no matter what the business. Whether in brake linings or consulting, in aircraft design or food flavorings, any investment in R&D must be based upon specific revenue targets within finite periods. The Times Mirror Training Group actually had a policy of funding their new product development operation out of capital, meaning that there was no accountability for ROI. In fact, we counted a $12 million dollar investment over a couple of years that produced no discernible revenues, nor were there any projections indicating that it would. Every R&D officer in the land should be held accountable for commercialization, and every line request for R&D investment should include that line officer's estimate for revenues on his or her watch.

▲ End the role of support functions as independent silos, and move them to the front lines. Many organizations have moved away from huge corporate staffs to smaller, nimbler staffs within each business unit. At State Street Corporation, human resources people report to their business unit head, not to a centralized HR function. Some organizations are outsourcing support functions altogether, opting to focus full-time resources only on full-time business issues.

Headquarters doesn't need protection, but the front-line troops need ammunition. Human resources, finance, MIS, marketing, and planning should be close to the customer, actively engaged with sales and service personnel. When staff functions are contained in home office silos, by definition they become protectors and guardians, not innovators and expanders. They tell you why you can't do something, rather than help lubricate the system to enable something to happen. The current horror shows featuring Chief Financial Officers, Chief Human Resources Officers, Chief Information Officers, Chief Learning Officers, and every other chief under the sun all serve to add sclerosis to the system by hardening its communication and action arteries. *Every manager had better be a chief human resources officer, or we've got more trouble than we think.*

LULLABY AND GOOD NIGHT: THE CULPABILITY OF COMATOSE BOARDS

There are precursive indicators that we ignore at our own risk, but sometimes ignore deliberately. Actions (or inactions) of boards of directors are clearly among them.[6] Early in my term as a board member for a woman's shelter that was—as do all these organizations—struggling for money, a director brought up the issue of board members doing business with the agency. The dozen people on the board represented a variety of product and service providers who could, theoretically, sell their wares to the organization. The board chair was a lawyer, and I assumed the response was a no-brainer, until she opened her mouth.

"There's nothing wrong with our doing business with the shelter," she explained, "as long as the transactions are documented and voted upon by the board if the expenditure level requires it."

Two of us—out of a dozen—lunged for her throat. "Are you serious!" we shouted. "How can we make objective decisions

---

6. And this applies no less to the local parent teacher association, scout group, community theater or fund-raising event. This isn't a matter of professional versus amateur, it's a matter of standards versus every person for themselves.

about the conduct and future of the organization and its management if we are profiting personally from its actions? No board member should be permitted to make one cent from their association with this organization."

The attorney was aghast. This had never occurred to her. "Why do you think we take our time to serve on these boards?" she asked rhetorically. The two of us managed to shame the rest into accepting a "hands off" policy, but it wasn't easy. No one thought there was anything wrong with the concept, and they positively salivated at the prospect. You don't have to work in Hollywood for Megapictures, Inc. to be greedy. Nor is greed reserved for the stereotypical "masters of the universe" of the private sector. However, there is a "greed" in protecting executives at the expense of shareholders that is uniquely a large organization phenomenon.

For example, downsizing is usually a response to poor bottom-line results, which are in turn almost always caused by poor strategic implementation. What starts as a proper accountability of executives and boards of directors—the formulation and assessment of the nature and direction of the enterprise—becomes lost or distorted when the translation isn't effectively made into tactical realities. When profits slip, bodies go.

Starting with the first Neolithic hunting cooperative, strategies usually don't fail on the basis of a poor formulation. They usually fail because the implementation is shoddy, misguided, subverted, or nonexistent. The good strategies aren't executed properly by the operational managers (an executive responsibility), and the bad ones aren't audited or monitored (a board responsibility) so that they can be changed and revised. Most organizations suffer from two chronic chasms that no one seems anxious to bridge:

1. Strategy is not translated into operational reality, with accompanying operational objectives for middle management, accountability for business unit heads, and measures of progress at least quarterly. (I'm waiting for the bumper sticker for executives that says, "Strategy Happens.")

2. Senior executives' performance is not evaluated by the board of directors against longer term goals (and, often, even shorter term goals). Top managers are able to dance around per-

formance shortcomings for so long that, ultimately, drastic measures such as mass firings seem the only logical remedy to keep
the ship afloat. Just when did all those leaks appear, anyway?

Board members usually confine themselves to the bridge and
upper dining saloon, so they seldom see either the leaks in the
lower decks or the condition of the crew and passengers.

How can conscientious, well-meaning, experienced, sometime diverse, and intelligent board members countenance the
human misery and horrible publicity of mass firings? Apparently,
much easier than we would think.[7] Here is what often transpires:

Lack of Independence

Many boards lack independence, which results from a board
having too many insiders (existing officers), outsiders who are
beholden to the CEO, or family members. This is why Archer Daniels Midland became so deeply embroiled in price fixing allegations and FBI surveillance before the mess exploded. The board
was nothing more than a rubber stamp for the CEO. It was composed largely of company insiders, with a few outsiders who were
beholden in one way or another to the CEO. At Humana, the
CEO's son sits on the board. There's simply no way to justify such
an appointment. At Warnaco, half of the six-member board is
composed of insiders. Rollin Environmental is a publicly held
company that apparently holds the record in this category: every
single board member is an insider.

Lack of Stakeholders

Members own little or no stock in the enterprise, so poor
performance doesn't affect them personally—their retainers and
fees are unaffected. (In the public sector, this includes a lack of
passion and involvement in the organization.) For example, at
giants such as Champion International, Unisys, K-Mart, Brown-
ing Ferris, and Bausch & Lomb, directors own relatively little
stock. They personally have nothing at risk, and they, themselves,

---

7. For actual ratings and commentary on many of the examples
listed below, see "The Worst Boards of Directors," *Business Week*, 25 November 1996, 85.

are not paid for performance. Unisys is a chronically poor performer, but senior meetings were often held near Lake of the Ozarks, Missouri, not far from where, coincidentally, the CEO had a lavish retreat.

In the public sector, it took both the United Way and NAACP boards nigh unto forever to discharge their CEOs, and only then in the face of overwhelming threats to contributions caused by lavish personal living, inappropriate expenses, and sexual harassment payoffs. (A potential cutoff of funding is the equivalent of a hanging in the morning for nonprofit directors: it immediately focuses their attention.)

Sclerosis

Directors serve too long and become too inured to the status quo, or they stay on long after mandatory retirement ages for employees and officers. At H.J. Heinz, as of this writing, six directors are over seventy years old. At Ogden, four are over seventy and one is eighty-four. There is nothing inherently wrong with either age or long tenure, providing that performance is superior. However, often that relationship is inverse. I advise all nonprofit and closely-held clients, for example, to limit board tenure to finite durations (usually less than six years) and to apply the same retirement ages to board members that pertain to the organization.

Conflicts of Interest

Conflicts of interest exist that wouldn't be tolerated in a bad novel. I described earlier the nonprofit board chair who was amazed that I was appalled at her acceptance of directors doing business with the institution, and in Challenge 2 discussed the trustees at Adelphi who profited from their board membership while the organization declined on their watch. Unfortunately, they are not alone. W.R. Grace, for example, paid $420,000 to a director's consulting firm, and provides pensions for its directors, almost all of whom would be either receiving or in a position to receive pensions from their "day jobs." The pensions for board members are little more than extravagant "sops" that help to make directors happy and quiet. Quaker Oats, suffering from the multibillion dollar loss from its terrible acquisition and subsequent sale of poor-performing Snapple, provides its directors with pensions. (Imagine the difference if it had provided them with shares of Snapple in lieu of their fees.) At Disney, two directors receive fees from the organization for other services provided.

Gluttony

Directors are too busy serving on boards to be of much service to boards. There's a limit to how much detailed financial information, performance evaluation, market strategy, and acquisition/divestiture debate anyone can engage in (which is why, presumably, boards form subcommittees). Multiply that by participation in three, five, or eight boards, and you have someone who is merely filling a seat and cashing a check. There are actually people making over a half million dollars a year solely on the basis of board membership. This is exacerbated by the "celebrity" board member, be it Henry Kissinger or Colin Powell, who is there merely to add some luster, or the "politically correct" appointee who is there solely to broaden the demographic. Can some of these people contribute to deliberations, nonetheless? Certainly. Are they the best available choices to fill a limited seat? Invariably no. At Time Warner, one director sits on sixteen different boards. I suppose he might serve on more, but occasionally he's asked to vote on a motion. At RJR Nabisco and Westinghouse, directors *average* more than five boards each. AT&T directors historically serve on a multitude of boards.

Incestuous Business Relationships

Reciprocity eviscerates rigorous analysis. I go over there and serve as chair of your compensation subcommittee, and then you come over here and play the same role on mine. Just how hard are we going to be on each other? In a related horror, insiders at H&R Block, a very poor performer that saddled itself with a CompuServe operation it's never understood or managed decently, sit on both the nominating and compensation committees (the former screens new directors). At Advanced Micro Devices, the CEO chairs the nominating committee. The CEO of Champion International serves on the boards of two of his directors.

Lack of Smarts

Lack of business acumen and understanding of the industry. There were some all-star names on Apple Computer's board, but they allowed a company with perhaps the finest technology in its industry—and a rabidly loyal customer base—to flirt so close with disaster that its independent future was in doubt. They took forever to fire CEO Spindler, who was a vacillating, uncertain embarrassment. They paid a fortune for Amelio, his formal replacement (also fired), and Jobs, his informal replacement, without much to show for the investment (performance not being the issue, since both men received huge, immediate payoffs for agreeing to step onto and off of, if needed, the ship). Apple earnings have continued to decline and management has downsized another 25 percent of the workforce. The cost of jettisoning one CEO and the acquisition of two people to replace him equals the jobs of 10,000 or so employees. (Only recently has Apple shown indications of solid performance.)

Bausch & Lomb's board didn't take action quickly enough on its former CEO. Astra Pharmaceuticals (showing this is not strictly an American phenomenon) allowed their AstraUSA CEO, Bildner, to run amok, sinking the organization into a morass of sexual harassment suits and resulting in other allegations against Bildner of millions in embezzlement. Morrison Knudsen filed for bankruptcy after CEO Bill Agee, running the company from a far-removed luxury retreat, ran it right into the ground. Until his termination, there was virtually no board oversight of his performance or expenditures. The K-Mart board witnessed huge losses before it managed the courage to replace the CEO.

AT&T's board, charitably, is not filled with telecommunications or electronics expertise. While it's true that boards should focus on governance and not try to run the business, the former is easier to attain and the latter simpler to avoid if directors have a passing knowledge of what the business—and the competition—are about. Prudential, a mutual company whose policyholders "own" it, allowed transgressions at both the insurance and securities operations that deeply hurt its profitability and, worse, public trust. More recently, it has decided to convert to a stock company from a mutual company, to the distinct disadvantage of existing policyholders. The list goes on.

Downsizings stem from frantic efforts to cut expenses in organizations that view their human resources as expenses and not assets. Downsizing is a last resort that occurs because the business is out of control, replete with forecasts that aren't met, performance that isn't achieved, and costs that aren't contained. Those bucks stop at the executives' desks, and it's the responsibility of the board to hold those Gucci-shod feet to the fire. However, at most board meetings, there is commiseration about the sad state of affairs rather than condemnation of the desultory senior performance. Confrontation tends to ruin the party, and it's tough to confront the one who invited you.

Some boards, of course, perform superbly well.Say what you will about the "New Coke" fiasco, but both executives and board members handled the debacle rather well (a refusal to panic, no scapegoats or heads rolling, a reassurance to the public that they were being heeded, rapid reintroduction of the original product), and anyone who sold their shares because of it would rue the day they did. Gordon Bethune and the board at Continental have done a remarkable job in turning around an operation that was once no one's carrier of choice into a stellar, on-time performer.

NONPROFIT SHOULD NOT MEAN NONPERFORMANCE

A few words are in order about nonprofits. For the sake of this discussion, I'm going to include charities (e.g., United Way), fund-raising groups (committee to restore the Old Town Theater), social groups (the Junior League), civic groups (Smithtown Light Opera), national groups with local operations (Boy Scouts), social work groups (Alcoholics Anonymous), professional trade associations (AMA), and preparedness groups (Red Cross, volunteer firefighters) in that group.

Any organization has a business plan it must meet. While Ford's plan includes a profit and return to shareholders, the local theater group must operate within its budget, stage its projected performances, and continually recruit new members. Just because profit is not part of the motive doesn't mean that there isn't a business plan. *Success* is always part of the motive. Sustainability and self-perpetuation are almost always a tacit part of the plan. (Yes, there are some nonprofits that deliberately sunset themselves, but they are few and far between. The March of Dimes didn't disband when their original cause, polio, was cured.)

Another reason to focus on nonprofits is that they are prolif-
erating. The government retreat from the social welfare and artistic sectors that began under the Reagan administration has never
been reversed. More and more former government services (suicide prevention, alcohol abuse, substance counseling) have fallen
to privately organized or community-sponsored organizations.[8]
Increasing leisure time and retirement populations have created
more arts, recreation, and sporting groups. Entrepreneurs have
generated still more need for individualized interests and avoca-
tions (investment clubs, sports activities). Nonprofit status also
alleviates a great many tax concerns for the organization. For
these reasons and others, the increase in nonprofit organizations
will undoubtedly continue.

Nonprofits, however, have organizational missions, and their
boards have fiduciary responsibilities to contributors, employees,
customers, members, and the environment in which they operate.
The most egregiously overlooked problem with nonprofit organizations is that their boards don't seem to realize that the organization exists for a reason that lies outside of the board meeting
room. Here are the concerns plaguing the nonprofit world:

Ignorance of Governance

The board is too often a tool for the CEO or executive director, rather than a governor and overseer. Nonprofit boards should
do three basic things:

▲ Establish the mission of the organization.
▲ Determine what measures will determine success in that
   mission.
▲ Select, evaluate, and develop officers and senior managers.

Instead, the boards are often established and meet only at the
whim of the CEO, and merely sanction and rubber-stamp the

---

8. When I served on a suicide hotline for the Samaritans, I found
myself fielding calls for help with alcohol, drugs, teen pregnancy, abor-
tion, sexual dysfunction, and every type of discrimination. When I asked
the director why 80 percent of our calls were non-suicide related, he told
me that the Samaritans were one of the few places left that people could
turn to. Virtually all of the former government help lines had gone out
of business.

CEO's decisions. In over half the boards I've served on, proper rules of order are unknown; motions, seconds, and votes are often illegal under the organization's own bylaws; and the officers often make decisions independent of the board's votes in any case. This occurs so easily because of the next point.

Poor Choices for Board Membership

The most common criterion I've heard for prospective non-profit board members is: Can they raise money? Fund-raising and governance are two separate requirements, and one individual rarely possesses both sets of skills at equal levels. Sometimes a "name" is sought, such as a present or former politician, local executive, or even executive's spouse. These are inevitably poor choices, because they may be willing to lend their names but are seldom willing to lend their time.

Board members should, amongst them, represent experience and expertise across the following gamut: business management, public relations, finances, law, human resources, volunteerism, and nonprofit experience.

Inappropriate Size

Virtually every nonprofit in the land errs on the side of too many board members. This is because board members are chosen not only for governance (which is, in fact, the least of it), but also for name recognition, reward, potential donations, contacts, cachet, and personal friendship. Also, various special interest groups seek to be served and accommodated.

The board size that then results is unwieldy and dysfunctional. I've seen local charter schools and a major national trade association such as the American Institute of Architects both try to stumble along with over fifty board members. Neither does it very effectively.

Ironically, while most of the board members simply don't show up often, they do show up often enough to frustrate the activists who are trying to get something accomplished, and they lead the cry of "Hidden elites!" when the dutiful minority tries to push something through in their absence.

Poor Self-Regulation and Discipline

I was sitting next to a veteran board member at a local charity who seemed to be against any motion, movement, or momentum suggested by anyone else. "How long have you been on the board?" I asked. "For twenty-four years," she responded proudly.

Nonprofits need board terms even more than for-profits, because there is less external incentive and internal upheaval likely to cause turnover in the former. Many of the members do serve for the passion of the cause, not for financial remuneration or ego, and that passion can be undimmed after decades. But all boards need renewal, fresh air, and new blood.

There also needs to be an attendance requirement. I've seen attempts to create them voted down vociferously at my share of board meetings, but there really is no excuse to miss more than two monthly board meetings over a year. If meetings are quarterly, meaning that important business is discussed on these precious and rare occasions, then attendance should be mandatory to retain one's board seat. (I greeted a "new" board member after six months of service on that charity, only to find that she predated my appointment and was making one of her rare appearances.)

Board members should be required to learn about the organization, interact with employees, and take in-service education on board responsibilities. There is an increasing number of courses around the country dealing with board accountabilities and requirements, and at least one board member should be responsible for attending and disseminating the information to colleagues between meetings.

I'm often called in to provide a workshop on board responsibilities, conduct of meetings, conflict resolution, and related areas that can enhance the board's effectiveness in working together as a team. These are the planners and healthy people. There are other situations where I'm called in to facilitate a hopelessly deadlocked or dry-docked board, which can no longer get out of its own way. These are the procrastinators and the dysfunctional people.

Every year, the board should review and rate its own effectiveness. It should evaluate its strengths and weaknesses right down to committee performance, and take appropriate action. Few do.

Lack of Interim Actions and Poor Committee Work

No one can provide governance by working only once a month, much less once a quarter. Committees and subcommittees need to be active in the interim. These are the Achilles' heel of most nonprofit boards, because they rely almost exclusively on the initiative, energy, and competence of the committee chair. In many cases, unwilling people have been stuck with unfamiliar roles, unwanted committee members, and unknown problems. Otherwise, the system works great.

Subcommittees work best when they are given specific goals, time lines, and resources. Example: The human resources subcommittee will interview 15 percent of all employees and 10 percent of all current volunteers to determine why our fund-raising initiatives are always late. This will be done in the next sixty days, and reported at our March 1 meeting by the chair, John Jones. Six interns from the local community college are available to help with the interviews as the subcommittee sees fit.

Committees are actually a very good alternative to get work done in nonprofits and avoid the weight of a board that's too big and too ponderous as a whole. But leadership is everything, and these assignments are seldom made with the essential discipline: who, what, when, where, and how.

Insufficient Distance From the Organization Leadership

Since the board must evaluate the organization's leadership, there has to be an arm's distance relationship. Too often the executive director or president is a close friend of the board chair and/or key board members. Sometimes this coziness grows to the extent that the board chair and CEO often change places, or one is seen as a stepping-stone to the other.

I recently had to facilitate a session during which the board was forced to hear from the organization's executive director as well as employees in a state of rebellion over harsh treatment, obscene language, and abusive treatment. The board had to vote to fire the executive director as a result of an objective airing of the facts. I was relieved to see that there were no die-hards, defending the director to the last. The buck has to stop with the board. I was convinced that, had the board done nothing, thereby failing in its governance responsibility, the employees in question would have filed lawsuits. What many volunteer board members don't realize is that they have liability in such actions, and there is seldom—especially among smaller nonprofits—any board liability insurance coverage.

All the more reason to take governance seriously.

Ignorance of the Bylaws

As archaic and ancient as many of them appear (and frequently are), the bylaws are the legal basis for operating the enterprise. They are ignored with shocking regularity.

Boards need a parliamentarian (hence, the need for the legal skills noted above) to keep them on the straight and narrow. I was once party to a board meeting where the newly nominated board members seconded their own nominations and promptly voted themselves into office!

When it comes to expenditures, ability to borrow, types of investment, frequency of meetings, voting requirements, and a host of other organizational issues, most bylaws provide significant constraints on a board's actions and restraints on a board's members. Ignorance is no defense. This is a litigious society and anyone who can sue generally does sue.

Bylaws should be required reading for all new members, need to be taken up in review form at least annually by the full board, and should be updated and revised as current conditions warrant. The best boards assign a person as the watchdog to make sure these requirements are met. The worst can't even find their copies.

Micromanagement

Boards of all types chronically confuse the "what" and the "how." This is bad enough in for-profits, where business acumen and consultants are in more abundant supply, but in nonprofits the problem is lethal. When you typically ask a nonprofit board a question such as, "What type of organization do we want this to become?" the answer is, "We should create a major fund-raiser for the end of the year," or "We need to expand our accommodation space." These responses are specific alternatives. It's like answering the question "What do you value in life?" with "I need better tires for my car." It's cognitive dissonance raised to an art form.

Nonprofit boards act, most of the time, as if they were the senior management team. Their job is not to implement, not to execute, not to oversee daily operations. Their job is to set long-term goals and evaluate progress toward those goals. Telling a poorly performing executive how to do his or her job differently is like leaving the landing lights on for Amelia Earhart: A nice touch, but a tad too late. The board should be replacing that executive, not helping to do the job itself.

Boards have to have the confidence in their management selections to trust that they will find efficacious ways to meet the board's long-range plans. However, once governance and management get bollixed up, neither is done well at all.

The Great "Campaign" Debacle

The most legitimate gripe I've encountered from nonprofit staffs is the annual change in "theme." Many nonprofits elect a new set of officers from the membership every year who are supposed to give guidance to the day-to-day management and staff. Unfortunately, a quasi-mystical phenomenon has developed in which each successive set of officers believes it must have a "vision," or "theme," or "campaign," or anything else that enables a cute motto and logo to be attached to it. "Soar on the wings of words" is the current melodic piece from the National Speakers Association, replacing such never-to-be-forgotten lines as "The privilege of the platform" and "Share the vision."

With each succeeding theme, the staff has to make changes. Some are merely cosmetic, such as changing letterhead, answering the phone differently, or printing new brochures. But some are substantive, such as reallocating resources to the current mission (e.g., attracting new members versus gaining greater public image), spending money on advertising, and lobbying in a different direction.

The trouble, of course, is that strategy should never be solely a twelve-month affair, and constant theme changes can easily disrupt long-term strategy, making a mockery of any attempts to achieve longitudinal objectives. While bylaws often require a change of elected officers each year, they certainly don't require a change in direction that is not dictated by strategic need or environmental events. The best arrangements occur in those non-profits whose bylaws specify a president-elect, and sometimes even name a first vice president who is third in line for the throne. In that way, current and future leadership can work together on longer term plans, incorporating new leadership gradually each year.

Misunderstanding the Value of Volunteers

The most waste to be found in any nonprofit is in the squandering of volunteer resources. Boards tend to look at volunteers as so much cannon fodder, not comprehending the tremendous asset they represent, the fact that the resource is not nonrenewable, and the financial fact that there is a return on investment equation that applies to volunteers.

First, volunteers cost money. They have to be found, trained, monitored, nurtured, and, one hopes, rewarded. If one attempts to save money and time by doing this poorly and haphazardly, the resultant resources are poor.

Second, volunteers have a qualitative component. Simply assigning them, without thought or management, to whatever priority is on the table, is wasteful and inefficient. Their individual skills and behaviors need to be matched to the job at hand. This is why there needs to be a hierarchy of volunteers. For example, those who are good a fund-raising are of the most valuable kind. The skills are relatively rare, and the results are critical to the organization. Those who can tend bar or prepare food are much less essential, because the skills are in greater supply and you can always use a caterer.

Third, volunteers are nonrenewable in this regard: If you use their energy for five or six minor projects, they will have commensurately less energy for a major one. (Interestingly and critically, the same dynamic holds true for donors. It's better to pursue them once for one large contribution instead of asking for a series of tiny ones.) Hence, an overall strategy must be completed that not only matches talents with tasks, but also accommodates top priorities with appropriate energy levels.

It's no accident that most nonprofits hear the echoing complaint that "the same people are always doing everything." That's a board problem, since volunteers are a key organizational resource. The path of least resistance is simply to return again and again to those who will say "yes" until they're unable to speak due to exhaustion. Nurturing volunteers in a nonprofit is no different from raising trees at Weyerhaeuser. The natural resource has be nurtured and constantly renewed.

SOLUTIONS: NONEXECUTIVES ARE VALUABLE ASSETS, TOO

The rubric that downsizing is a necessary evil to protect shareholders' interests is like saying that amputation is a prudent step after the doctor allowed the scratch to become infected through negligence. Downsizing is not part of corporate destiny. It is an aberration created by the combination of inept leadership and inadequate governance. Shareholders' interests are best protected by investment in assets, composed primarily of the human talent and energy of the enterprise, and the long-term growth of the revenues of the company. Profit is acceptable only as a result of increasing business, never as a result of stagnant (or declining) business camouflaged by slashed investments.

How do we avoid corporate anorexia? Herein, six recommendations:

1. View People as Assets, Not Expenses

The traditional view has been topsy-turvy. No matter what the balance sheets created by the accountants may state, people comprise the heart and soul of the business, its source of ideas, and means of execution of those ideas.

All managers—particularly senior executives—should have performance goals that include:

▲ Investment in the development of subordinates
▲ Measurements of improved subordinate productivity
▲ Clear and comprehensive succession planning progressions
▲ Comparisons of hiring with subsequent actual performance
▲ Personal accountability for return on the people investment (ROPI)

It's not numbers that matter so much as the right talent aligned with the right challenges. Senior people should bear responsibility for ensuring that the corporate "talent bank" is properly invested. That generally includes lean staff positions, accountability thrust forward to the point of customer interaction, and promotions and selection made not on the basis of *past* performance, but on the basis of projected *future* performance.

Investment in people should minimally include skills development, at least quarterly performance reviews conducted interactively, career analysis and developmental choices, and an opportunity to pursue varied career paths if talent warrants.

If senior people aren't aggressively managing the nature and disposition of the human investment, then I can assure you that no one is, because no one else has the power to effectively do so.

2. Apply a Basic Ethical Mind-Set

No executive should ever receive incentive compensation for profits derived from reducing existing jobs. It is antithetical to every behavioral standard that a company would wish to create or support, either with its people or with its public.

Executives should be rewarded for growing the business, for leading it upward, not overseeing its reduction. The notion that "without me, it would have been worse" hardly calls for reward, and well might call for therapy for narcissism. There are two things inherently wrong with rewarding profits through expense reduction. First, the cuts inevitably damage the future of the business, because they are made in the absence of strategic thrust and in the presence of tactical pressure. Second, downsizing creates an inescapable human misery that, even if somehow unavoidable, should not be exacerbated by the profit of the people orchestrating it. If you need someone to slash jobs, I assure you it can be done at lower level and less cost.[9]

Executives have long tossed around an informal template for assessing whether their actions pass a "stink test": How would they feel if their decision appeared on the front page of the *Wall*

---

9. In fact, one of the worst cases I've seen was documented in "He's Gutsy, Brilliant, and Carries an Ax," *Business Week,* 9 May 1994. Robert Thrasher, a mid-level manager at NYNEX, became known as "Thrasher the Slasher" while cutting tens of thousands of people at that company. He admitted to the "pressure" he felt in recommending who got cut, but also allowed that he couldn't remember a Sunday when he hadn't worked.

Street Journal the following morning? In a time of callused public reaction to mass layoffs, I'd suggest another set of questions to evaluate ethical propriety:

▲ Would I like it if my family were treated this way?
▲ Would I join a firm that has done this?
▲ What effect will this have on our top-priority recruits?
▲ What will the employees who remain think of our actions?
▲ Is this why I aspired to this job and can I be proud of my actions?

3. Consider the Longer-Term Pragmatics and Real Productivity

People who are trusting in their leadership and believe they are treated honestly direct most of their talents outside of the circle I've noted earlier. UPS people, despite the notorious strike the company endured, are basically positive and constructive people, which is what keeps them polite and helpful through the course of an arduous and hectic average day. (Virtually all managers came up through the ranks.) Unhappy employees have no energy or empathy left to lavish on customers—they're too busy indulging in it themselves. We discussed above the three immediate casualties of downsizing who were still on the payroll, and the consequent productivity decline.

Firing people to improve profitability is a short-term palliative that the early, longitudinal studies have begun to depict as a chimera. The survivors' short-term productivity drops; initiatives and projects with mid-term payoffs are delayed or abandoned, sacrificing competitive edge and money already invested; and long-term planning is undermined by a reduction in resources and elongated "recovery time" from the cutbacks (not to mention increased difficulty in attracting top talent into the chaos). Invaluable customer loyalty, forged over the consistency of carefully nurtured relationships, can be lost overnight.

Downsizing makes very little economic sense, no matter how favorably Wall Street might react for the moment. It is the panicked reaction of a small mind, at a low metabolism, with limited vision of the larger future. If that's the same mind as the person occupying the executive suite, you're in trouble on the bridge, not in the engine room.

4. Some People Have to Be Fired

A paradox? Not at all. Downsizings are usually the aftermath of poor performance, caused by too many poor performers who have never been confronted, helped and/or discharged. Proper termination for poor performance should be occurring regularly. In organizations of tens of thousands of people, not every hire or promotion is going to be perfect, and some will be abysmal. Corporations have to clean up after themselves.

The proper termination of scores of nonperformers, done rigorously and systematically, prevents the need for mindless termination of thousands of good performers by the time the water has overwhelmed the pumps. Executives have to stop quaking every time a staff attorney mentions the threat of wrongful dismissal or an interest group arrives at the door shouting discrimination.

There is no discrimination in firing people for poor performance, theft, or sabotage, and there is no lawsuit so expensive that it ultimately justifies retaining poor performers who endanger the viability of the entire enterprise. Executives should *listen* to the lawyers, which is why the latter are paid. Then they should *act on* what is ultimately best for the long-term success of the business, which is why *they* are paid.

5. Boards Must Cease Being Enablers

Passivity on a board is the exact equal of endorsement. Executives who are paid well for mediocre performance and/or not scrutinized for suspicious actions will drift toward a perpetuation of that performance and a continuation of those actions. Just as there are audit committees for finance, there should be audit committees for human resources, strategy implementation, and executive performance.

Boards should set strong performance criteria that are not solely related to share price or profit, but include revenue, growth and expansion. Multiyear incentive plans for top people are hailed as longer term rewards, but they are highly misleading and often disingenuous. After all, if you tell an executive [in his or her late 50s or early 60s] that they will be measured on profit over a three- or five-year span, what real incentive do they have for longer-term growth? That executive can hold together an operation for three to five years, maximize profit, fudge the growth, collect a fortune, and retire, leaving the mess to his or her successor.

Moreover, performance criteria shouldn't be met through expense reduction gained by downsizing. If boards allow the bottom line and subsequent incentive compensation to be gained through the layoff of people, they are establishing a scenario for slaughter. The bond between employee and employer appears to have been permanently broken at IBM, Kodak, Sears, AT&T, Apple, and the other organizations in which financial recovery was achieved through massive cuts in the workforce.

6. Shareholders, Public Watchdogs, and the Media Must Scrutinize Board Performance

If most people could see what I've seen during board meetings (let alone become the fly on the wall at the meetings I haven't been able to see) they would alternate between falling down laughing and being scared out of their minds. I've seen board members, appointed for "show" and name recognition, who smile pleasantly and never disagree with a single issue or position of the CEO. I've seen old pals approve compensation packages for performance that would merit a severance package in other organizations. And I've seen gross misunderstanding of regulatory requirements, reporting obligations, and basic ethical practices.

There are directors who never utter a word. There are those who don't understand the least iota of the organization's business. There are those who could care less and are searching their calendars for their next appointment. There is the emotionalism, politics, uncertainty, ambiguity, and deceit that are to be found at all meetings, at all levels, in all departments of any organization on the planet. Merely paying people more, providing exalted titles, and assigning rich perquisites does not create profound decision making, or even vaguely accurate guesses.

We need to hold our boards directly accountable for corporate performance. If they are not there to approve strategic direction, evaluate executives' performance in achieving short- *and* long-term goals within that direction, and independently auditing key segments of the business, then they have no useful function at all. Effective boards should follow a set of guidelines like these:

▲ CEO pay linked to short and long-term performance goals.

▲ No direct or indirect business between organization and directors.

▲ Directors must own at least minimum stock amounts.

▲ Compensation, nomination, and all audit subcommittees composed solely of outside directors.

▲ Maximum of two inside directors.

▲ External consultants evaluate board performance annually.

▲ Strategic direction approved by board.

▲ No reciprocal directorships.

▲ CEO is not present during his or her evaluation.

▲ Retainers for board paid predominantly in company stock or options.

▲ Retirement for directors consistent with retirement for employees.

▲ Board term limitations.

▲ Individual terms not to exceed three years without re-elections.

▲ Directors may serve on no more than three boards in total.

Downsizing is nasty work. It's doubly heinous when it's the result of executive stupidity, board neglect, and public apathy.

I was asked by a large utility to help them with a reduction in force of almost 15 percent of the total employment. As I headed for the door, I told the CEO that I didn't believe in downsizing and mass layoffs. He told me that's why they wanted me for the job.

"We've just finished our best year ever," he said, "and we've known for some time that we've grown too fat due to advances in technology, increased efficiencies, and virtually no turnover. We're now in a position to humanely and carefully reduce our employment without having to take drastic action. Help us do that."

We implemented a plan which, over two years, either produced voluntary early retirements or placed everyone else into a position with other companies. At one point, we produced a "book" of talented people whose résumés we circulated to other firms with strong endorsements.

Every single person was handled with care and treated well. Every single person remaining, despite some early skepticism, commented in our surveys that they were impressed with the process and respected the company more than ever. It was the only "downsizing" I've ever helped occur.

Challenge Seven

End Executive Compensation Plans That Reward Mediocrity

The Bigger They Are, the Softer They Fall

We have lowered the bar the most for the people who earn the greatest amount. Instead of demanding the highest performance from the most richly rewarded, boards seem to think that merely sitting on the throne is sufficient to demand the riches of the land. Rather than act as owners of the enterprise, thereby identifying with the shareholders, too many CEOs act as if they are Wall Street traders, seeking short-term, dramatic returns from their company's stock price.

As in baseball, where desperate general managers spend millions on weak-hitting second basemen who have had a couple of good years and a great agent, boards spend millions seeking the all-star CEO who can solve all their problems. Like the ballplayer, the executive often turns out to be someone who has had a couple of lucky years, a lot of media attention, and a strong search firm in support.[1]

---

1. An interesting phenomenon these days is the otherwise unknown executive who creates his or her own celebrity. Harvey McKay, who has run a largely unheard of envelope company in Minneapolis, has created national attention with a series of books and unabashedly brazen self-promotion. He is on the lecture circuit speaking not about how to run businesses, but about how to network and achieve celebrity. This is a new wrinkle: CEO as stepping-stone to celebrity!

Are CEOs leaders, or have they become major investors, reaping profits from short-term stock movements? It appears that their role has become mixed.

Mixed-up management sends mixed messages. Michael Ovitz stepped down from his post at Walt Disney, having accomplished precisely nothing, for which he was paid approximately $90 million in cash and stock. Mr. Ovitz was a personal friend of Disney CEO Michael Eisner. It was as though Mr. Eisner had produced a bad animated film and was writing off the losses, except the losses weren't incurred until Mr. Ovitz received his windfall. Who paid? The stockholders, of course (and consumers, since Disney's price structure has to reflect these giant expenditures).

Mr. Ovitz has something of a bad rap here, since he merely had a better friend and a stronger contract than most. He's actually in a sizable fraternity within the media industry,[2] which includes:

Executive	Company	Departure Payout
Frank Biondi, Jr.	Viacom	$25 million
Michael Schulhof	Sony	$20–40 million
Michael Fuchs	Time Warner	$20 million
Douglas Morris	Time Warner	$30 million
Robert Morgado	Time Warner	$40–50 million

We can add to the list the large departing packages of other industries' dismissed executives: two consecutive CEOs at Apple, two consecutive CEOs at AT&T, CEOs at Delta Airlines, Club Med, IBM, and scores of others.

What do we learn from this? First, the bigger they are, the softer they fall. We fire salespeople every day for poor performance, and they're lucky to get a few months of severance based upon a $50,000-a-year job. Second, there seems to be a level of hierarchical success in this country that supersedes actual performance. In other words, if you attain a certain income level, you're guaranteed to receive more of it, *no matter what your actual record*.

New York City is an expensive place. Here is what some of the people who work in the area earn:

---

2. See Bruce Orwall and Joann S. Lublin, "The Rich Rewards of a Hollywood Exit," *Wall Street Journal*, 16 December 1997, B1.

Gas station attendant	$9,360
Harpist	$20,000
Cable television installer	$25,000
Elementary schoolteacher	$26,000
Topless dancer	$39,000
Limousine driver	$50,000
Bus driver	$52,000
Police detective	$141,000
Former CEO of AT&T (Robert Allen)	$2,677,000[3]

We've mentioned to Mr. Allen earlier. It's safe to say that he did not have as good a year as most of the people in the professions listed above. Nonetheless, he earned 103 times what a city schoolteacher earned. Alas, Mr. Allen is not alone by a long shot. The average compensation of a CEO in the United States is 209 times the salary of a factory floor employee, by far the highest such multiple in the industrial world.

EATING OUR WAY UP THE COAST: SEVEN EXECUTIVES WHO DEVOURED CINCINNATI

The excesses of the executive suite can border on the obscene. Unfortunately, there is a plethora of examples to prove the point. We've chosen the following seven for their sobering and diverse appeal:

1. For 1995, Lawrence M. Coss, CEO of Green Tree Financial Corporation, received a bonus of $65.1 million. The shock of digesting that one had barely worn off when Mr. Coss received an astonishing $102 million bonus for 1996. That's over a quarter of a million dollars for every calendar day, in addition to his $433,000 annual salary. What might he have done to have earned about $279,000 every time he awoke? Did he cure cancer? Did he ensure world peace? Has he alleviated all suffering?

Green Tree provides financing for mobile homes. For the five-year period ending in 1996, the company's stock generated a return of nearly 53 percent and its market value climbed from $460

---

3. These statistics as of 1997, from Haidee Allerton, "Other People's Incomes," *Training and Development*, January 1997, 71.

million to $5 billion. Despite that very impressive growth, Mr. Coss's income is so huge that it actually dwarfs the performance. Using a compensation versus performance formula, *Business Week* evaluated him as the third worst CEO in terms of providing shareholder value for their investment.[4]

2. In 1997, Nolan Archibald, CEO of Black & Decker Corp., received a $75,000 salary increase, raising his base compensation to $900,000, and a $600,000 increase in his bonus, raising it to $1.4 million. His long-term incentive payments increased by $250,000 to $1.4 million, and he cashed in prior options that netted him a profit of $2.9 million. Add it all up, and Mr. Archibald had a $6.7 million year, which would tell you that his leadership and decision making must have been nearly flawless.

That same year, Black & Decker shareholders experienced a decline from $26 to $23 per share. What would Mr. Archibald have earned had the share value—novel thought—*increased*?

3. At Dominion Resources, Inc., the Richmond, Virginia, utility, Chairman Robert E. Capps missed his targets of earnings growth and return to shareholders. In fact, share price declined for the year. The company directors decided that this performance merited a $300,000 pay increase, to $1.4 million.

4. At CSX Corp., Chairman John Snow received an 11 percent salary increase to almost $1 million, and a $1.5 million bonus paid in company stock. The board also provided a long-term compensation package valued at $1.6 million, and options of $2.8 million. Then Mr. Snow requested and received a below-market loan to buy an additional 679,000 shares of CSX stock. Finally, using totally inexplicable arithmetic, the board voted to calculate Mr. Show's retirement package as if he had spent forty-four years at the company, despite the fact he actually joined it in 1980. That will add $1 million to his retirement pay *annually*.[5]

5. Stephen Case, the CEO of America Online, oversaw a year in which his company was charged with improper financial reporting, his system broke down under poorly planned expansion

---

4. Jennifer Reingold, "Executive Pay," *Business Week,* 21 April 1997, 58–64.

5. Black & Decker, Dominion, and CSX reported by Steven Pearlstein, "CEO pay often rises even when company's stock takes a dive," *Providence Sunday Journal,* 6 April 1997, F5. Reprinted from the *Washington Post.*

that denied hundreds of thousands of subscribers access to the Internet and their own E-mail, and the company was forced to offer refunds and concessions to make up for the sloppy service and poor planning. Both the company value and the stock price declined.

Mr. Case was paid over $33 million for his leadership. Relative to his compensation, the shareholder value, and the company results, Mr. Case is one of the two worst-performing CEOs in the country. On his watch, America Online produced a negative 413 percent return on equity. Quite a performance. Mr. Case holds another $116.5 million in unexercised stock options.

6. Jill Barad, CEO at Mattel, wasn't eligible for a 1996 bonus for the logical reason that she missed her personal performance targets. So the board instead granted her $280,000 as a "special achievement" bonus, perhaps for not missing her targets by an even greater amount. Further, if Barad is dismissed, or even leaves with "good reason," she'll receive five times her last salary plus average bonus, become vested in the executive retirement plan at age fifty, *and be forgiven a $3 million loan.*

7. Drew Lewis, CEO of Union Pacific until 1997, received $21.5 million, in addition to a $3.75 million, five-year "consulting contract" requiring him to work one week a month. More about Mr. Lewis a little later.

When was the last time you saw a salesperson fired for non-performance—or departing for a "good reason"—who was forgiven a company loan, provided with five times salary as severance, or vested in the retirement plan of the company he or she was leaving?

CURRENTLY, CEO PAY FOR PERFORMANCE USUALLY ISN'T

The average salary for a CEO in 1996 rose 39 percent to $2.3 million. Outside of the highest echelons of entertainment and sports, I challenge you to find another position that has enjoyed such growth in average income, because I couldn't. And that's only salary. If you add retirement benefits, short- and long-term incentive, stock options, perquisites, loan guarantees, and other lagniappes, we're talking astronomical sums. Total CEO compensation, when including that range, rose a mind-boggling 54 percent to nearly $5,800,000.[6]

The average factory employee received a 3 percent raise in 1996. The average white collar worker received 3.2 percent.

Even when organizations have stellar years, it's seldom the lone efforts of the CEO that created the success. Yet often, in a poor year, it can be the incompetent decisions of the CEO alone that cause it, as when AT&T's Bob Allen lost $300 million in an ill-advised foray into the computer business. (Mr. Allen was granted $10 million in stock options in 1995–1996 as part of his restructuring that included an announced 40,000 job eliminations.) There is seldom a downside to the CEO "pay for performance" philosophy. The CEO gets paid *anyway,* no matter what the results and no matter who is responsible for what.

There is no argument that the people at the top are exposed to inordinate risk. There are the ineluctable ambiguity, crises, technology explosions, and government interference that make the oversight of a huge organization extraordinarily difficult, if done well. However, it's not difficult to do it poorly, and we seem incapable of discerning the difference.

While CEO pay is superficially performance based (only 23 percent is fixed salary, according to a survey by Pearl Meyer, a New York executive pay consultant), the fact is that so many guaranteed goodies are added to that base that the safety net has actually been strengthened considerably. For example, receiving stock options is totally risk-free compensation, since there is no downside, in that the shares haven't been purchased and needn't be unless a guaranteed profit is available (because the share value has increased). If the options have a sufficient volume, slight improvements in share price can yield huge windfalls, so that the shareholders see a blip while the CEO sees bullion. Those slight improvements are often the result of downsizing employees, which creates a quick "hit" on the bottom line through expense reduction. Stock options, therefore, help create the perverse behavior that reduces or destroys worker compensation while commensurately improving executive compensation. That's because options provide so much potential profit, the CEO is tempted to act not like an owner but like a broker, profiting mainly from short-term performance rather than long-term equity.

---

6. And that follows a 30 percent increase in total compensation the year prior. See "Executive Pay," above.

Magellan, the Godzilla of mutual funds, turned over its portfolio last year at the rate of 155 percent. Its managers are seeking quick profits. If you want Magellan's managers to invest in your company with that mentality, then you want to show them quick profits. There's nothing wrong with Magellan's practices as a mutual fund, but a lot wrong with that philosophy if you're trying to lead a company.

Options are also illusory for the investors: they camouflage earnings. Organizations show higher earnings if compensation is in the form of options rather than base salary. While direct compensation appears as an expense, reducing the profit line, options do not. Although, when exercised, the options cost the company money, they are not an expense that detracts from earnings when they are granted. For example, if Microsoft had reported options as an expense in 1996, its net income would have been $1.8 billion ($2.85 per share) instead of the $2.2 billion ($3.43 per share) actually reported. That means that its Nasdaq stock price would reflect a higher earnings multiple. Only since March of 1997 have companies been required to reflect the differences in net earnings that would result if options were treated as an expense—in a footnote in their annual reports. That difference will probably average 10 to 30 percent.

Among other perks are lucrative relocation deals. PepsiCo CEO Roger Enrico received $777,000 to cover his costs and taxes to move from Dallas to Purchase, New York. That's in addition to his $2.2 million compensation and options on $1.7 million shares. Mark Willis, CEO of Times Mirror, received shares worth nearly $872,000 as a "housing differential allowance" to move from Minneapolis to Los Angeles, as well as over $300,000 to cover his relocation costs.

These relocation packages are obviously used to increase total compensation while avoiding embarrassingly high salaries and bonuses. The typical transferred employee is a married, 38-year-old male earning about $53,000. An average of $45,000 is spent to move him if he owns a home. For new hires, the average investment was only $35,000.[7]

Finally, we have guaranteed exit packages, like Ms. Barad's, above. In fact, her predecessor, John Amerman, also didn't qualify

---

7. Statistics from Joann S Lublin and Joseph B. White, "More Companies Relocate CEOs in Style," *Wall Street Journal*, 7 April 1997, B1.

for a bonus in his final year, for failing to meet *his* goals. Instead, he was rewarded with $1.1 million to be a "senior advisor" to Ms. Barad, an amount exactly matching his prior CEO salary. Thus, Mattel managed to pay for two CEOs in a single year, and both missed their performance goals. Quite a coup.

Phillip Rooney, pressured into departing as CEO of struggling WMX Technologies, Inc., received $2.5 million for five years for allowing himself to be kicked out. Michael Orvitz, cited above, drew over $90 million for fourteen unproductive months.

Occidental Petroleum Corp. Chairman Ray Irani has a deal that pays him 50 percent of his highest annual compensation (salary, bonus, and stock) *for life.* This will be a not-insignificant drain on Occidental's earnings when the CEO is retired and fishing, because his most recent earnings are $6.6 million, which include $1.2 million bestowed beneficently to atone for California's high personal income tax rate.

David LeVan, Chairman of Conrail, will take home $22 million if Conrail and CSX merge. The aforementioned Drew Lewis, CEO at Union Pacific until last year, received $4 million when it merged with Southern Pacific, in addition to a $1 million salary, a $2 million bonus, and that $3.75 million, five-year consulting contract noted above.

BellSouth's stock fell 7 percent in 1996, but CEO John Clendenin received $3 million to retire early (at age 62) in addition to his $2.7 million in pay and options.[8]

THE CONCEPT OF MULTIDIMENSIONAL REWARDS AND TRUE PERFORMANCE

Remember when Lee Iaccoca reduced his salary to $1 a year until Chrysler was profitable again? At the time, Chrysler stock had descended to $3 per share and there weren't many takers at that price. In early 1999, Daimler/Chrysler was trading at over $100.

Iaccoca gained the trust of shareholders, the public, employ-

---

8. Some of the negotiating strains credulity. Michael Pickett, CEO of Merisel, a computer wholesaler, didn't have his contract renewed, which tells you something about his performance. Nevertheless, he successfully managed to keep his company Porsche with cellular phone, crystal chess set, and popcorn maker.

ees, and vendors, no mean trick for a company that analysts claimed would close down or be sold. (For the younger readers, I know that's hard to believe, with Chrysler minivans, Prowlers, and Vipers pouring off the assembly line. However, it was also impossible to believe about Pan Am or Eastern Airlines. Picture Intel or DuPont threatening to go broke tomorrow.)

His performance was multidimensional:

▲ He gained loan guarantees from Congress.
▲ Chrysler reintroduced the convertible.
▲ The unions agreed to wage concessions.
▲ Vendors agreed to new terms and conditions.
▲ He became the personal "guarantee" in TV commercials.
▲ Dealers were re-embraced.
▲ Engineering and styling improved.

Chrysler paid back its loans early. No one lost a penny. Those who bought stock made a fortune. And people who buy Chryslers today are driving fine cars. The actions in the list above are both strategic and tactical, long term and short term, financial and nonfinancial. What might have been a tortuous route back to profitability became a steady, straight drive under Iaccoca's leadership.

From a position of poor strategy (bad investments, poor positioning, declining R&D) and poor execution (poor quality, late deliveries, unprofitability, etc.), Iaccoca moved the organization to superb performance along both axes. He received a fortune in compensation in subsequent years. He deserved every penny.

In an age of exorbitant compensation for basketball players, rock stars, and retired politicians, it's hard to support a blanket condemnation of anyone making "too much" money. But it is both easy and proper to condemn those individuals and companies that have created the ultimate executive piggy bank: stratospheric pay for poor or no performance. Six- and seven-figure compensation packages shouldn't be offerings bestowed by an awed board of directors, nor presents from admiring friends. They should be earned through the multidimensional growth of the organization.

Anyone can fire people or "downsize." CEOs are inordinately rewarded for throwing people out the door. The Institute for Policy Studies found that CEO pay at the thirty corporations with the largest layoffs in 1996 rose an average of 67.3 percent. The CEO pay at America's top 365 corporations overall rose 54 percent.[9] Compensation consultant Graef Crystal has found that all companies want to pay their CEO slightly more than average for the industry. This creates a continuing salary inflation. Moreover, rewards and punishments are far from equal, says Crystal:

> If you read these reports from the directors, when things are going well it's always because of the brilliance of the CEO. But on the downside, it's those damn politicians in Washington or it's Wall Street or it's the drop in oil prices—somehow it's always someone else's fault.[10]

IF YOU FLAUNT IT TOO MUCH, THE TIDE WILL TURN

There is a determined resistance to the excesses noted above. It's not overwhelming and is rarely in the news, but it is growing. We might actually be treated to reports of CEOs being held at least to the same standards of performance that are used for salespeople, secretaries, editors, underwriters, and tellers.

Bausch & Lomb shareholders recently voted two nonbinding resolutions to shorten directors' terms and create a shareholder rights plan, both of which were opposed by company management. Shareholders also supported a proposal to discontinue the "poison pill" plan, in place since 1988, which supposedly protects the company from takeover by making such an act too difficult. Among the proposals defeated was one seeking to eliminate lucrative officer severance contracts and another demanding minimum ownership requirements for directors. The *Wall Street Journal* termed these actions "discontent but not revolt."[11] Perhaps they should have been more heavily armed.

Consultants at William M. Mercer, Inc., claim that about 58 percent of companies currently tie some aspect of executive com-

---

9. "It's a tough job," *Providence Journal,* 16 May 1997, E1.
10. Steven Pearlstein, "CEO pay often rises even when company's stock takes a dive," *Providence Sunday Journal*, 6 April 1997, F5. Reprinted from the *Washington Post.*
11. "Bausch & Lomb Votes By Shareholders Go Against Management," *Wall Street Journal*, 30 April 1997, B7.

pensation to performance. However, that performance is often strictly financial, and even then (as we've seen above) an adept CEO can weasel out of poor results with the assistance of the board.

Compare that with a latter-day Iaccoca, James Barksdale of Netscape Communications. He tied his compensation to his performance, and forswore both salary and other cash compensation for 1997, tying his personal success to that of the company. The organization's stock has lost more than half its value since Mr. Barksdale joined in January 1995, at which time he was granted options for eight million shares. In 1996 he was paid $100,000 and received no additional options.

Let's return to CEO Lewis of Union Pacific. That company's stockholders faced some very upset Teamster members at the annual meeting, protesting the Lewis package described earlier in this chapter. In fact, unions, religious groups, and large retirement fund investors are beginning to exert pressure on the largesse of the executive suite. Almost twice as many (112) proxy resolutions were filed over this issue in the first half of 1997 as compared to the year before.[12] The AFL-CIO has launched a Web page[13] revealing CEO pay and how to file proxies, and the United Farm Workers are planning attacks against Monsanto on this issue, whose CEO, Robert Shapiro, earned $4.4 million in 1996. Monsanto, it seems, owns strawberry farms that pay workers less than $10,000 per year. Do the math: Mr. Shapiro is earning the equivalent of 440 workers' salaries with his reported compensation alone.

Florida's $80 billion pension fund has been voting "no" on executive pay packages. The United States Trust Co. has an investment operation focusing on socially responsible organizations. When our friend Mr. Allen of AT&T was granted his $10 million in options at the same time he announced 40,000 job cuts, a group of investors sponsored a resolution to freeze executive pay in times of downsizings.

The entrenched company management almost always wins these battles, as did AT&T. However, there are sometimes victories. The Teamsters—with a $60 billion pension fund—filed to

---

12. See Aaron Bernstein, "An Embarrassment of Riches," *Business Week*, 21 April 1997, 64.

13. http://www.ctsg.com/ceopay

prevent Nabisco from repricing executive stock options when the stock price falls. In 1995 Nabisco allowed executives to swap options priced at $50 for new ones priced at $27 after the stock dropped to—can you guess?—$27. This means that the executives' inability to improve corporate performance, and thereby not profit in the marketplace as any normal investor would not have profited, was "rewarded" through the reduction in option price to the executives' level of ineptitude. They could still make a lot of money if they raised the company from the pit in which they had placed it.

Where I come from, this is called "a sure thing." Nabisco agreed not to do it anymore, which is probably a smart move when faced with Teamsters armed with $60 billion. Unfortunately, that's the degree of persuasion required.

SOLUTION NUMBER ONE: TREAT EXECUTIVES AS IF THEY ARE EMPLOYEES, NOT GODS

The solutions to excessive and unmerited executive largess are simple and difficult. They are simple because what needs to be done is clear. They are difficult because to do the right thing requires a very strong sense of volition and a clear value system. Here are my guidelines for executive compensation.

No Reward for Profits Made Through Layoffs

No executive should ever receive discretionary incentive for profits derived from cost cutting, and particularly those gained from reducing employment. Even when these actions are wholly merited, they should not result in an executive's pocket being filled through the loss of other people's jobs. In addition, the AT&T resolution doesn't go far enough (to freeze CEO pay during layoffs): the total compensation of a CEO should be reduced by the same percentage that the company workforce is reduced. A 5 percent downsizing would decrease CEO pay by 5 percent; if a quarter of the workforce goes, so does 25 percent of the CEO's pay. Discretionary incentive compensation should be reserved for business growth, not expense reduction.

Report Total Compensation as Expense

Total executive compensation should be reported—including stock options, relocation packages, deferred income, club memberships, and all other perquisites—in all appropriate company reports and should be reported as an expense item in its totality, affecting earnings and stock price commensurately. Shareholders have a right to know how much the CEO's earnings are affecting the share price in any given period. They may think it's well worth it, but that's for them to decide, not the corporate accountants.

Maximum Salary Determined by Multiple of Average Salary

Boards should implement a policy calling for a maximum on the multiple of CEO pay as compared to the average company salary. That's not as onerous as it appears, since we're not talking about the lowest salary (as with Monsanto CEO Shapiro being "worth" over 400 manual laborers). However, it is reasonable that a multiple of somewhere between 50 and 100, depending upon the industry and the organization's position, be applied. Hence, an average salary of $35,000 still results in over $2.5 million for the CEO if the multiple is 75. Presumably, the higher paid the staff, the more difficult the work and the leadership job.

(I've been tough on Ben & Jerry's earlier for their disingenuous use of values in running the business, so I'm happy to provide some balance here by pointing out that their CEO receives a multiple of only about eight times average worker pay.)

Limits on Payout of Golden Parachutes

No form of golden parachute should be allowed if the executive leaves via resignation and/or personal volition, for any reason whatsoever.

No Rewards Attached to "For Cause" Departures

No form of severance whatsoever—other than vested retirement benefits and reasonable accommodation (i.e., transition of insurance benefits)—for any executive fired for cause, be that incompetence, malfeasance, corruption, or any other objective standards. (Yes, incompetence can be judged if performance standards are in place. It's done every day for those farther down the food chain.)

No Insiders on Key Committees

No insider sits on the board's compensation committee, nor does any outsider with an "interlocking" relationship (someone from the company sits on that director's board). The CEO is never present during debate about his or her performance or remuneration.

Use Objective Outside Data

The board acquires external, objective assessment on an annual basis of equivalent CEO pay in the industry and the nation, including corresponding returns to the shareholders in both share price and earnings.

At Least 50 Percent of Incentive Based on Nonfinancial Criteria

CEO incentive compensation is never more than 50 percent reliant on short- or long-term financial return. The remaining percentage is based upon the factors described below, especially succession planning, exemplifying desired values, and development of people (and behavior during a crisis, should one occur).

SOLUTION NUMBER TWO: ADD NONFINANCIAL ACCOUNTABILITIES TO CEO'S PERFORMANCE MEASURES

In any organization, the CEO should be rewarded for accountabilities in addition to financial objectives. These accountabilities are those that guarantee longevity of success, continued innovation, retention of talent, and similar goals.

Develop the Bench

A CEO should develop "bench strength" and a succession plan for all key positions. Jack Welch is an excellent example of a CEO who creates great depth below. Lawrence Bossidy, a direct report, saw that he probably wouldn't succeed Welch any time soon, and left GE to become CEO of Allied Signal, for example. GE didn't suffer, because it had and has a surfeit of highly capable executives waiting in the wings. Young GE managers are increasingly rotated through overseas assignments in anticipation of their need to be global thinkers and leaders as they progress through the ranks. It's no accident that, in one of the largest and most complex of all major businesses, GE's directors could probably find replacements for all significant positions by tomorrow from within the company's own ranks.

Be a Role Model

The CEO should be the exemplar for values and behavior in the company. People only believe what they see, and that applies to both employees and customers. Iaccoca understood this, and took on the role of company representative personally. Lawrence Tisch was a poor leader at CBS, selling off valuable assets, downsizing without regard to quality, and appearing to be out of touch with both CBS's history and its purpose. His focus was short term, bottom line (which, ironically, wasn't enhanced during his tenure). As a result, morale deteriorated, talent left, and mediocrity took over. When CBS was sold, it brought a fraction of the price that ABC did in a contemporary sale. In the late 1990s, CBS is unprofitable and in serious straits. It was once "Paley's House" and the gem of the broadcast industry.

Boards can "bench mark" this exemplary behavior and measure it by talking to employees and observing organizational behavior. I've mentioned earlier that a "human resources audit" is as important as a financial audit, and a director should be responsible for overseeing one annually. By listening to people, tracking their performance in times of stress and ambiguity, and learning how they are informally rewarded, the impact of the top exemplar will be evident.

Most people do not cheat, steal, or commit unethical acts for themselves. They do it on behalf of their organizations. The top person advertently or inadvertently gives the signal as to whether such behavior is acceptable. When the "Texaco tapes" were released, revealing biased language and thinking on the part of several top officers, it was an indication that such language and behavior were generally condoned by the organization. To speak openly in that manner with other officers present demonstrates that it was acceptable, and despite the disavowal and prompt remedial actions by the CEO, it was too little, too late. The CEO's responsibility is to *prevent* such acts, not merely to punish them when they are caught and become public.

Foster Effective Communication and Encourage Innovation

I've found small companies that are very bureaucratic and stifling, and large companies that are quite open and risk taking. Innovation and effective communication aren't functions of size, but of *intent*. This comes directly from the top. I sat in an executive meeting at Fleming Foods some years ago when one of the participants actually addressed the CEO as "Mr. President." That doesn't promote communication, accessibility or team work. In the previous chapter, I mentioned Bill Klopman's profanity sending six-figure people scurrying from the room at Burlington Industries. I once listened to the senior corporate vice president for human resources at Mallinckrodt inanely dance around a direct question from his CEO because he was too scared to give an opinion.

When a CEO is surrounded by "yes people" then that's what you'll find further down the line. When the CEO encourages open debate and honest feedback, then that's what you'll find below. (And these are the behaviors a "human resources audit" will find.) The top gun is the ultimate determinant of the levels of innovation and candor in the organization.

Forge an Effective Executive Team

I frequently serve as an executive coach, both to individuals and the teams they comprise. Most executive teams are, in actuality, committees. A true executive team contains individuals who usually represent major functions, such as research, sales, or marketing (see Figure 7-1). These executives will represent their areas and fight for the budgets, staffing, and resources required to meet their business objective, *but they will also willingly surrender power and resources to team members if that exchange will further the goals of the entire team.* For example, as head of marketing, I might agree to a budget decrease or give up some personnel slots so that both can be provided to my counterpart in charge of Asian sales, a market that we are trying to build significantly to meet our overall business strategy and two-year plan. The entire team will be rewarded if that Asian growth takes place.

In a committee, those functional heads fight for their turf and power, period. There is little voluntary sacrifice—in fact, it's seen as a sign of weakness, hence the political infighting that marks so many enterprises—and only the CEO is in a position to make final determinations and serve as Solomonic distributor of "wins" and "losses." A dictatorial CEO will do this, creating a fawning and/or politicized organization around him or her. A weak CEO will try to avoid the arbiter role, creating a divisive, turf-conscious set of fiefdoms. Both models are dysfunctional. Yet the vast majority of organizations contain top committees, not top teams, despite what the organization chart calls them.

Be Visible and Decisive in Times of Crisis

Jim Burke's leadership at Johnson and Johnson during the Tylenol crisis set the standard for responsibility and courage. Lawrence Rawl's literal disappearance as CEO of Exxon during the first 48 hours of the Exxon Valdez disaster established the nadir. What most people don't realize is that Burke had established a strong code of ethics and integrity that J&J people observed every day. With that foundation, it was "easy" to do the right thing in the Tylenol case.

Figure 7-1. Team versus committee approaches.

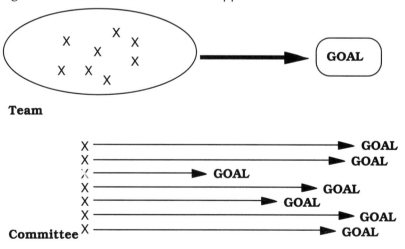

Many CEOs defer to their public relations and legal departments when stuff hits the fan. The superb ones ride out in front of the troops. A few years ago, Merck suffered an explosion in its Puerto Rico pharmaceutical manufacturing plant. One life was lost and several people were hurt. Then-CEO Roy Vagelos was in California at the time. He immediately changed his itinerary, flew to Puerto Rico, visited with the families involved, and pledged a company-wide audit of its manufacturing procedures.

When minor crises hit at lower levels, guess what the difference in actions are between Exxon and J&J or Merck?

Are these conditions onerous? Having observed hundreds of CEOs on the job, I don't think so. With a continuing opportunity to earn seven figures in the short and/or long term and a full range of perquisites, it's not unreasonable to expect that we hold the top people to at least the same standards of performance and measurement to which they hold everyone else.

Once, in my younger days, I was walking along a countryside road with a friend who was an attorney. We came to a particularly pretty patch of land.

"What's to stop us from taking those plants and transplanting them to our property? They don't belong to anyone."

"Alan, everything belongs to *someone*," he informed me. "It's either private land that's not developed or it belongs to the government, or to some nature preserve. But I guarantee, it belongs to someone."

Similarly, executive compensation comes from someplace. It might be from the company's earnings and, therefore, stockholder value, or it might come from development funds, or employee raises, or new hires, or plant expansion.

It should come solely from the profits derived from increased growth.

Challenge Eight

Communicate as a Consumer

A Customer Offensive and an Offensive Customer Are Two Different Things

For many years, the family that owned the Syms discount department stores advertised their goods on local television with the tag line, "An educated consumer is our best customer." The Syms family simply meant that they wanted their customers (and prospective customers) to understand their discount system, so that there would be no mistakes about how to find the best bargains in the store. I think that the slogan has potential far beyond knowing how to get 40 percent off retail.

Just as I've cited the need for self-esteem among employees and their organizations, customers need to develop a renewed sense of self-worth. We are too often supplicants, arriving at the seller's door with our hats in our hands and our credit cards in our pockets, hoping to capture some tiny scrap of merchandise or paltry bit of service. We will pay for almost anything, and complain about virtually nothing. We are serfs appearing at the castle keep, providing our harvest as tribute and hoping to be granted some entertainment or slight pleasure in return. We have become, in current terms, wimps.

We have allowed service providers to adopt the lowest common denominator in terms of guaranteeing that service. The cable television company, washing machine repair service, and electric utility all grandly offer to "be there sometime on Tuesday." Unless, of course, it turns out that they just couldn't get there on Tuesday. Occasionally, we can extract "between noon and five," but without a real assurance that the proper people with the proper equipment and expertise will actually materialize on the doorstep. What we've accepted as "emergencies," "unexpected traffic tie-ups," and "absences among the staff" are, in reality, excuses for poor planning, overbooking, lack of discipline, and slothful enforcement of standards by the purveyors. The emerging cable TV systems, ostensibly a private sector, high-growth, entrepreneurial business, have provided such abominable service that they are the butt of jokes from talk shows to movies. Yet, their customer sign-ups go marching on.

The computer hardware and software industry has excelled in abusing its customers. Can you imagine, for example, the auto industry engaging in practices similar to computer software and hardware firms? Your new car purchase and experience would look something like this:

If Cars Were Like Computers

▲ There is an "acceptable" defect rate of about 10 percent, and the manufacturer and dealer can't understand why consumers can't simply accept that "fact."

▲ If you turn on your car's radio and it fails to play, the entire car stops and has to be restarted.

▲ Starting your car requires several minutes while all of its systems sequentially warm up. Sometimes, to get certain systems to work, such as the lights, you have to arrange for other systems, such as the windshield wipers, to be shut down.

▲ Any repairs require weeks, and you do not get a loaner. The car cannot be fixed locally, and must be sent to California, unless you live in California, in which case the car must be sent to Minnesota.

▲ Cars are aggressively sold before they are perfected, and customer complaints are eagerly expected in order to build better successors. The industry strategy is to learn from actual breakdowns, and if that means that accidents and possible loss of life occurs, it's a small price to pay for product improvement.

▲ The car's guarantee expires in ninety days, or before you've had a chance to try all of its features and understand those that aren't working, whichever comes first.

▲ Although improved features are created for the car, they are incompatible with the model you own and an entirely new vehicle must be purchased in order to accommodate them. Your model is effectively obsolete in three to five years, when it can no longer provide contemporary transportation.

▲ The company stops making replacement parts after three to five years, and refuses to service the car after that time. You are forced to pursue obscure ads in the back of magazines and do business with unlicensed suppliers if you insist on trying to keep the car running.

▲ Your car phone cannot communicate with any other phones except those exactly like it. Your car does not fit into parking spaces designed for other cars. Your car cannot be driven by others who do not have licenses explicitly acquired for your type of car. Not all gasoline can be used in your car, and even gasoline that is specified might not work since those providers have frequent quality problems themselves. There is no such thing as "self-serve."

▲ When you call the dealer for assistance, you are kept on hold for half an hour, then find that the technical expert you require is not available, or the company can't find anyone who is familiar with your type of problem. The people on the phone lines speak a strange technical language, and openly mock you for not knowing what the "fuel-inject fuse bus linkage paradigm" means.

▲ The car's indicators and diagnostic system frequently provide you with data that means nothing to you. Sometimes the data simply disappears without adverse affect, but sometimes they presage the car's complete breakdown. You have no way of determining which data indicate the former or latter condition.

▲ The car often stops for no apparent reason, sometimes placing you in danger, sometimes placing others in danger, and always resulting in your luggage being lost.

▲ The controls sometimes freeze, and sometimes result in varying direction. The car often takes you someplace you haven't intended on visiting, and promptly forgets how it got there. The only way to resolve this situation is to call for help and proceed immediately home, starting your trip all over, no matter how far you've previously gone.

▲ There is virtually no trade-in market or equity in the car once you've had it for a few months.

We've accepted shoddy service and products from software and hardware manufacturers, and thereby "educated" them the wrong way. They do not invest in rigid quality control as does Toyota, or spend lengthy time on mock-ups and concept prototypes, as does Daimler Chrysler. They know that a poor product will not seriously affect market share, and that poor technical service isn't even a factor in consumers' minds.

The most horrific consumer scenario I can envision is computer repair being subcontracted to the local cable TV station. We'd all have to quit our day jobs.

The worst thing about lowering our own standards and expectations is that we fail to recognize quality service, excellent products, and outstanding relationships when they do occur.

MEDIOCRITY EXISTS BECAUSE WE ACCEPT IT AS THE STANDARD

Eschewing mediocrity is a two-fold endeavor. We must exhibit zero tolerance for it as consumers and customers, and we must provide exemplary leadership to prevent it as managers and business people. Most of us spend time on both sides of that equation. It is a double-edged sword.

What are we believing in and supporting every day? Is it the slow clerk, the late delivery, the damaged product, the indecipherable directions, and the inconsistent performance? Or is it a demand that products and services live up to their billing, that service people be responsive and courteous, and that guarantees be observed?

Passivity is an action. Apathy is a point of view. The mere acceptance of the status quo perpetuates the status quo. I arrived at O'Hare Airport in Chicago three hours late one night on a weather-delayed American Airlines flight from San Francisco, en route to Providence. The plane to take us to Providence was available (it had been similarly delayed), the beleaguered but full crew was assembled, and the remaining gate agents and luggage handlers were making what was clearly a halfhearted attempt to get us on our way at 2:30 in the morning. From a window, I saw the baggage handlers stop loading and reverse the conveyer to unload bags. I approached the gate agent, the senior flight attendant, and the first officer, all standing in the jetway.

"Look," I said, "I know it's late and everybody's weary, but unless there's a legal reason not to fly this airplane then I expect everyone to do everything possible to get us to Providence. Your baggage handlers are apparently deciding to shut down, and that's not their decision. Now, who's in charge?"

"That would be me," said the pilot emerging from the cockpit. "And we will have you out of here in the next thirty minutes if it is humanly possible."

It was, and I know that I was personally responsible for averting the public address announcement that was going to ensue about how much the airline regretted the flight being cancelled. If I can make an airplane fly, what can you do? You never know until you try, but I'll tell you this: Passivity will encourage—not allow, but *encourage*—the status quo to continue. If you want to change something, then get in its way.

The leadership authority John Gardner said once that we have to learn to honor excellence in any activity, no matter how humble, and scorn mediocrity in every activity, no matter how exalted. He said that we need excellence in our plumbers, no matter how humble that pursuit, and that we can't tolerate mediocrity in our philosophers, no matter how lofty that calling, or else neither our pipes nor our theories will hold water. Yet we have corroded our standards and learned to live with pernicious undercutting of our organizations and professions because, just maybe, some day we'll have our turn at the trough of slops.

Do you know why it is that the local phone company, gas company, cable operator, furniture store, carpet outlet, and appliance store can get away with telling you that their delivery and/or service will occur on Wednesday, but not have to tell you when on Wednesday? Because we allow them to do so. Service and installation calls can be scheduled, and unanticipated problems can be dealt with on a contingency basis. Years ago, Eastern Airlines ran a shuttle service among Boston, New York, and Washington, D.C., on which they guaranteed everyone who showed up a seat, with no reservations required. How did they do it? Quite simply: If a plane filled up and there were more passengers waiting, *they rolled out another plane.* If Eastern could do that with airplanes,[1] why can't the appliance people do it with deliveries, or the cable company do it with service calls?

The answer is that they can, but management is too lazy to think it through and has no urgency to do so as long as customers sit in their homes like prisoners gratefully awaiting the jailers. Simply pay for the new dishwasher on a credit card and, at scheduling time, tell the retailers that if they can't guarantee delivery within a two-hour period in the morning or afternoon, you'll cancel the sale and not honor the charge. You'll find that these folks can schedule sufficiently tightly to make the Normandy invasion seem loosely organized by comparison. Inform the gas company that you'll file a Public Utilities Commission complaint if the repair crew isn't there during a specified period. Tell the cable company that you'll switch to a satellite dish if they can't install at a time convenient to you. You just might find a whole new dimension in customer responsiveness.

Do you know what happens when your auto dealer might not complete your repairs on time and may be forced to provide you with a loaner car? Unless your engine has fallen out, they finish the repairs rather than risk an unhappy customer in a competitive environment (repairs and servicing are far more profitable than new car sales themselves) and incur the expense of a loaner out for another day.

There are no differences among a consumer, a manager, an executive, a seller or a buyer. We all play many roles but one overall mentality will prevail. In other words, a consumer who feels he or she must tolerate shoddy service will tend not to be a manager who is insistent on premium service from his or her operation. I've known many managers, running mediocre units, whose motto is, "I have to tolerate delays, so why shouldn't our customers?" And that attitude permeates those in the work force. Managers are consumers. Many consumers are managers. What we accept in one role we are prone to accept in all roles.

I once asked a top service manager why she was so zealous about providing top-flight responsiveness. "Because," she said emphatically, "I wouldn't accept anything less myself."

---

1. Eastern Airlines went out of business because of intractable labor problems and a lack of trust in management, largely perpetuated by the CEO, Frank Borman. Their actual operations were often innovative and quite efficient.

We have to stop enabling lazy management by accepting shoddy service, slow responsiveness, and inferior products, in our lives and in our work. "Close enough for government work" cannot be a performance standard.

AM I MISTAKEN, OR DID YOU JUST TREAT ME VERY WELL?

We have all experienced exceptional service and long-lived products. I remember writing to Texas Instruments years ago to tell them that I had used one of their calculators for twenty-three years, it had just failed, and I was rushing right out to buy their latest model. A woman in customer relations wrote back telling me not to buy a new Texas Instruments calculator, but to accept one with their compliments, and would I mind returning the one that broke so that their technicians could determine why it had failed? When I returned the calculator, but told them not to send me a free one because I had already purchased their current model, the same woman sent me a check for the retail price and thanked me for my loyalty![2]

Yet these actions are notable by their exceptional nature. They are not the norm. Those levels of service and performance *are eminently achievable by any enterprise and by any performer*, but only if they are used as the standards and everyone's performance is evaluated against them, and not as the exceptions recognized as rare achievements. We have to acknowledge that, and let them know it.

Treating the consumer well does not always mean pampering or responding to serious problems. It simply means being honest about what's to be delivered, and then delivering it. Southwest Airlines is hardly a luxury operation. It provides cattle cars with wings, but it's honest about the offering and does what it says: For the lowest price around it gets you where you want to go, almost always on time.[3] It has rabidly loyal employees, faithful

---

2. Actually, the check was for a few bucks more than the retail price, but I was afraid that if I returned the change there would be more letters, stock options, and so on. . . .

3. One of the wonderful and, perhaps, apocryphal stories of Southwest is that of a flight attendant, rushing down the aisle throwing peanuts left and right, asking the passengers, "Does anyone have change of a twenty?" The reply from a middle seat, "Honey, if we had change of a twenty, do you think we'd be flying this airline?"

customers, and a wonderful profit line, _even in times when the rest of the industry has struggled._ Passengers have recognized the quality of the airline and its service commitments. There is no full-service airline in the United States that provides a similar level of honesty and dependability. Poor service has become institutionalized in often bizarre ways. For example, a plane ticket doesn't always get you a ride on a plane. At the moment, in fact, passengers on both United and Continental holding connecting tickets, are often bussed between two of the cities (i.e., if you're going from San Jose to Boston through San Francisco, the initial leg is on a bus). Who could make this up?

It is both faster and cheaper to go from Chicago to Milwaukee, for example, by Amtrak than by airplane. Yet Amtrak doesn't aggressively market this advantage and the airlines don't seem to care. They keep flying the route, and keep taking money from the apathetic customers.[4] I asked an airline executive seated next to me on one flight why passengers still choose air travel on those routes, and how he marketed to maintain that niche.

"Market?" he scoffed. "We don't do anything for those routes. The bottom line is that people are lazy." Apparently, so are Amtrak executives.

At the moment, an inordinate amount of many Americans' savings are gathering dust in very low-interest bank savings accounts, providing a bonanza for the banks and small payback for the savers. Ask any honest banker, and he or she will tell you that it's simply consumer apathy, and it would be crazy for the banks to try to educate those investors. I feel differently, and I advise my clients accordingly: If your customers aren't taking advantage of the best deal, let them know proactively and often. Don't wait for the competition, government regulators, the media, or serendipity to "expose" an unfavorable relationship.

If customers choose to keep their life savings in low-interest accounts despite being reminded regularly and clearly that there are superior options for them, then the organization has done the right thing. But if they keep those savings in desultory vehicles

---

4. If you compare travel from Chicago to Milwaukee by air, with attendant expenses and time to travel to and from the airports, against traveling by train, via the central-city stations, the train wins every time, and in inclement weather it's no contest whatsoever. In fact, it's quicker to drive from Chicago to Milwaukee than it is to fly.

through the benign neglect of the organization, that's a travesty. (One of my clients at Fleet Bank, the nation's eight largest, calls these deposits "dinosaur accounts.")

Treating the customers well means going out of the way to inform them, or as the Syms family said, "educate" them, about their best interests. Sooner or later, someone will.

I'M MAD AS HELL, AND I'M NOT GOING TO TAKE IT ANYMORE

Peter Finch's character's famous admonition in the movie *Network* represents the degree of outrage that has finally overcome consumer torpor in the past. Sometimes there are mechanisms in place that allow the rage to be vented. The Federal Aviation Authority, for instance, does receive hundreds of thousands of complaints about airline cancellations, lost luggage, and poor service. But that's a rare government watchdog necessitated by clear issues of public safety. And many FAA critics claim that even that agency has blunted teeth, vacillating and waiting too long to mandate such things as cargo compartment fire suppression systems, which probably would have prevented the ValueJet crash of several years ago.

There are only three categories of impetus for a company to consistently "do the right thing" for its customers:

1. A set of corporate values and a corporate philosophy, as discussed in Challenge 4 in this book, that mandates unremitting quality and absolute responsiveness to legitimate customer need.

2. Customer feedback so excruciatingly annoying, so relentlessly shrill, that it's easier to accede to the demands than it is to keep fighting them.

3. Appeals to those whose self-interest is, itself, endangered by consumer outrage, and who possess weapons that frighten the offenders: namely, politicians.

Nordstroms is, perhaps, the poster child for category 1, offering the finest service in its industry, training and incenting its salespeople in unqualified customer service, and accepting almost any consumer excuse to justify returned merchandise. The added expense of a nearly universal return policy is more than offset by the reputation generated as a safe and supportive place for customers to patronize.

Category 2 is represented by the dizzying return of "Classic

Coke" in the wake of "New Coke's" debacle.[5] The fashion industry, bruised and battered, terminated the "midi skirt" look after
women simply refused to purchase it. Texaco exploded into action
in the wake of the "Texaco tapes" and their alleged racial bias,
following the merest threat of a nationwide boycott. Intel reversed itself about the Pentium chip's shortcomings when even
technological consumers had been riled beyond their normal state
of meek submission. This occurred again in early 1999 over a chip
that could reveal private details about visitors to Web sites. Intel
bowed to the consumer outrage.

The television industry has long been held captive itself to
the arcane ratings system, in which, presumably, consumer interests are carefully tracked and acted upon in terms of program-
ming and scheduling. (This may be theoretically true, but how it
explains programs such as "Veronica's Closet," "Caroline in the
City," or "Men Behaving Badly" or the success of a personality
like Roseanne is beyond my comprehension.) Consumer advocacy
groups have been responsible for the voluntary recall of toys because of potential danger to children, and of household electrical
appliances because of potential danger to adults. This pressure
can be highly effective whether organized or simply the sum total
of individual feedback.

Outraged consumers, working through their elected officials,
generated the "lemon laws" now on the books in many states,
which protect consumers from the costs and time incurred in
poorly manufactured automobiles, a good example of category 3.
This alternative is also represented by movie and television ratings indicating the intended audience levels and describing vio-
lent and/or sexual content. (You don't have to have a law passed
to achieve corporate action; the mere *threat* of a law is usually
sufficient to galvanize executive attention.)

"No smoking" areas, which have given way to entire
"smoke-free" facilities in both public and private accommoda-
tions, are category 3 results. Access for the disabled and equal
opportunity hiring are even more dramatic examples of effective
use of the political process to engender change.

---

5. Of more than minor interest is the fact the most rabid supporters
of "old Coke" couldn't tell it apart from "new Coke" in blind taste tests.
This wasn't about product quality, but about consumer emotions that,
when enflamed, are nothing to fool around with.

In all candor, however, category 3 is usually reserved for either politically sensitive issues (e.g., Americans with Disabilities Act) or such widespread unhappiness (and mammoth corporate stupidity) that virtually all constituents are, or can be, affected (as in the case of the lemon laws). Category 1 is largely unaffected by consumers or, as we've seen earlier, even shareholders and boards. It is reliant upon the inherent principles of the organization and values of the leadership. In some cases those attributes are in place in sufficient quality and quantity. Too often, they are not.

That leaves category 2. And that is where most of our solutions reside. An educated consumer is *your* best customer.

The only way for consumers to effectively vent their rage is to provide direct communication to the offending company. But unless this is done repeatedly and consistently, the total effect is slight. Ten thousand angry customers represent only 1 percent of a million-customer base. I'll appease them with a small staff and a modest offer, but why do anything more?

SOLUTIONS: PAYING CUSTOMERS HAVE A FUNNY HABIT OF AFFECTING PERFORMANCE

What is the reason that one firm settles for "good enough," and another doesn't? The reason is you and me. There really isn't any "they" representing influence in the marketplace that we can't control. *We* allow the system to operate the way it does. *We* deserve the kinds of government, sports, and business that we experience. *We* are responsible.

What can we do as individual or groups of consumers to display our intolerance for mediocrity and our support for excellence? A lot more than we think.

Pursue Excellence, and Do Not Tolerate Mediocrity

Author Robert Heinlein once noted that "luck" is the term applied by mediocrities to try to explain away genius. Saints might engage in introspection, but it is we sinners who run the world, like it or not.

The tolerance of mediocrity—whether in shoddy products, poor service, failed commitments, or missed deadlines—is actually a corrupting philosophy. As we allow expectations to decline we simultaneously encourage standards to decline. Once one person drives on the shoulder to avoid the traffic jam, others quickly follow suit, until there is a long line justified by someone else's actions. The cumulative effect of accepting poor (and, worse, declining) performance from our businesses, manufacturers, service providers, and agencies is a degradation of our lives.

If we don't strenuously object, standards seldom improve on their own. It took MCI to make AT&T even vaguely customer-friendly. If we stop patronizing poor performers, they will either change or go out of business, both of which are desirable outcomes.

Calpers, the huge California state employees' pension fund, is one of the major institutional investors in the country, responsible for billions in investments. The Calpers directors have taken quite a proactive and aggressive position about which organizations receive their funds. For example, they have created standards about boards of directors (i.e., limits on numbers of boards, no interlocking directorships, preponderance of outside directors, etc.)[6] that must be met to merit investment consideration. They will pull their funds from organizations that depart from those standards. Many boards, which prize the capital infusion that a Calpers can provide, have taken the standards very seriously.

Consumer boycotts have brought previously aloof giants to their knees. The civil rights movement pioneered the use of economic power to create changes leading to increased objectivity and fairness in hiring and promotion standards. Attempts by airlines to raise prices are often rebuffed by activist passengers. Women soundly scuttled designers who produced the unflattering "midi" look.

The increasing popularity of the Internet, coupled with the existing power of the media, create potent weapons for consumers to generate mass influence over providers of goods and services. There is a plethora of sites dedicated to consumer outrage and solidarity. Just enter "consumerism" or "consumer complaints" in any Web search engine.

Create Accountability

"We are as gods, and might as well get good at it," stated *The Whole Earth Catalog*. Like it or not, we are accountable, so we

---

6. See Challenge 5 for many of the very guidelines they are enforcing.

might as well create and reinforce the proper standards. When we leave the standards to the providers, we get things like tail fins on cars and constant busy signals at our Internet providers. Buying Japanese cars with excellent quality and gas mileage marvelously focused Detroit's attention.

Anyone who picks up a phone in an organization should "own" what follows, which is usually the resolution of a concern. "That's not my job" is an oxymoron, because resolving those issues is everyone's job. A customer demanding to talk to someone in management who will provide a credit for a late delivery is an attempt to force accountability, even if that customer must end up talking to the president.

When the cable television provider's service representative tells you that "we'll have someone there sometime on Tuesday," simply respond that you'll need a specific appointment because you're taking time off from work, you have other appointments, or it's simply too inconvenient to wait around all day. If the rep tells you that there is no provision for specific times, ask to speak to a supervisor. If the supervisor echoes the company "policy," ask for the manager. If the manager is of no help (or is unavailable and doesn't call back), go to the vice president of operations. The odds are that, sooner or later, someone is going to apply some reason and comply with your needs, so long as you remain polite but firm. When enough people do this in concert, we create the rare but increasing "change in policy." There are now cable companies, in the aftermath of horrible publicity and unremitting criticism from the media and public, that guarantee installation between limited hours or the service is free. Don't tell me you can't fight city hall.

Escalating a reasonable request up the hierarchy has the remarkably salutary effect of moving away from employees who are disempowered to help you even if they wanted to do so (making debate futile)[7] and moving toward people who are much more inclined to grant your request. That's because the higher you go, the more the manager or executive you've pursued:

---

7. I once dealt with a Delta Airlines reservations agent who, in trying to explain why it was cheaper to fly to Europe from New York than to Dallas, simply stated, "Look, there is no good reason for it, it's just our policy." The people on the front lines are seldom the enemy, and they wish the system was more user friendly just as much as the customer does.

▲ Has the legitimate corporate power to make the change.

▲ Understands the need to keep customers happy.

▲ Is so busy that it's easier to concede than to engage in long debate.

▲ Is an expensive resource, realizing it's costing more money to resist than to agree.

▲ Wants to set an example so that this doesn't land on his or her desk again.

▲ Appreciates the importance of judgment over blind rules and policy.

▲ Is no longer "faceless," and doesn't want to be the particular target of your anger or unhappiness.

▲ Can solve the issue with a single decision, without further approval.

▲ Is sensitive to—and affected by—the political repercussions if you pursue his or her boss.

▲ Knows that the "buck" has to stop somewhere.

▲ Actually knows that you're right.

I will accept unavoidable problems from any organization. There will always be mechanical failures, unforeseen breakdowns, inventory errors, unanticipated emergencies, and inevitable human error. It's silly to become enraged at the power company because a squirrel shorted out the neighborhood. It's appropriate to become assertively concerned if it happens weekly. I will not accept shoddy service or poor products that are a result of repetitive error, stupid policies, or simply poor planning. In those cases, I escalate right to the CEO's office. Ninety percent of the time that I do wind up there, I'm successful in achieving my goals. (By definition, I'm successful 100 percent of the time when I don't have to go that far.)

Some of those CEOs, like Robert Booth of Hammacher Schlemmer (whom I mentioned in Challenge 1), go on to become active correspondents. Let's give them all the benefit of the doubt. They need to hear from us.

Confront Nonsense and Diversions

Whenever I answer the phone and hear someone say, "Alan, how *are* you today!?" I know I'm talking to someone who is trying to sell me securities. I'm not about to buy securities over the telephone. The technique is a dead giveaway, and the industry is too dumb to change its ways.

Similarly, when you're confronted by an employee who immediately uses your first name, empathizes with your plight, and tries to explain why he or she would feel the exact same way, you're being conned and diverted. I don't want a friend, I don't want empathy, and I certainly don't want someone telling me that the status quo is good for me. I want the circumstances changed, and if you can't do it, find me someone who calls me "Mr. Weiss" and can.[8] In my experience, companies spend more money on this "relationship" training drivel than they do on effective problem solving. Phone representatives, in particular, are trained to immediately use a customer's first name in an attempt to create an atmosphere of friendliness rather than actual remediation of the problem. Call me an elitist, but I'm appalled by a company representative whom I've never met immediately calling me "Alan." This standard-lowering decline into informality also creates a misconception of attentiveness and concern. But it's really a subliminal attempt to influence *your* behavior, and a studious attempt not to change *their* behavior by having to deviate from policy or, heaven forfend, actually resolve an issue on the phone or in person.

Poland Spring, the water supplier, recently delivered our six-gallon water bottles to a neighbor a quarter of a mile away. Their service representative, Ronald, who answered after the obligatory phone menu, holds, and voice mail information, finally told me, "Alan, I'll have to contact the driver. It's his route, his commissions, and any adjustment would come out of his pocket."

"I'll tell you what," I replied, "first, it's *Mr.* Weiss, or *Dr.* Weiss, take your pick."

"All right, sorry, Dr. Weiss. Most people don't mind."

"Most people probably feel it's hopeless to expect common courtesy. Now, I don't care about your internal reward system.

---

8. Twice now, I've heard a flight attendant on American's Providence-Chicago route go through the cabin after takeoff saying, "Hi, my name is Maryann, may I call you Nancy?" or whatever the passenger's first name is. Some passengers nod and continue reading the newspaper, some look in mild surprise and then agree. One gentleman finally said to her, "I really think it would be more professional if you called me '*Dr. Johnson*,' if you don't mind." There seems to be deliberate effort to use first names as a pseudo-relationship-building device.

I'm not paying for a delivery that we had to go fetch ourselves. I'm not talking to your driver, or anyone else."

"You don't understand, Dr. Weiss, that I must get fifty calls a week like this. This is how they're handled, always through the driver."

"You don't understand that I don't care about your internal problems, which seem to be severe. Either credit my account for this entire delivery, or cancel my service. You have two competitors who would sign me up tomorrow. If you feel you have to do the latter, I want you to know that I will write the president and tell him why I've left you, using your name, Ronald."

The account was credited and the deliveries have been unerring ever since. The entire call took about ten minutes. If we don't provide feedback, nothing will ever change. And if enough of us don't "push back," there is no incentive to change. Don't be waylaid by friendship and recordings that intone, "Your call is important to us, please continue to hold." If your call *were* that important, *the system would be designed and staffed to prevent the need for that recording.* Anyone who uses an impersonal recording to tell you how important you are is pulling your leg and, perhaps, taking advantage of you as a customer.

Align the Rewards You Bestow With Your Long-Term Values

We have to let organizations know when they've done it right. As difficult as it is to prompt consumers to communicate, when they do it's predominantly because they have a complaint. People are usually moved to action by pain, not by pleasure. The former makes us active, the latter complacent. Yet we can't be merely chronic complainers, as comforting as that can be at times. We have to provide positive feedback to support and reinforce those behaviors we truly cherish.

Organizations reward—with recognition, promotion, visibility, incentives, appointments and, oh yes, money—what they truly cherish. No amount of signage on corporate walls will change a culture that demands "get the business at any cost" if the only reward is for top-line revenue growth, period. As one client vice president commented, "No one who worked here and hit their numbers was ever chastised, even if that accomplishment meant they also happened to stomp people into the ground."

People react to rewards and punishments (more pristinely referred to as "consequences" in polite consulting society). Everyone wants to make a profit (even in a nonprofit—only the measures are different). It's the *how* that is problematic. Long-term success is seldom, if ever, directly or exclusively correlated to the current quarter's results. What does the organization stand for, how will employees' behavior manifest it, and how will we know it?

When an organization has used judgment to make policy exceptions, provided special services, narrowed time frames, reduced waiting, or expedited requests, someone was responsible. A post card, phone call or E-mail can't hurt, and I know from experience they are always read at significant levels because those below in the organization's bowels pass them up with great alacrity.[9] I was sitting with the CEO of a Midwestern manufacturer, a $450 million business division. He was reading six letters of praise for a new return policy.

"How much influence do these have on your decision making?" I asked.

"Probably more than they should," he admitted. "But I know that letters of support and endorsement for our policies are rare, given human nature, and that these represent a lot more satisfaction out there than simply that of the six people who took the time to write. You have to multiply these a thousandfold, whereas a complaint might represent nothing more than that one disgruntled customer."

When my firm conducts customer focus groups, interviews, and surveys, we always find positive things about our client that the client didn't sufficiently appreciate. That's because people do have a lot to say about what's working well, but don't proactively take the time to say it. If they're asked, they'll respond. But every company-sponsored survey, no matter how well done, is always tainted somewhat by the process itself: The respondent is being pursued (sometimes with an inducement for participating), is "forced" to come up with examples, and often feels obligated to

---

9. Although I'm making the opposite point, if you ever want to get an executive's name and people are loath to provide it, simply make it clear you're trying to write to compliment the behavior of a person or performance of a unit. You'll find that the CEO's home address and unlisted phone number are suddenly available.

say something nice. The spontaneity and, hence, the truth, is often lost.

We have to ask ourselves to provide that feedback more often, so that the companies that are meeting expectations and raising standards can continue, confidently, to do so.

On the second day of the Battle of Gettysburg in July 1863, the Union commander, Major General George Meade, was no longer sure of his troop dispositions after a series of attacks and counterattacks. He turned to a staff officer, Major General Gouvernor Kimball Warren, an engineer by trade, and told him to find some vantage point and report back on what he saw.

Warren got on his horse and rode to the extreme left flank, where he found a small hill, unoccupied, called Little Round Top. After dismounting and climbing the height, he found to his astonishment that the entire Union line could be flanked from that position. Then, looking over his other shoulder, he saw to his horror Confederate troops laboriously pushing artillery up the other side of the hill.

Racing down the slope, and on the authority of the two stars on his shoulders, Warren ordered the closest Union troops to take the heights and hold at all cost. That unit was a volunteer regiment, the Twentieth Maine, commanded by a volunteer colonel by the name of Joshua Chamberlain.

Chamberlain's men made it to the top minutes before the Confederates, who had stopped to rest believing that the hill was still unoccupied. A furious fight ensued. Three times the Confederates charged, and three times they were repulsed by the men of the Twentieth Maine. Finally, just enough light and just enough Confederates remained to make one last attempt, and once more they came up the hill.

This time they were met with an eerie silence. The Twentieth Maine had run out of ammunition. The men looked at their colonel, expecting to be ordered back down the hill. After all, they had done everything they could.

Joshua Chamberlain watched the advancing Confederates, and issued one of the great commands in the history of the United States military.

He said, "Charge!"

The remainder of the Twentieth Maine fixed bayonets and dutifully ran down the hill into the Confederates screaming like wild men. The brave Confederates reached the only logical conclusion available: The Union lines had clearly been reinforced and had gone on the offensive. The Confederates broke and ran, and Little Round Top, the Union lines, the battle of Gettysburg and, perhaps, the Union were saved.

Joshua Chamberlain later received the Medal of Honor.

Isn't it time we all went on the offensive and charged?

Challenge Nine

Make the Choice: Decline or Excellence in Business and Society

Our schools are graduating students who can't locate Peru on a map, calculate the square footage of a room, or name one of Shakespeare's plays. The choice is not solely between excellence and mediocrity. It is also between excellence and decline, because acceptance of mediocrity as a standard is an inherently corrupting position.

We often seem to miss the exquisite irony of the sports figures on the motivational circuit. Sports were once a metaphor for business: sacrifice, strive for excellence, break records, build motivation, give 110 percent, and so on ad nauseam. It's still a metaphor, but hardly for excellence. Athletes are routinely tested for illegal drugs, and many sports figures are in the news more for spousal abuse, illegitimate children, weapons possession, and rampant egomania than for any exploits on the track field or in the stadium.

It is no accident that with the growing acceptance and toleration for mediocrity in sports, politics, and society, we also suffer through increased corruption: athletes taking drugs and using illegal equipment;[1] politicians in the news for everything from illegal fund raising to illicit sexual conduct; and juries that seem to

---

1. Corked bats have been discovered in the midst of major league games. A football player was disqualified on the high school level when it was discovered that his father had sharpened his helmet fittings so as to cause more damage to the opposing players who were hit with it.

have lost the ability to separate fact from fantasy. Make no mistake: the abandonment of the high ground of excellence for the safer ground of mediocrity is not merely a change in altitude. It is an acceptance of corrupt behavior and a breakdown of order. It is the fixed result and phony showmanship of professional wrestling replacing the honest toil and rigorous preparation of the amateur gymnast. You can't fake a perfect balance beam routine.

We've reached an age in which cartoon characters are dispensing the wisdom that becomes the bromides of our society. Dilbert, by Scott Adams, has become the modern-day troubadour of the business community, using both amateurish art and metaphor to parody the empty headedness of contemporary organizational leadership.[2] He has taken the baton from Walt Kelley and Pogo, whose immortal observation, "We have met the enemy and he is us" has rivaled "Give me liberty or give me death" as a modern adage to live by. Nevertheless, we've come a long way from Upton Sinclair and Lincoln Steffens. Intellectuals and "muckrakers" attacking shoddy business practices have given way to three-panel cartoon strips and jokes about computer illiteracy amidst a general sense of overwhelming ennui.

Pogo's observation can be reexamined as we have suggested earlier in this book: There is no "they." We are they.

WHO'S TEACHING WHOM? THE AVATAR MUST BE BUSINESS

Ted Williams, the great Boston Red Sox Hall of Famer, and the last man in baseball ever to hit over .400, reached the final day of the 1941 season right on the edge of .400. His manager offered to let him sit out the final game, preserving the rare average, because if he batted and went hitless, Williams would finish the season at .398 or so. Williams wouldn't even consider it, played the game, got two hits, and finished at slightly better than .400, a record that still stands. He did it by facing the challenge and letting talent prevail. Fifty years later, another Red Sox player, pitcher Roger Clemens, also headed for the Hall of Fame, refused to pitch in the final game of the season because it wouldn't affect the

---

2. It's always been vaguely ironic to me that Adams began the strip while on the payroll of his then-current employer who, presumably, was paying him to be doing something else entirely.

standings and he didn't want to run the risk of injury, since he would be negotiating soon with other teams for a better pay package.

Who says the game's gotten better?

Sports role models are still with us, but the standards they set are one of stock deals, deferred compensation, ego gratification, and personal control. The range of their influence is as wide and pervasive as ever, but the message is quite different. We're not in this for the team, we're in this for ourselves. Just a few years ago, the great Chicago Bulls basketball player Scotty Pippen took himself out of a game in the final, decisive minute, because the coach called for a play to win the game that did not involve Pippen attempting the shot. He was offended, and decided not to help. (The coach's call was effective, and another player made the basket, winning the game.)

Years ago, Notre Dame's football coach, the late Ara Parseghian, played for a tie in the season's final game in order to clinch the then-mythical national championship. Notre Dame had a clear chance to win outright, but the coach demanded that the team run out the clock, despite decent field position, taunts from the opposing Michigan team, and howls of his own team. He said later, trying to defend the timidity, that he didn't want the team to lose its big opportunity through a careless, last-minute error. Of course, he was really talking about *his* opportunity to have coached the national champions. So he actively played for the tie. More recently, the Minnesota Vikings coach, Dennis Green, instructed his quarterback to "take a knee" and run out the clock in a championship game in which his team was tied with the Atlanta Falcons. Instead of trying for a last-second win in regulation, Green tried "not to lose," with the result that he lost in overtime and the Falcons went to the Super Bowl.

Every day, I see business management not playing for the "win," but playing for themselves. In these growing times of ambiguity, lack of precedent, and increased urgency, instead of "doing what's right" they "protect their turf," "make their numbers," or "blame *them*." Delegation has been replaced by "passing it up the line." E-mail is used not so much as a convenient communication device but as a method to blanket everyone in the organization with otherwise irrelevant information and copies, thereby protecting oneself, since if everyone knows, then the originator can't be blamed.

Individual deals have become far more important than corporate advances. In fact, departing deals for poor performers often are more lucrative than existing deals for stellar performers. In an era of weak-hitting mediocre shortstops earning $4 million a year, and the phony antics of the World Wrestling Federation filling arenas with paid ticket holders, we also suffer a business climate in which lousy leadership is richly rewarded (whether to stay or to leave), and we're all witness to the phony antics of pyramid marketing schemes and "get rich quick" hucksters.

We seem to have lost the connection between reward and value in contemporary society. For example, only in modern America could "multilevel marketing" take on a respectability, as though simply recruiting new members under the pyramid below you adds any value, worth, dignity, or lasting contribution to our business climate or society. We condescend to empathize with the Albanians and the Ponzi schemes they've endured, or the Russians and the impossible chances provided in their fixed lotteries, but are we really any better in supporting "multilevel marketing" as a legitimate endeavor?

WITH NO PORT IN MIND, NO WIND IS FAVORABLE: THERE IS NO SUBSTITUTE FOR LEADERSHIP

If business is to be a leader in establishing standards and aggressively raising them, who is to lead business? Fortunately, there is a pantheon of leaders in this country, even if it's not exactly standing room only within its confines. Some of my nominees among contemporary (or recently retired) executives and where they've made their mark:

- ▲ Gordon Bethune, Continental Airlines
- ▲ Jim Burke, Johnson & Johnson
- ▲ Elizabeth Dole, American Red Cross
- ▲ Ray Gilmartin, Merck
- ▲ Lee Iaccoca, Chrysler
- ▲ Frank Olsen, Hertz
- ▲ Lew Platt, Hewlett-Packard
- ▲ Colin Powell, chairman, Joint Chiefs of Staff
- ▲ Ann Richards, governor of Texas
- ▲ Robert Schaeffer, mayor of Baltimore

- ▲ Fred Smith, FedEx
- ▲ Roy Vagelos, Merck
- ▲ Jack Welch, GE

What are the hallmarks of excellence in leadership, if leadership is responsible for excellence at large? Can we all engage in a heuristic journey to reach a common destination of superior performance and constantly improving standards? Herein are my nine criteria for excellence in leadership. How well does your leadership (or do you) measure up?

1. Impeccable Integrity and Fairness

Meeting the numbers at any cost is a superficial approach to any business. The people above and others like them are notable for long-term, consistent successes (albeit amidst the inevitable setbacks that ongoing innovation will always create). Leaders are fair. They make judgments based upon facts, not favorites, and select people based upon character not charisma. They don't have to be reminded about diversity initiatives and woman's rights, because they are constantly seeking and developing talent irrespective of origin, appearance, and whether or not they resemble the current leadership.

Test: Does the leader base his or her positions, repute, and responses upon what is right ethically rather than what is expedient financially or politically?

☐ *Yes*   ☐ *No*

Leaders should be consistent in the application of their value system. Jim Burke stood tall and visible during the Tylenol tampering crisis, and thus enabled his entire company to stand tall and do the right thing.

2. Prudent Risk-Taking and Support for Innovation

Organizations do not grow by correcting weaknesses. They grow by building on strengths. Protectiveness and defensive positions are for the also-rans. No great movement ever had an armadillo on its battle flag. Leaders must support the behaviors that result in new ideas, creative initiatives, and bars being raised.

Sometimes they will lead to failure, but there's no disgrace in failing in a good cause. There should be more concern for proper, innovative behaviors than for "victories" representing only the latest quarter. Employees require and deserve something more than "the freedom to fail—once." Superb leaders encourage innovation and support the prudent risks that are inherently part of it.

Test: Does the leader provide visible reward and recognition to people who fail while trying to do the right thing?

☐ *Yes*   ☐ *No*

Outstanding organizations appreciate their problem solvers, who restore conditions to past levels of performance, but truly treasure their innovators, who create new levels of performance. Lee Iacocca decided not to try to be a stronger third to GM and Ford, but to be first at being Chrysler. As a result, the convertible was repopularized, the minivan was launched, and entirely new concepts and styles emerged from a firm that has become #1 in its new configuration with Daimler-Benz.

3. Unerring and Unintimidated Selection of Talent

In some organizations, senior executives come and go as if on round-trip airline tickets, because the closer they get to assuming the CEO's position, the more dangerous they become to the entrenched, mediocre hierarchy. Building "bench strength" and tolerating strong, sometimes oppositional, personalities is a characteristic of confident, sound leadership. Just as talent should be selected without discrimination, solely based upon ability and potential, it should also be rewarded and developed based upon those same criteria. "Being one of the boys" is no longer good enough (and it's a shame so many otherwise talented women have been lured into that trap). Leaders develop talent to the point that they propel the leader to new heights through the sheer force of their pressure from below.

Test: *Does the leader avoid and root out "yes men"?*

☐ *Yes*   ☐ *No*

The top team should be comfortable in opposing the leader's views in open and candid discussion. While the team bands together to support initiatives arising from consensus, the members should be free to disagree and debate strenuously without any issue becoming a personal affront. After the disagreements and debate, the team members support the consensus. The sure sign of a weak organization is when senior executives blame the CEO for unpopular decisions.

4. Clear and Relevant Values and Vision

Vision, mission, and values have been overdone to death. No annual report is written without them, but virtually no front-line employee is operating with them. They tend to be idealistic, vanilla, Zen-like statements that can neither cause dissension nor provide discernible help in running the business. Real leaders provide a compelling message, built upon sound values, that can be readily translated down through the ranks. Improving shareholder value at a corporate banking level becomes rolling over IRA accounts at a branch level. Providing the best scientific research and resulting products for human suffering at headquarters level becomes a policy of voluntary disclosure of all side effects at the sales level. When there is lack of precedent, policy, and procedure, people will rely on their leader's values and vision. If it doesn't exist, is ephemeral, or doesn't relate, they will move to the default position, which is usually self-protection.

Test: Throughout the organization, can employees articulate in their own words the uniform values that influence their behavior every day?

 Yes ☐ No

Top-level decisions as well as front-line actions are circumscribed by those common values and vision, which create the common "playing field" for all employees, at all levels. At Hewlett-Packard, Lew Platt has been extraordinarily successful as the founders moved away from the daily business by exemplifying and promulgating "The HP Way," which is that organization's inherent intolerance of anything short of fair treatment, honesty, and ethical conduct. "The HP Way" doesn't have to appear in banners in the cafeteria or on lapel pins because it's simply how the company lives—and succeeds—every day.

5. Focus on Results and Not Tasks

Leaders work backwards from the end point of customer satisfaction and loyalty, eliminating those processes that are simply in place to justify the off-site retreats of corporate functionaries. If every customer is deemed a potential crook, then the processes in place will curtail thievery as well as alienate the legitimate customer. Organizations reward only what they truly value. The leader must ensure, both through example and alignment of processes, that the organization is rewarding the results that support corporate goals, not corporate bureaucracy.

Test: Periodically, does the leader "shop" his or her own organization, and determine if it is easy to do business with?

☐ *Yes*   ☐ *No*

The leader should reach down to gather information from those employees closest to the customer, product, and service, and use that information to determine how to improve the operation. Ask any employee at random, "What's your job?" and the response should be framed in terms of meeting basic business goals (i.e., not "make sales calls" but rather "bring in new business"). I've encountered a high-level Delta executive flying random routes to experience his company's service.

6. Avoidance of Fads, Crazes, and Quick Fixes

In Challenge 3, I described the Marine Midland Bank human resources operation so preoccupied with personality profiles and behavioral types that it couldn't focus on a primary goal: helping employees meet customer needs. Every time one fad seems to have mercifully been shot (i.e., left brain/right brain learning), another rises from the ashes (reengineering). Leaders don't tolerate bromides and aphorisms as substitutes for action. They insist that every manager is a human resources manager and place as much emphasis on legitimate employee development, evaluation, and placement as they do on any other area of the business. Leaders understand that any internal initiative that does not ultimately impact the quality of the product, service, and/or customer relationship is pointless. During one meeting years ago, a GM training officer said to me after listening to my description of how an intervention might be measured for effectiveness, "You don't seem to understand. We're not looking for the best developmental experience, we're looking for the least expensive."

Test: Is there consistent avoidance of "programs" or "events" that employees are forced to attend that attempt to blanket the entire organization with a single tool, technique, or typology?

☐ *Yes*   ☐ *No*

The development that does occur should be tied closely to job performance and measured by line and staff management, not by human resources specialists or external consultants. Development is not involute, but rather pragmatic and immediately applicable to the job. Motorola has long maintained one of the premier development institutes in the country, focused on improving quality and performance as they directly impact the customer.

7. Employees Receive the Trust, Tools, Information, and Support to Do Their Jobs

Call this "empowerment" or "enabling" or anything that suits you, but the point is that leaders instill authority in others. They do not derive their power through numbers of people, control of information, or volume of press releases. Their power and contribution emanate from leveraging the talents of others. Leaders ensure that the latitude for action is clear, the requisite skills are developed, the incentive is appropriate, and the systems support the performer. Decision making and accountability are constantly pushed lower in the organization, so that the great preponderance of tactical decisions are made as close to the customer as possible.

Test: Do requests and complaints to the organization get addressed and solved by the first person contacted, and are not continually shifted up the line to staff at higher and higher salary levels?

☐ *Yes*   ☐ *No*

Do multiple layers of supervision and management become involved in a single consumer complaint? At Ingram, the wholesale book distributor, virtually every problem or request is handled by the agent on the phone, from alternative warehouse deliveries to incorrect freight charges, from damaged books to unique order requests. Ingram phone representatives seem genuinely happy to be of service, and have the tools to be of service. I've never seen any organization with unhappy, unempowered employees and happy customers.

8. Creation and Maintenance of a Sense of Urgency

Productivity suffers at two equally odious extremes: very low anxiety, when a sense of entitlement and complacency dominates, and very high anxiety, when a sense of fear and paralysis dictates behavior. At the midpoint, however, is the adrenaline rush and challenge that represent organizations with high metabolisms. They perform well to the background of a systolic beat. The leader is the organization's heart pumping, providing the appropriate levels of incentive, challenge, consequences, personal accountability, and stimulus to keep the blood flowing right to the extremities. Organizations should launch initiatives regularly, jump on problems, argue over their own techniques, and continually move toward higher ground. When a profit or nonprofit enterprise begins to resemble any large government agency, it's time to regroup.

Test: Does work move with high velocity, or are there piles of papers and projects standing visibly on desks like stagnant water?

☐ *Yes*   ☐ *No*

Does it take four weeks to produce a check or issue a contract, not because of the technical needs but because of the approval levels, lack of accountability, fear of making a decision, or general lassitude? Does corporate E-mail copy everyone in existence not on a need-to-know basis, but so that the senders feel their rear ends are protected and all bases covered? The service commitment in my firm is to get back to every caller within ninety minutes, respond to every piece of regular or E-mail within the same day, and provide every proposal within twenty-four hours of the request. When the prospect says, "No one has ever responded this rapidly before!" we know the battle is almost won.

9. Leadership Takes Place From the Front

In an insurance company headquarters in Keene, New Hampshire, employees told me that most of them would not recognize several of their own top officers. When the Exxon Valdez hit the rocks, CEO Lawrence Rawl couldn't be found forty-eight hours. At Southwest Airlines, CEO Herb Kelleher is a familiar face all over the operation. Leaders ride at the head of their troops. They are recognizable, both by their intent and their actions. There is access to them without retribution for employees, and without hesitation for customers. One of my favorite responses from an American Express representative was, "You can't speak to a manager. Our managers don't speak to customers." That culture can't exist without tacit endorsement from the very top levels.

Test: Do employees ever see senior officers? Are they on a first-name basis? Do senior people take the heat (from the press, the public, the investors) and set an example for how to accept accountability?

☐ *Yes*   ☐ *No*

At Fleet Boston, COO Bob Higgins regularly takes the time to address departmental and functional meetings. He conversationally discusses the organization's current status, and takes direct, uncensored questions from the audience.

WHAT WILL HAPPEN TO EXCELLENCE?

Is it the end of the world as we know it, or the beginning of another "American Century"? The issue is far more important than an esoteric philosophic question. It is a question of the quality of our lives, the values of our society, and the efficacy of our businesses.

There are winners amongst us. I've tried to present a balanced picture of those whose performance is stellar and reaching upward and those whose performance is desultory and confused. Oscar Wilde remarked once that "We're all in the gutter, but some of us are looking at the stars."

At this writing, the economy is thriving and the stock market is booming, but both conditions are on the heels of a downsizing, job-destroying binge that is unparalleled in its destruction of both careers and the traditional bonds between organizations and workers. Increased employment is too often the result of increasingly menial jobs created to tend to the detritus of a culture whose standards are collapsing. Creating four new fast-food positions does not offset the loss of four underwriters, editors, or service representatives.

While economic conditions are supposedly improving for many of us, you would think it to be the time for a vibrant and confident society and business community to tackle the challenges raised in these chapters. Yet I hear no clarion call, only the empty boasts of politicians about how well we're doing and why they're responsible. I disagree. Many Americans are not doing well. Their career choices are limited, their aspirations are being curtailed, and their sense of belonging—to our businesses, our neighborhoods, and our values—is being shattered. The American Dream is still in place, but for an increasingly smaller number of us.

Everyone will not be successful in clearing each new height. But that shouldn't stop us from the attempt. Once we're in the air, we've got a shot at it, we're higher than we were before, and the view is far better anyway.

What happened to excellence? Well it's still there if we look. The excellent organizations I've used as examples have set the pace. But the competition is often weak and the fans don't always show up.

What's happening to excellence? It's been undermined and sabotaged by trite bromides, complacent leaders, and apathetic consumers. Too many people have sneaked under the bar and been ignored, too many have circumvented the system, and too many have been rewarded for lackadaisical effort and mediocre performance.

What will happen to excellence? You tell me.

> Many people make a great racket screaming about how unfair life is and how deplorable conditions are. However, a relative few are quietly going about their business constantly improving whatever they can.
>
> Which are you? Are you lighting candles, or cursing the darkness?

Index

Merit increases, 33
Meyer, Pearl, 201
Microsoft, 20, 162, 202
Mind Masters, The, 97
Mission, 125–128
Monsanto, 206
Morgado, Robert, 197
Morison Knudsen, 180
Morris, Douglas, 197
Motivation
  compensation as, 151–152
  conducive environment for, 106
  success cycle of, 106, 107
Motivational rallies, 105
Motivational speakers, 103–107
Motorola, 162
Multilevel marketing schemes,
  108–110, 236
Myers-Briggs Type Indicator, 100

Nabisco, 206–207
National Westminster Bank, 50
Netscape Communications, 206
Noble, Barbara Presley, 88, 173
Nonaka, Ikujiro, 111
Nonprofit boards
  and annual theme revision, 187
  excess membership of, 183
  inexperience of members, 183
  lack of effectiveness of, 184–185
  role confusion of, 186–187
Nordstrom's, 12
Northwestern Life Insurance, 156
Nynex, 72–73, 190

Objectives, alignment of, 8
Occidental Petroleum Corp., 203
Olsen, Frank, 236
Open meetings, 84–86
Organizational energy, external
  focus of, 86–87
Organizational success
  and content, 3, 4
  keys to, 7–20
  and process, 3, 4
Orwall, Bruce, 197
Our Emperors Have No Clothes, 27

Outdoor experiences, as manage-
  ment fads, 89, 93
Output, focus on, 17–18
Ovitz, Michael, 197

Pacific Bell, 91
Parcells, Bill, 5
Parseghian, Ara, 235
Pearlstein, Steven, 199, 205
Performance, management focus
  on, 134
Performax, 98
Peters, Thomas J., 7
Pickett, Michael, 203
Pipe, Peter, 80
Pippen, Scotty, 235
Platt, Lew, 5, 7, 236, 239
Pogo, 234
Poland Spring, 228
Ponzi scheme, 108, 109
Poor performers
  elimination of, 14
  protection of, 24–29
Positional power, 76–77
Powell, Colin, 104, 236
Power
  positional, 76–77
  real, 68
Pride, and productivity, 149,
  150–151
Process, and organizational suc-
  cess, 3, 4
Productivity
  effect of downsizing on, 170,
  171–172
  effect of increased investment
  on, 173
  and stress, 148–150, 153
Providence Gas Company, 97–98
Prudential Insurance, 130, 180
Punishment, as leadership power
  source, 74–76

Quaker Oats, 178–179
Quinn, Mark, 145

Raising the bar, 36–44
  instructions for, 46–49
  to raise performance, 39–41